HOME & DRY

A practical guide to insulation, damp-proofing and exterior home repairs

HOME & DRY

A practical guide to insulation, damp-proofing and exterior home repairs

Edited by Rick Ball

ORBIS PUBLISHING·London

Acknowledgments

Bax, Don pp 26, 96 (top)–98, 106–107; *Bielicki, Andrzej* pp 122–123; *Blue Hawk Ltd* p 105; *British Gypsum Ltd* p 36 (inset); *Camera Press* p 116; *Cape Insulation Ltd* p 33 (top); *Easter, Bill* pp 63 (right)–65, 117–20; *Fidor* p 36; *Fleury, Eugene* pp 28–29, 80–86, 94–95; *Hayward Art Group* pp 17–19, 21–22, 31–32, 39 (right)–40 (top), 60–62, 102 (right); *Mansell, Dennis, courtesy of Crittall Warmlife Ltd* pp 39 (left), 40 (bottom); *Marley Retail Supplies Ltd* pp 2, 45; *Matthews, Tony* pp 113–15; *Megafoam Ltd* p 33 (bottom); *Rentokil Ltd* pp 9, 13, 14 (left), 15–16, 20; *Orbis Publishing Ltd* p 27; *Orbis/Angelo Hornak* pp 94–95 (top), 99, 121; *Orbis/Bill Mason* pp 7, 43–44, 54, 63 (left); *Orbis/Derek St Romaine* p 96 (top); *Orbis/Langham Studios* pp 78, 100–102, 112; *Orbis/Terry Trott* pp 1, 23–24, 41–42, 48, 52–53, 103–104, 111; *Stanwell-Smith, Juliet* pp 8, 10, 14 (right); *Studio Briggs* pp 11–12, 34–35, 37–38, 46–47, 49–51, 55–57, 66–77, 79, 87–93, 108–110; *Sylglas Co* p 30.

First published in Great Britain by Orbis Publishing
Limited: London 1980
© Orbis Publishing Limited 1980

Printed in Czechoslovakia
ISBN: 0 85613 254 3

50121

Contents

Introduction

Life in a damp house is miserable. When you lie in bed at night listening to the music of drips through the roof hitting an array of old pans in the loft, while the wind whistles through warped and ill-fitting doors and windows, you know the time has come to take action. But the wise man tackles the job before damage is expressed in such a dramatic way and the time to act is at the first sign of trouble.

Our homes are under constant attack by the forces of nature. While wind and rain try to batter a passage through roof and walls, a more subtle invasion may be taking place in the damp, still air under the floorboards. There the spores of dry rot could be gaining a first foothold before spreading out to overwhelm the entire building. Meanwhile, wet rot could be digging in where paintwork defences are left to peel, leaving timber unprotected, while rust eats inexorably through neglected metal.

Before we can claim to be 'home and dry' in a sound house, we have to eliminate all these menaces, and then make sure they don't return. Since rising damp can quickly spoil our wallpaper, care of the structure of the house is obviously a sensible first priority for the home handyman. When the structure is secure, we can set about the more creative aspects of home improvement, ranging from building fitted wardrobes to complete interior decoration.

Home and Dry examines these threats one by one, and provides detailed instructions on the right steps to take in the campaign to make the structure secure. We begin by examining damp, a major problem for the British householder, marking internal walls and making the air feel chilly. The possible causes of damp are many, from condensation to a bridged damp-proof course, but the points of penetration are largely predictable. Having located the source, remedial action can take two basic forms – internal or external. Penetration of damp can be sealed off from inside the house, by waterproofing the walls, but this often proves inadequate in the long term.

Home and Dry suggests simple yet effective remedies to the damp problem and tackles such major projects as a DIY installation of a damp-proof course, which should banish rising damp forever. The junction of earth and house wall is one of the weak points in the house's defences, needing extra attention. While damp rises there, it could be falling in from the top of the house. Roof structures require regular examination and occasional repair. The approach to a roof problem will vary with the roof design and the materials used in its construction. The flat roofs which have been used increasingly in recent years, for example on home extensions, are a perennial source of trouble, while the problem with a traditional pitched slate roof can be one of access.

Not all of us relish exposing ourselves to the elements on top of a precarious roof. It is vital to take adequate safety precautions before any roof repairs are contemplated, even if the repair is limited to mending the guttering. A break in a cast-iron gutter can lead to constant damp on the walls below, and this damp can soon penetrate a solid wall. If you have decided to replace the cast-iron with modern plastic guttering, don't be tempted to remove the iron from an insecure ladder. Cast-iron is extremely heavy, and you can easily overbalance when you take the full weight. A proper scaffold will give you the security you need.

Even with proper protection, many will not wish to spend their Sunday afternoon feeling nervous on top of the roof. For different reasons there are those who will not feel prepared to tackle the installation of a complete damp-proof course or replacement of the whole window frame, believing such major jobs to be beyond their capabilities. However, even if you decide to leave the work to a professional builder, time spent studying the relevant chapter of *Home and Dry* will not be wasted.

First of all, the detailed instructions may give you the necessary confidence to tackle the work yourself. Secondly, you will gain an understanding of how your house is constructed, which will help in identifying the precise nature of any fault. This could save you money in two ways. You may be able to avoid an expensive replacement by carrying out a judicious repair, for example repairing an ill-fitting window rather than replacing it entirely. If the builder is called in, you will be better able to brief him, and with your knowledge of the task, you will be in a position to judge whether he has carried out a thorough job.

If replacement of a window frame may be too daunting for some to contemplate, the DIY enthusiast with limited confidence and limited time at his or her disposal can easily replace a broken pane of glass. Even this relatively simple task can be spoiled by an incorrect approach to the job. Our step-by-step instructions should prevent any blunders.

When windows, walls and roofs are in good repair and keeping the elements out, there are other odd jobs which may need attention before the structure of the house can be given a clean bill of health. The ravages of time may have left all manner of scars on the house. The final section of *Home and Dry* is therefore devoted to such jobs as repairing cracked or fallen plaster, repointing the brickwork or dealing with an uneven or inadequate floor. When all the work is carried out, you can turn to the decoration with confidence, knowing that damp and rot are unlikely to make the paper peel or bulge as soon as your back is turned.

Perhaps the best investment any householder can make will come at this stage, when the structure is basically sound. A dry house is desirable, but a warm house is even better. With the present cost of fuel, none of us can afford to be wasteful with energy, and even if fuel were free, sitting in a gale of draughts is an unpleasant way of spending the evening. For this reason, insulation makes sense, and DIY insulation makes extra good sense. Although a major job such as cavity insulation is best left to a professional contractor, there are many inexpensive yet effective measures the handyman can take to keep out the cold and keep down the bills.

Money and time spent now on securing your home will not be wasted. The benefits of insulation will be reflected in your next fuel bill, while the other jobs explained in *Home and Dry* will all prove to be long-term money savers. After all, a damp wall is a less effective insulator than a dry one. Decorations, too, will have a longer life in a dry house, and the life of the house itself should be prolonged by attention to the points covered in the book.

No house should manifest all the faults detailed in *Home and Dry*. However, few can hope to escape all the possible afflictions that make a book such as this so useful. A look at the contents list is enough to indicate the wide range of problems discussed in the book, while a glance at any chapter will show the thoroughness of the approach to the problems. Backed up with clear illustrations, the text is designed to take you step by step along the road to a house that is truly home and dry.

Damp and rot

Inside

Outside

cracked pot

defective flaunching

damaged mortar joints

defective chimney
and roof flashings

missing, broken or
displaced tiles or slates

leaking cistern
or pipes

choked, broken or
leaking gutters

cracked downpipes

rainwater penetration
round windows

eroded or dislodged
pointing on walls

leaking plumbing

cavity bridged with
mortar droppings etc

choked or buried
airbricks

solid floor   timber floor

bridged or defective
damp proof course

Dealing with damp

Every house is prone to damp, both inside and out.
Rain and snow batter the roof, walls, windows and
doors, while moisture in the ground attacks the
walls and floors from below. Inside the house, the
plumbing pipework conveys water under floors and
down walls as it travels to radiators, taps and tanks.
To remain unaffected, a house must be structurally
sound and well maintained; if it is not, damp will
set in and bring plenty of problems with it.

The effects of damp may be manifested in
relatively simple ways, such as wallpaper peeling off
a wet wall or a wet patch appearing on a ceiling. In
these cases, if prompt action is taken to cure the
underlying cause of the problem, then all that
remains to complete the repairs is a relatively
straightforward decorating job. Where damp is
allowed to remain untreated, more serious problems
arise. There may be a dampish atmosphere throughout the house, mildew will form on clothes and a
stale smell prevail. The occupants of the house may
suffer ill health as a result of living in a constantly
damp environment. Structural timbers such as
floor joists and roof timbers may develop rot,
making repair work complicated and expensive.

Protection against damp
Houses built in Britain since the 1920s are generally
far less susceptible to damp than older properties
since they have damp barriers incorporated into the
structure which stop moisture working its way up
through walls or floors (rising damp). In the concrete ground floor there is a damp proof membrane
consisting of waterproof material stretched across
the building from wall to wall to intercept moisture
rising from the ground. The external cavity walls
have a damp proof course laid in a mortar joint,
usually between the second and third or third and
fourth courses of bricks above ground level. This
dpc, installed to prevent moisture creeping up the
walls, is a strip of thin, impervious material, such
as slate or bituminous felt, which stretches right
round the external walls of the house to protect
both the outer and inner leaves of brickwork.

Houses with suspended timber floors on the
ground floor are generally far less prone to damp.
Where there are problems, they are usually caused
by a faulty dpc laid on the walls supporting the
joists (sleeper walls) or by blocked up airbricks in
the outside walls of the house. These bricks are
designed to ensure a constant flow of air under the
floor to keep the timber well ventilated and dry.

As well as rising damp there is also rainwater
ingress or penetrating damp; this is prevented in
modern houses by the air space in cavity walls.
Rainwater which soaks through the outer leaf of
bricks cannot cross the cavity and reach the inner

1 Faults in the house structure which can
give rise to damp. Damage to chimney pots
and the surrounding area should be repaired
as soon as possible

leaf of bricks which form the outer walls of the rooms.

Faults in damp proofing Assuming the roof and gutters etc. of the house are sound, a modern house should remain free of damp. But problems may arise if faulty damp proof materials are used or errors occur at the building stage. For example, a split in a floor membrane or wall dpc will allow moisture through; and if mortar is allowed to fall into the cavity during building it could land on and set across one of the metal ties linking the walls to form a perfect bridge for moisture to cross over to the inner leaf of the wall.

Older houses Where there are no purpose-made damp proof barriers incorporated in the structure, the thickness of the materials used may prevent moisture creeping right through solid walls and floors. The density of some of these materials means moisture takes a long time to soak in and will dry out in settled weather without damp ever showing inside the house. On the other hand, with walls made of very porous material, moisture may well soak right through and, in severe weather conditions, tell-tale wet patches appear on interior surfaces.

Damp or condensation?

While damp is easily confused with condensation, since both produce similar wet stains on walls, it is important to differentiate between the two since remedial treatments vary. Condensation is readily recognized when it causes misting on windows or beads of moisture to drip from water pipes or the WC cistern; identification problems arise when a wet stain shows on other surfaces. Usually the weather will pin-point the problem; on a wet muggy day or during periods of prolonged rain, wet stains indicate rising damp or rainwater ingress. On a cold, dry day wet stains on walls, especially when accompanied by the more familiar signs of misty windows etc, point to condensation.

Checking for damp

Normally any wet patches caused by damp which appear inside the house can be linked to a structural fault nearby. For example, a wet patch high up on an upstairs wall could be the result of a leaking gutter or downpipe and one at skirting board level on the ground floor is probably caused by a defective or non-existent dpc. Random patches on walls point to rainwater ingress, while wet stains on ceilings could be traced back to a cracked roof tile or leaking plumbing.

Chimney stack Damp appearing on chimney-breast walls can indicate rainwater ingress in the chimney stack area. This problem is often created or accentuated by blocking off the air supply to the flue after removing a fireplace. A broken or loose chimney pot may need to be removed or replaced; if the flue is no longer used, you can fix a special capping pot which allows for ventilation but keeps out rainwater. Other common faults in chimneys are cracked flaunching (the sloping layer of mortar securing the pot), crumbling mortar joints between the brickwork of the stack, which should be re-pointed, and defective or loose flashings (the materials, usually zinc or lead, which seal the joint between the base of the stack and the roof). These can be stepped, with one edge secured in rising mortar courses of the chimney stack brickwork, or a straight band around the base of the stack, known as apron flashing.

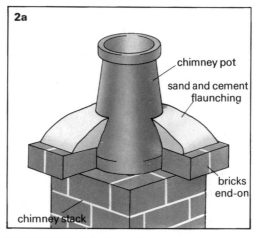

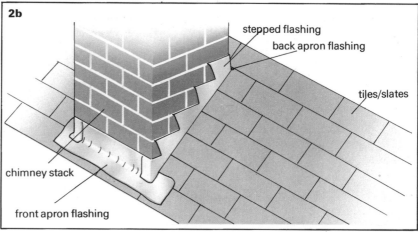

2a If damp appears on chimney-breast walls, check the condition of the chimney pots, flaunching and the chimney stack
2b Check also the flashings round the chimney stack are sound and there are no loose or missing tiles or slates

Roof Slipped or missing tiles or slates will admit rainwater to the felt beneath, which will sag, eventually split and allow water to drip onto the loft floor and show on the ceiling of the room below. Loft timbers kept constantly wet by dripping water will rot quickly so you should replace the missing roof covering as soon as possible. Fine cracks in tiles or slates will allow rainwater to seep inside; it may be difficult to spot cracks from the ground and the best way to find them is to climb into the loft during heavy rainfall and look and listen for drips. You can then trace these back to their source which could be some way from the dripping water.

Gutters and downpipes Where the rainwater drainage system is working properly, water falling off the roof is collected in the gutters from where it flows steadily into the downpipe to be discharged to the drain below. If the system fails, a large volume of water may drain onto one area of a wall, causing the brickwork to absorb an excessive amount of moisture.

Walls Where a wall has a solid covering of rendering, roughcast or pebbledash and is kept well painted with a good quality exterior paint, damp problems from rainwater ingress should never arise. However, if the wall covering is cracked or loose and the mortar joints in the brickwork behind are in poor shape or there is no decorative paint finish, then rainwater can soak through.

Treating damp

Plain unpainted solid brick walls rely completely on the density of the material and sound mortar joints to keep out rain, so any loose or crumbling joints should be repointed. If walls are in good

3a Installing a damp proof course using the liquid method is a job you can tackle yourself — as long as you are prepared for the large amount of work involved
3b With the strip method, the dpc is inserted in slots cut in the mortar with a power saw
3c Electro osmosis treatment involves inserting electrodes in the wall and linking them through a copper strip; this is connected to a terminal buried in the ground
3d With the capillary method, porous ceramic tubes are set into the wall

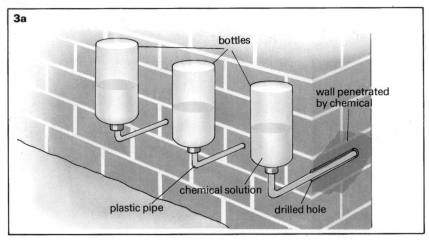

3a

bottles

wall penetrated
by chemical

chemical solution

plastic pipe

drilled hole

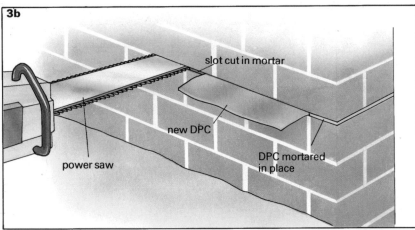

3b

slot cut in mortar

new DPC

DPC mortared
in place

power saw

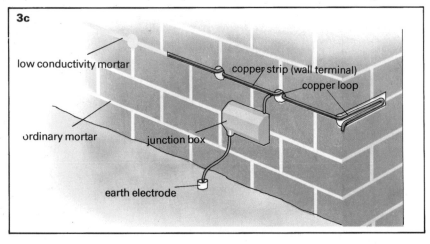

3c

low conductivity mortar

copper strip (wall terminal)

copper loop

ordinary mortar

junction box

earth electrode

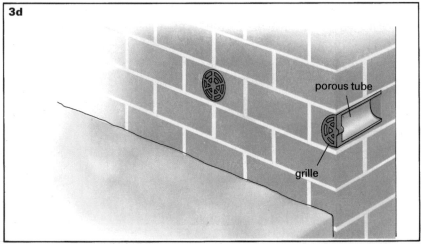

3d

porous tube

grille

repair but damp shows inside, a brush coating of a silicone water repellent liquid applied to the outside of the house should cure the trouble. These colourless liquids keep out the rain but still allow moisture vapour trapped in the wall to escape. There are also liquid treatments for internal application; but these are simply sealers which prevent moisture from affecting decorative materials and are not intended to cure the damp problem. Similarly, you can apply a dry lining to walls using materials such as bitumen-backed aluminium foil or steel corrugated sheets before decorating, but again these do not cure the damp itself.

Rising damp in walls can be treated by one of four methods of installing a dpc. With one exception they are probably best left to a specialist.

Liquid treatment A chemical liquid is fed into the wall and diffuses through the brickwork to form a damp proof barrier. The liquid can be injected under pressure using special equipment or be left to soak into the wall from a number of special bottles located in a series of pre-drilled holes. This treatment is one you can carry out yourself and will be covered in greater detail later.

Dpc strip method A power saw is used to cut through a mortar course right round the outside of walls and a damp proof material such as lead, copper or polythene is slipped into the saw cut. (Slate is not normally used since saws generally do not cut a wide enough slot for this material and laborious chipping out is needed.) Fresh mortar is then inserted to complete the process.

Electro-osmosis The difference in the electrical charge between the wall and the ground causes damp to rise in the wall. The electro-osmosis system involves fitting electrodes into the wall and linking them through a copper strip which is, in turn, linked to an electrode driven into the ground. Minute electric charges in a wet wall are then discharged down the link to prevent moisture rising.

Capillary Holes are drilled into the walls, either from the inside or outside of the house, and porous ceramic tubes inserted; these are bonded into the holes with special porous mortar and then fitted with a protective evaporation cap. Moisture from the brickwork or plaster is drawn through the pores in the tube and then evaporates into the air. The installation of this process involves the minimum amount of disturbance to the structure.

Warning Before going to the trouble and expense of installing a new dpc, check that something more basic is not causing the trouble. The existing dpc may be perfectly sound but could have been bypassed by earth or a rockery piled against the wall. Paths beside a wall should be 150mm (6in) below dpc level or rainwater will constantly splash above the dpc; in times of torrential rain, water on the path could soak the wall above dpc level.

Solid floors Normally a suitable damp proof barrier can be applied by brushing or trowelling on a damp-proofing liquid such as pitch epoxy sealer or rubberized bituminous emulsion, though sometimes a plastic membrane sheet can be used instead. Remove the skirtings temporarily and take the damp proofing material up the wall to link with the wall dpc. Where the problem is more acute, a sandwich treatment is required. Apply two coats of damp proofing material, allowing the first to dry before applying the second. Sprinkle some clean, sharp sand over the second coat while it is still tacky to form a key for a finishing screed 50mm (2in) thick.

Detecting dry and wet rot

Dampness can lead to dry and wet rot which, if not properly treated, will cause a great deal of damage to the structure of a house. Dry rot, in particular, spreads rapidly and must be tackled immediately it is discovered. So it is important you can recognize the presence and extent of the problem in your home – and, where necessary, take appropriate action.

There is only one way to deal with dry and wet rot – cut out and replace the damaged timber, apply a fungicide over the nearby areas and make sure you correct the cause of the damp. Before you can treat it, however, you must diagnose what sort of rot has set in. Wet rot, caused by a combination of dampness and lack of ventilation, is symptomatic of a poorly designed and constructed building. The basic difference is that wet rot is restricted to damp timber, while dry rot can transfer itself from wet to dry timber. While wet rot is twice as likely to occur as dry rot, it is rarely as serious.

The householder can often treat both types successfully, but serious attacks affecting the structure of a building will require the advice and assistance of a specialist.

Above and left Examples of the more advanced stages of dry rot, which must be recognized and treated immediately
Top left Old timber which has been seriously affected by wet rot and must be removed and replaced wherever it is discovered

Dry rot

This is caused by a fungus which grows on damp wood then spreads – if not caught – throughout the building. The first sign is a covering of matted fungal strands on the surface of the timber. These appear with a silvery-grey skin, which could be tinged with patches of lilac or yellow.

In humid conditions the covering grows rapidly and takes on the appearance of a soft, white cushion with a cotton wool type texture. If the edges of the cushion contact drier air or become exposed to light, they will become bright yellow. In damp conditions, where the growth is still active, many globules of water will be present. The decayed wood darkens in colour, becomes lighter in weight and will crumble when rubbed between the fingers.

In advanced cases, a fruiting body or pancake will appear; it will begin as a pale grey colour, white around the edges, with the centre portion corrugated. Later a covering of rusted spore dust will appear, accompanied by a strong mushroom smell.

The dry rot fungus has an ability to produce pencil thick water-carrying roots which transport the disease to dry wood elsewhere. Simply cutting out this timber will not cure it because the strands – or roots – will have reached dampened timber elsewhere and can pass over brick, stone and metal.

Checking for rot

Once there is an indication of dry rot, check all vulnerable parts of the house, looking for defects that allow damp to infiltrate through the roof, walls and floor. Examine the chimneys, downpipes and gutters, pointing, rendering and masonry. Check the level of soil in relation to the damp proof course and airbricks. If the house has been flooded or burst pipes have soaked timbers, be sure to check the wood has dried out.

Inside the house look for damp patches on walls, ceilings and floors. Often the problems are caused by a faulty damp proof course. By the time it becomes evident, damp patches will have penetrated structural timbers below floor level. If you suspect a defective damp proof course or blocked airbricks, it is essential to look beneath the floor. Lift the boards and look for brown discoloration of timber, cracking and 'cotton wool' or matted strands. These will reveal the extent of the problem. If fruiting bodies or rusted spore dust is present, the dry rot is of considerable maturity.

Wet rot

A number of fungi cause wet rot, which normally remains in the original area of attack although dry rot can take hold nearby. Wet rot is revealed in its early stages by discoloration around decayed wood. Look for yellowish-brown streaks or patches. Later the wood becomes lighter in weight and brownish-black in appearance. Fungal strands, thinner than those of dry rot and resembling string or twine, may grow in a fern-like shape on the surface of the timber or across damp plaster. Outdoors, a thin, olive green fungus is often seen. As wood dries, it will shrink and crack along the grain. There is sometimes cross-cracking and the individual pieces into which the wood breaks will be smaller. In severe cases, the wood becomes so brittle it crumbles between your fingers.

The difficulty in spotting wet rot is that all the damage may be taking place under what appears a sound surface – a skin of paint, for example – and will not be discovered until the skin finally collapses or is prodded with a sharp knife. Timber attacked by wet rot may also be supporting dry rot. Even wood that has dried out sufficiently to kill wet rot could still be harbouring dry rot. So always suspect the presence of dry rot.

Areas to associate strongly with wet rot are bathrooms, kitchens, the roof, cellars, fence posts, sheds and garages.

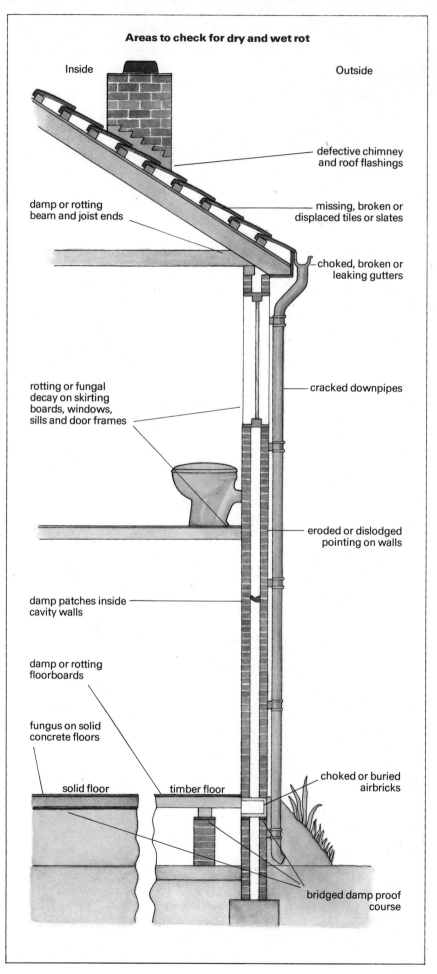

Areas to check for dry and wet rot

Inside   Outside

defective chimney and roof flashings

damp or rotting beam and joist ends

missing, broken or displaced tiles or slates

choked, broken or leaking gutters

rotting or fungal decay on skirting boards, windows, sills and door frames

cracked downpipes

eroded or dislodged pointing on walls

damp patches inside cavity walls

damp or rotting floorboards

fungus on solid concrete floors

solid floor   timber floor

choked or buried airbricks

bridged damp proof course

Treating dry and wet rot

Once you have detected wood rot (as we described previously) and have decided whether it is dry or wet rot, you must act quickly to prevent it spreading. An enormous amount of work can be involved and you will have to decide whether you have the ability and technical expertise to do it safely and efficiently or whether you need a professional.

Remember if you find evidence of rot you must regard that as being the centre of a sphere of rot and you should examine thoroughly all areas within a radius of at least 1m (or 3ft) around the discovered spot. Inspect not only timber, but also plaster, brickwork, masonry and similar materials. If you find more evidence of decay, inspect a similar size area around it and continue to do so until you have discovered the complete area of attack and

Below Clean away all traces of rot from affected areas on the wall with a wire brush

Far right Drill angled holes into the wall before inserting fluid
Right Irrigate the wall with fungicidal fluid to treat inaccessible rot

traced the structural defect causing the rot. With dry rot the defect can be a long way from the evidence of attack.

Dry rot

There are several stages involved in curing dry rot. The rotting timber has to be removed, other affec-

ted areas dealt with, surrounding areas sterilized, new timber cut in, decorations made good and the cause of the problem remedied.

Removing rot

Cut out all timber showing signs of attack for at least 1m (or 3ft) beyond the last visible evidence of fungal decay, but make sure you are not weakening the structure of the building while cutting away diseased timber. Hack away any plaster, renderings, skirtings, panellings or ceiling that have been penetrated by strands of dry rot. You must be prepared to trace the damage through or over adjacent brick, block, concrete or timber surfaces, raking out mortar joints and so on. If structural timbers – such as rafters, beams or upper floor joists – are involved, a firm of wood preservation contractors should be called in.

If the ground floor of the building is laid over an earth sub-floor and you find a covering of spore dust together with heavy growths of 'cotton wool' or matted strands, you should excavate about 100mm (4in) of soil.

In short, the entire area of concentrated dry rot attack – and beyond – must be opened up and the decayed material removed from the building by the shortest possible route. All affected timber and debris must be burned as soon as possible to prevent it being taken back into a building.

Sterilizing area

Next the affected areas should be sterilized. Using a fungicide, lightly spray all walls, partitions, sleeper walls, concrete, remaining timber and steel and pipework within a radius of 1.5m (or 5ft) from the furthest extent of suspected infection, having cleaned these areas with a wire brush and burned any dust and debris as before.

Working from the highest level downwards, apply the fungicidal fluid to all brick, block, concrete and earth surfaces until they are saturated. Refer to the manufacturer's instructions for the exact amount of fluid to use, but as a general guide apply it at a rate of 4.5 litre (1gal) to 5sq m (or 50sq ft). A coarse spray is best for this – either on a knapsack garden sprayer or a hydraulic pump.

Where dry rot strands have penetrated brickwork both sides of the wall must be treated. Using a power drill and a masonry bit, drill 13mm ($\frac{1}{2}$in) holes sloping down at 45 degrees for about 150mm (6in) at 600mm (or 2ft) staggered intervals and fill them with fluid. Irrigating the perimeter of the attacked area like this will form a 'toxic box' and any inaccessible strands inside it will die.

Replacing affected areas

Any new replacement timber must be thoroughly dry and well seasoned. Treat it with two coats of a fungicidal wood preservative (an organic solvent wood preservative or dry rot fluid complying with British Standards is ideal) and steep any sawn ends in the liquid for several minutes before fixing. If replacement timber is touching a wall, coat the wall with zinc oxychloride paint or plaster to provide an extra fungicidal barrier.

Apply two generous coats of fungicidal fluid to all timber surfaces adjacent to the area, up to 1.5m (or 5ft) from the extreme edges of cut-away timber. The second coat should be applied only when the first has been absorbed. The application rate for

timber is about 4.5 litre (1gal) to 60sq m (or 650sq ft) – but check carefully with the manufacturer's instructions. Before applying the fluid, coat any exposed rubber-covered cables with a polyurethane wood sealer to prevent the fungicide damaging the rubber.

Making good

Once the rot has been removed and new timber fitted, you can make good all decorations. Where wall plaster was hacked away, render the wall with a mix of one part cement, one part lime and six parts sand. As a precaution against further attacks you should apply a 6mm ($\frac{1}{4}$in) coat of zinc oxychloride plaster over the rendering coat to an area extending 300mm (or 12in) beyond the attacked timber. Render all surfaces adjacent to the zinc oxychloride plaster – which is now above the level of the surrounding plaster – with a further coat of the cement, lime and sand mix to level off the area.

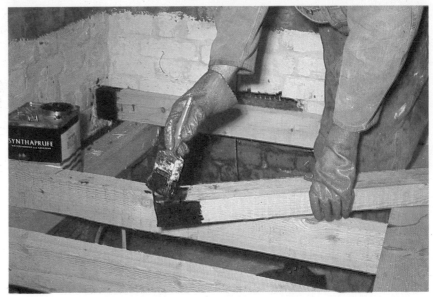

Replace skirtings or floorboards which have been removed and repair or replace other affected areas, such as window sills or door frames.

Removing cause

You may have to repair structural defects to correct the cause of the rot. Clear blocked airbricks with an old screwdriver or insert new ones. If the damp proof course is defective or non-existent, a new one should be inserted. Always seek expert advice before attempting repairs of this nature.

Wet rot

Less drastic treatment is needed to stop the spread of wet rot. The cause of dampness must be corrected and the timber allowed to dry out. The fungus will then die off.

Treatment is in three stages. First cut out any wood that is completely rotted, protect any attacked timber that still retains adequate structural strength and, finally, treat all surrounding timber.

Work outwards from the area of badly rotting wood and test all surrounding wood with a sharp penknife until sound timber is detected. Cut out and burn all diseased timber, together with dust, dirt and debris. When replacing timber, use only well-seasoned dry wood. After cutting it to size, give it two generous coats of a proprietary rot fluid or wood preservative and immerse any end grain in the fluid for several minutes before fixing. Use wood filler for minor areas.

Treat all adjacent timbers, brick, concrete and blocks with at least two liberal coats of fluid or preservative. Ends of joists being replaced should be painted with bituminous paint (for wood) or covered with bituminous felt.

Make good any decorations in the same way as for dry rot but, if you have to replaster walls, finish them with anhydrous (wall finish) plaster.

Above Coat the ends of new timber with wood preservative for protection
Left Remove floorboards and spray the fungicidal fluid underneath

Treating damp walls internally

Various damp treatments are available for internal walls in the home; they do not cure the dampness in the wall, but they will prevent the effects of damp ruining inside decoration. Although suitable for any room, they are especially useful in cellars and basements where access for external treatment is a problem. Before carrying out treatment, always check the manufacturer's instructions carefully.

Bituminous emulsion

This rubber-rich substance adheres strongly to a smooth surface to leave a black, waterproof, elastic film. The method of treatment depends on the extent of dampness in the wall; in moderately damp conditions with reasonably sound plaster, you will first have to strip off all loose distemper, paint and dirt and repair any damaged plaster.

Before use, and occasionally during use, stir the emulsion thoroughly. Put it on with a brush, working in one direction only to give an even coating. Before starting work, dip the brush in water and shake off the moisture. When you are working it is best to immerse the bristles only halfway into the emulsion. The type of brush you should use depends on how the wall is to be finished after treatment. Where a lining paper is to be used as a base for normal decorating, you will need soft bristle brushes; where a plaster finish is required, use coconut fibre brushes. You will find you need two brushes to prevent hold-ups during the work because after five to ten minutes' use a brush should be placed in water and left to soften.

When applying the treatment, you must first dampen the affected surface with water. Put on three coats of emulsion, allowing each to dry thoroughly before applying the next. For each coat of emulsion, allow 5 litres (or 1 gal) per 11sq m (or 13sq yd). You can speed up the drying process by using a fan type electric heater. At the end of the day, suspend the brushes in creosote and next day wipe them dry and clean them off in turpentine or a proprietary equivalent.

Warning The fumes from this substance can be harmful, so make sure the room in which you are working is very well ventilated.

If the wall is very damp, a more rigorous preparation is needed. Use a cold chisel and a club hammer to hack the existing plaster back to the brickwork and spread a thin layer of cement mortar (six parts sand to one part cement and one part lime) over the brickwork. When this is dry, dampen the surface with water and apply three coats of emulsion. While the final coat is still tacky you should sand-blind it by throwing clean sharp sand at the surface with a shovel – wear protective spectacles or some other form of eye protection when carrying out this process. The sand-blinding provides a key for a plaster finish which you should apply in a layer at least 6mm ($\frac{1}{4}$in) thick.

Preparing for decoration Leave new plaster to dry out thoroughly (two to three months) before decorating, then prepare the surface to suit the kind of material you are using for decoration. For emulsion paint, allow the wall to dry then hang lining paper with heavy duty cellulose paste.

Emulsion paint can be applied direct to a plaster finish as long as the plaster is at least 6mm ($\frac{1}{4}$in) thick. You should apply a coat of plaster sealer (or a coat of emulsion thinned down with water) followed by two coats of emulsion. If you intend using oil paint, a plaster finish at least 15mm (or $\frac{5}{8}$in) thick over a sand-blinding is required. Apply two layers of plaster and allow it to dry – this can take up to six months. You can test for the degree of dryness by using a damp meter; repair the holes made by the prongs of the damp meter with cellulose filler. For wallpaper, hang lining paper horizontally over the bituminous emulsion with heavy duty cellulose paste; use the same paste to fix the wallpaper over it. For vinyl or washable paper, a 15mm (or $\frac{5}{8}$in) thick plaster surface is needed.

1a Before treating a very damp wall with bituminous emulsion, hack back the plaster to the brickwork and apply a thin layer of cement mortar

1b After dampening the mortar with water, brush on three coats of emulsion, working in one direction only; leave each coat to dry before applying the next

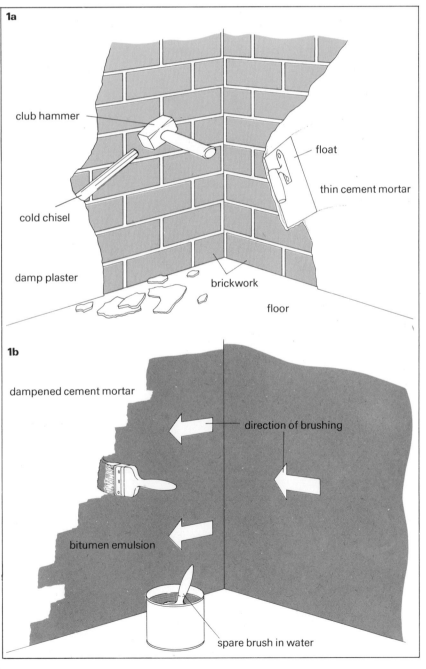

1a
club hammer
cold chisel
damp plaster
float
thin cement mortar
brickwork
floor

1b
dampened cement mortar
direction of brushing
bitumen emulsion
spare brush in water

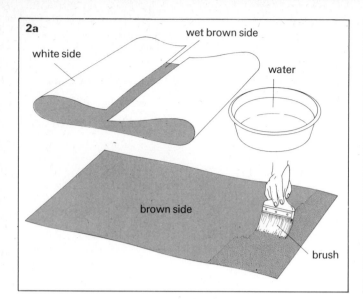

2a
white side
wet brown side
water
brown side
brush

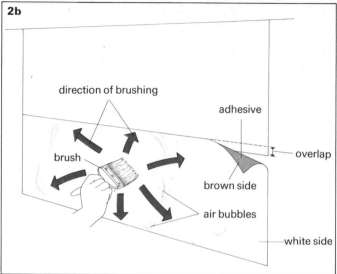

2b
direction of brushing
adhesive
brush
overlap
brown side
air bubbles
white side

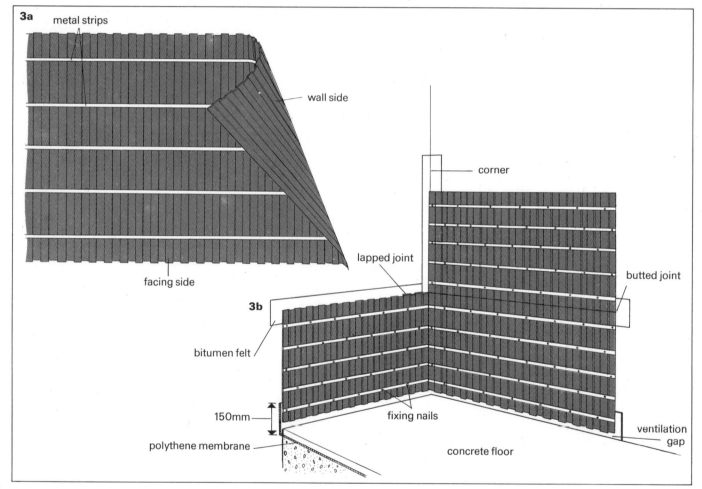

3a
metal strips
wall side
facing side

3b
corner
lapped joint
butted joint
bitumen felt
150mm
fixing nails
ventilation gap
polythene membrane
concrete floor

Waterproof laminate

This material comes with a special adhesive and produces a long-lasting barrier which stops both damp penetration and the appearance of efflorescent salts. It will adhere to moist surfaces.

Remove existing loose wallpaper, paint or distemper, repair damaged plaster, sand down any high spots in the wall and remove the skirting boards. Brush on a diluted coat of adhesive to prime the wall and allow this to dry for an hour. The laminate is hung in horizontal lengths, allowing a little excess for trimming. It has a white and a brown side; brush water onto the brown side of

each length and fold the ends loosely to the middle with the brown surface inside. Wait an hour, then brush adhesive onto the wall to cover an area to be occupied by one length of laminate; hang the laminate immediately with the brown surface against the wall. Brush outwards over it to remove air bubbles. Even after this there may be a slightly bubbly appearance, but this will disappear in time. Hang successive lengths of laminate so the edges overlap each preceding length by 13mm ($\frac{1}{2}$in). Use a sharp knife to trim off excess laminate at the wall sides and allow 24 hours before carrying out decoration and refitting skirting boards.

2a Dampen waterproof laminate, fold it loosely and leave it for an hour
2b When hanging, place the lengths of laminate horizontally on the walls
3a With corrugated pitch-impregnated fibre base make sure the metal strips face into the room
3b When fixing to the wall, butt horizontal joints and lap vertical ones

Pitch-impregnated fibre base

Any condition of damp wall can be treated using this material, since it forms an entirely new wall surface. It is available in 5 × 1m (or 16ft 6in × 3ft 3in) rolls and is corrugated with a dovetail key to provide for plaster on one side and insulating cavities on the other.

Remove the skirting and any cove and use a cold chisel and club hammer to hack damp plaster back to the brickwork of the wall and for about 1m (or 3ft) along adjoining party or partition walls in case damp has crept into these walls as well. Using a sharp knife, cut the rolls into lengths according to the width of bare wall. You may have to trim the width of the final strip of material to fit the remaining gap at the top of the wall; where there is a solid floor, the material should stop 25–50mm (1–2in) above floor level. (This provides ventilation and the gap can be covered by skirting later). On a suspended timber floor the material should be laid between the wall and the floorboards.

Place each length in position against the wall with the corrugations vertical and the metal strips facing into the room. Nail through the corrugations at intervals of 200–300mm (or 8–12in) with galvanized clout nails or hardened masonry nails, depending on the wall surface. Alternatively, on a very hard surface, use a cartridge gun (available on hire) to shoot nails through special rectangular washers which fix into the corrugations. Any polythene damp proof membrane on a newly screeded floor should rise 150mm (6in) on to the wall and be placed behind the material.

The material is flexible and therefore can be bent round corners. Try to avoid joining lengths at corners; if this is unavoidable, place a 100mm (4in) wide strip of bitumen felt behind the joint as reinforcement to prevent the plaster finish (which is later applied over the material) being pushed through to contact the damp wall. Vertical joints must be lapped, while horizontal joints are butted up and lined with 100mm (4in) wide strips of bitumen felt. If the material has to be cut to fit round pipework, the gaps should be sealed with waterproof mastic.

When the wall is fully lined a normal three-coat plastering can be applied. If necessary, you can use a render and setting coat to leave a joint flush with any existing plaster or adjacent areas. Drying out will take longer than usual, since the damp treatment material does not absorb water; so make sure of good ventilation to speed up the process.

Alternatively you can use panel boards to finish over the material. The boards can be nailed through into the wall or fixed by applying blobs of special adhesive at 350–450mm (or 14–18in) intervals to the back of the board. This adhesive can be obtained with the damp-treatment material; a 5kg (or 10lb) tub of adhesive is sufficient for 12sq m (or 18sq yd). Rest the boards on a level 50 × 25mm (2 × 1in) timber plinth to ensure a neat joint between boards and to give the required air circulation gap at the base.

The adhesive will set in two or three days and temporary support can be provided with one or two hardened fixing pins in the middle of the panel. These can be removed or driven home later. Use brown paper tape, masking tape or cellulose filler to seal the joints between boards. You can, if you wish, apply a skim coat of plaster over plasterboard panels. Wallpaper or lining paper and emulsion paint can also be applied to the boards.

Finally replace the skirting, having checked there are no signs of rot or decay, and cover the gap between the top of the lining material and the ceiling with cove. Fix the cove to the wall and flush with the top of the lining, or to the ceiling, leaving a slight gap between the cove and the wall to provide ventilation.

Levelling wall Sometimes it may be necessary to level an uneven wall before applying the damp treatment material. You can do this by lining the wall with battens – before fixing, treat these with a wood preservative. Use a spirit level to find true horizontals and fill any low areas behind the battens with timber packing.

Arrange the battens so all the edges of the damp treatment material will be supported – one or two intermediate horizontal batten supports should also be provided. Space the battens at approximately 330mm (or 13in) intervals and place the corrugations of the material at right-angles to the battens.

3c Fix panels over the fibre base with adhesive, using timber plinths to ensure the panels are held level and to provide a ventilation gap; remove the plinths when the adhesive has set

3d On an uneven wall you will need to fix a series of battens to ensure flush fixing of the fibre base. Pack any lower areas behind the battens with pieces of scrap wood

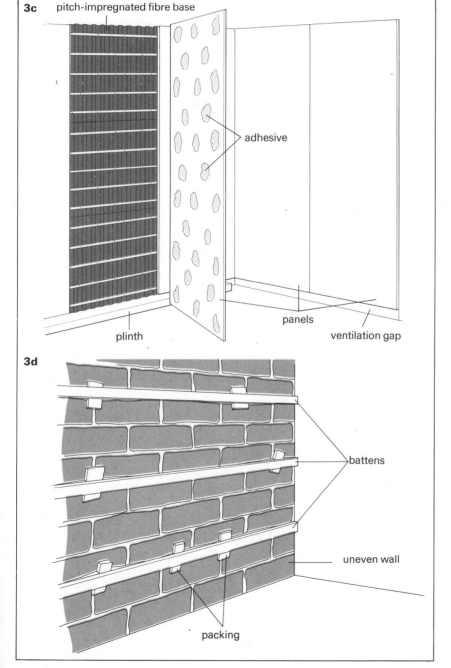

3c pitch-impregnated fibre base
adhesive
plinth
panels
ventilation gap

3d battens
uneven wall
packing

Installing a damp-proof course

Rising damp is indicated by a tide mark just above floor level on internal walls. It does not usually rise more than about 1m (or 3ft) up the wall. Its presence means either there is no damp proof course (dpc), which is common in houses built before 1875, or that an existing dpc has failed. A dpc that is not functioning should be regarded as non-existent.

Most methods of installing a dpc should be employed only by specialists. A method which you can use yourself, however, is the infusion into a wall of a special dampcoursing solution which gels within the wall and creates a continuous chemical barrier to prevent rising damp. The system is widely used by specialists, but you should be able to achieve equally good results provided you are very thorough. If the job is skimped, the dpc will break down in places and the rising damp will return. One specialist company provides detailed working sheets and a technical advisory service.

When selecting a DIY damp proofing process, check the company supplying the materials and instructions offers a guarantee which would be acceptable for mortgage purposes.

Warning The infusion system cannot be used for walls of more than 450mm (18in) thickness, or walls constructed of materials other than brick or soft sandstone.

Inserting the dpc

The job involves three processes: drilling the holes at a selected level, carrying out a preliminary run with water to test for damaged brickwork and the infusion of the fluid.

Selecting position The level at which the dpc is to be inserted depends on whether the ground floor of the house is of suspended timber construction or solid concrete. If it is a timber floor, the dpc should be immediately below the floor level; with a concrete floor it should be adjacent to the floor.

If it is impracticable to insert a dpc below a suspended timber floor – for example, where there is a patio – it will have to be inserted at floor level. In such a case, spray the floor joists and floorboards liberally with a good timber preservative to prevent attack by rot.

Where a house is on sloping ground, step the dpc to follow the line of the ground floor. In a semi-basement install the dpc above ground level to a height of about 150mm (6in). Internal rendering, carried out after insertion of the dpc, will prevent damp rising above this level.

Drilling Use a lightweight rotary hammer drill, obtainable from a hire shop, and fit it with a 16 mm ($\frac{5}{8}$in) diameter drill bit. The length of the bit needed will depend on the depth of the holes to be drilled, which in turn will depend on the thickness of the wall. Fix a piece of adhesive tape to the drill bit at the required depth to guide you.

In all cases holes should be drilled at an angle of 30 degrees downwards from the outside face of the brickwork and at 75mm (3in) intervals horizontally; start drilling just above a mortar joint. If working from one side only, use the side most accessible and convenient. Remove the skirting board before drilling on the internal wall. If you are drilling through a party wall, let your neighbours know what you are doing.

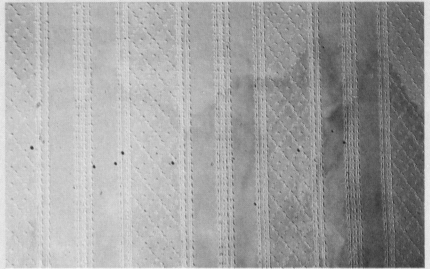

For 112.5mm (4½in) brickwork Drill to a depth of 100mm (4in), working from one side only.

For 225mm (9in) brickwork Drill to a depth of 200mm (8in), working from one side only.

For 337.5mm (13½in) brickwork Treat as for 225mm (9in) brickwork up to a depth of 330mm (13in). You may treat 337.5mm (13½in) brickwork from both sides if wished. In this case, drill 200mm (8in) holes one side and 100mm (4in) holes the other side.

For 450mm (18in) brickwork Treat from both sides, drilling 200mm (8in) deep holes.

For 275mm (11in) cavity brickwork Drill 100mm (4in) deep holes from both sides.

Water test If you inserted damp course liquid into a wall which was cracked or otherwise damaged, it would seep out of the cracks and be wasted. To prevent this, make a trial run with water to find out if there is any damage. Fill each hole to the brim, using a funnel. If the water disappears quickly, this indicates there are cracks. Fill the holes with a mix of two parts sand and one part cement to seal the cracks, ramming the mortar

Top The existence of damp in walls can easily be identified by the presence of mould growth
Above Rising damp will be detected inside the house when wall coverings become stained and start to peel away from the wall
1a If you are treating a wall behind which there is a suspended timber floor, the new dpc should be immediately below floor level
1b If you are working where there is a solid floor, make sure your new dpc is installed at the same level as that of the floor
1c If the area you are tackling includes floors of different levels, you will have to step the new dpc between the levels

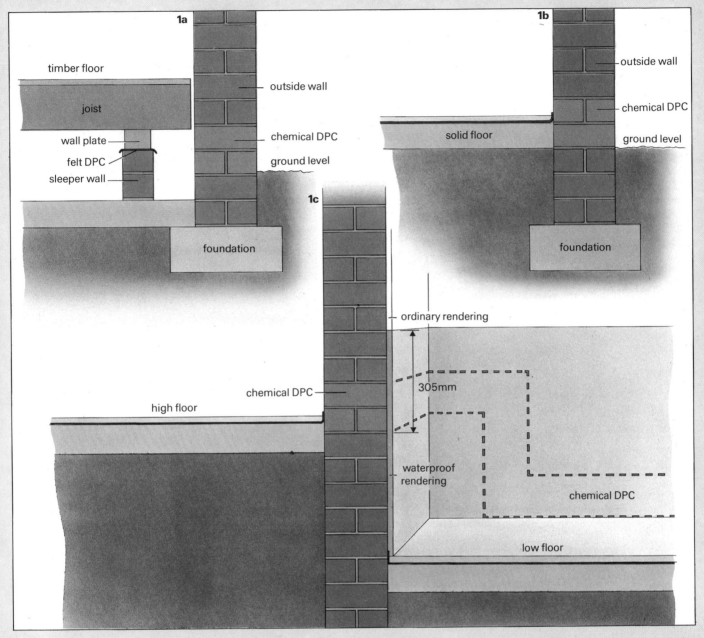

1a timber floor / joist / wall plate / felt DPC / sleeper wall / outside wall / chemical DPC / ground level / foundation

1b outside wall / chemical DPC / ground level / solid floor / foundation

1c high floor / chemical DPC / ordinary rendering / 305mm / waterproof rendering / chemical DPC / low floor

firmly into the holes with a length of dowel the same diameter as the holes; let the mortar dry before redrilling the holes in the same places.

Walls vary in porosity, so use the trial run to assess the absorption rate. This will enable you to judge how many holes you can fill at a time when you use the fluid.

Introducing the fluid Don't introduce the damp-proofing solution until at least six hours after the water test. You can hire special irrigation bottles for pouring in the fluid or use a jug and offset funnel. As a guide to the amount of fluid needed, a hole drilled in a 225mm (9in) wall will take about 190ml (⅓pt), which is about the same as filling each hole four and a half times. So use a jug holding 570ml (1pt) and allocate one jugful to three consecutive holes.

It is important not to allow a hole to empty or the liquid will start to cure at the mouth of the hole and prevent further saturation. If the absorption is particularly speedy, do not tackle too many holes at a time.

Fill the first three holes to the brim and keep the remaining liquid for topping up, doing this progressively and methodically until all the holes have been filled.

Leave the holes for a few weeks while the solution is drying out. Then fill with a mix of three parts sand to one part cement.

Finishing treatment
When the dpc has been installed, rising damp will cease but there will still be dampness in the walls due to the action of hygroscopic (moisture absorbent) salts, general condensation or water penetration. The finishing process stops the damp and eliminates the effects.

First remove the skirting boards so the walls can be treated down to skirting level. Where dampness has existed for a few years, hack off the plaster to bare brick; work to a point about 450mm (18in) above the highest damp patch.

Porous brickwork Where the brickwork is porous, you need to treat it to prevent water penetration. Before treating it, cut out and replace any damaged bricks and repoint defective mortar joints. Then brush or spray on two coats of a silicone-based waterproofer and sealer to the outside wall.

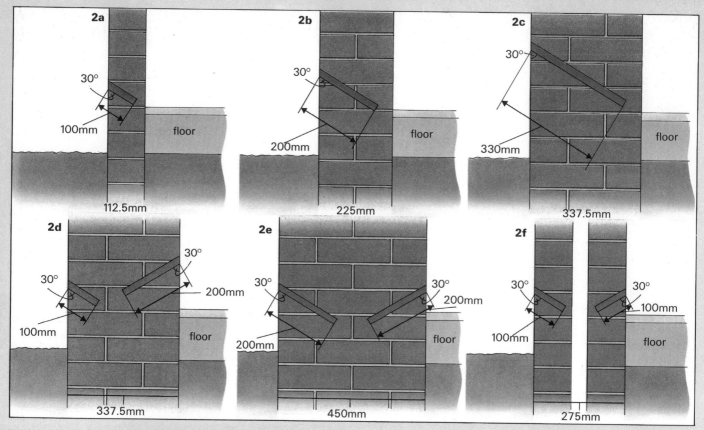

2a 30° 100mm floor 112.5mm

2b 30° 200mm floor 225mm

2c 30° 330mm floor 337.5mm

2d 30° 30° 200mm 100mm floor 337.5mm

2e 30° 30° 200mm 200mm floor 450mm

2f 30° 30° 200mm 100mm 100mm floor 275mm

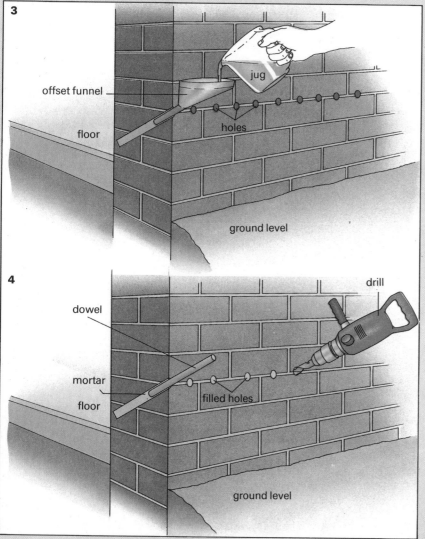

3 — offset funnel, floor, jug, holes, ground level

4 — dowel, mortar, floor, drill, filled holes, ground level

2a–f Drilling positions for different wall thicknesses. **3** Before adding damp proof liquid, pour water into the drilled holes **4** If it disappears quickly, seal the holes with mortar, ram down with dowel and redrill

Removing mineral salts Rising damp will dissolve some mineral salts from the brickwork, which will diffuse through the wall and plasterwork in damp conditions and, on drying out on the surface, will show as a whitish chalky substance (efflorescence). These salts are hygroscopic (moisture absorbent) and if sufficient water is absorbed. they will dissolve in it forming condensation.

Use a chemical neutralizer to treat the affected area. Apply the solution to the brickwork with a 100mm (4in) paint brush. Work quickly and make sure you treat all areas where hygroscopic salt and efflorescent action was evident on the plaster. The solution penetrates up to 150mm (6in) into the brickwork and forms a barrier to the soluble salts while the wall is drying out.

Rendering After at least 48 hours, render with a sand and cement mix (eight parts sand to one part cement) containing an integral waterproofer diluted with ten parts water. Add a mortar plasticizer to make the mix more workable. Apply the render at least 10mm ($\frac{3}{8}$in) thick and finish with a lightweight plaster skim. Leave a gap of at least 38mm ($1\frac{1}{2}$in) between the render and plaster and the floor; the gap will be concealed when you replace the skirting.

Where a high ground level was involved (for example, a semi-basement) and the dpc was installed 150mm (6in) above ground level, a slightly different treatment is required at the base of the wall. From a point 300mm (or 12in) above ground level down to floor level apply three coats of rendering. When refixing the skirting, use impact adhesive so there is no danger of the rendering being punctured by nails.

Coping with condensation

For most people condensation conjures up pictures of bathroom walls running with moisture, windows steamed up and water on the window sills. These more easily recognizable forms of condensation can be temporarily cleared up with a little time and effort devoted to mopping up. But there are ways of helping to prevent condensation forming in the first place.

Condensation is caused when moisture in warm air comes into contact with a cold surface and turns to water. Kitchens and bathrooms are the obvious places to suffer, but condensation will often occur in patches on walls or ceilings in living areas too.

Windows

Single glass windows are undoubtedly one of the worst offenders in causing condensation. In damp winter conditions few homes escape the problem – and bedrooms in particular suffer from its effects. This is the result of lower night temperatures reacting with the warm air we breathe out or warm air circulated by heating equipment.

The problem is made worse by the introduction of new moist air into a room by cooking, using hand basins or running baths. Probably the worst effect of condensation is the damage it can do in a short time to window frames and paintwork. Even when frames are correctly painted 3mm ($\frac{1}{8}$in) in on the glass pane, the lower beading quickly breaks down

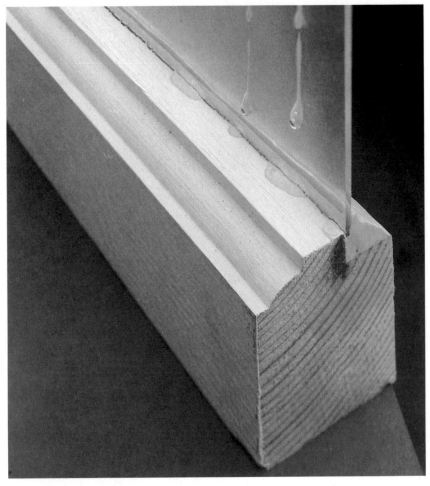

Above Condensation on window will break down paint surface and attack wood or metal frame

Far left When lining walls with expanded polystyrene, hang first length and overlap second length by about 13mm ($\frac{1}{2}$in). Check with your supplier on suitable adhesive
Left Trim halfway across overlap through both thicknesses of polystyrene

Far left Peel away both trimmed edges
Left Stick back edges, having applied more adhesive to wall, to give flush finish to join

23

To test for damp floor, place piece of glass on ring of Plasticine over affected area
Right Moisture on underside of glass indicates penetrating damp
Below right Moisture forming on top of glass indicates condensation present

and allows moisture to attack the timber or metal beneath.

One remedy is the installation of good quality double-glazing. Although condensation may not be completely eliminated, the build-up is reduced sufficiently to prevent moisture being a problem.

Bathrooms

Decorative materials with cold surfaces, such as ceramic tiles, are renowned for the rapid formation of condensation. The build-up can be quickly dispersed by opening the windows. An extractor fan set into the window or mounted on (or ducted to) an exterior wall will also help remove vapour quickly. You can reduce condensation in cold bathrooms by heating the room for a short time before running the bath water. But remember you must use wall or ceiling-mounted heaters of the type recommended for bathrooms. Try running a little cold water into the bath before you turn on the hot tap, as this will also help reduce condensation.

Other wall surfaces

The real problem areas are patches of condensation which sometimes appear in odd corners of the home. Often these go unnoticed until a patch of mould appears. Poor circulation of air is one of the prime causes and on a damp day a short burst of warm air from a fan heater, or a hair dryer, will help to check condensation.

If mould persists – and the surface is not wallpapered – rinse the wall with a strong solution of bleach. If the surface is wallpapered you will have to remove the paper and line the wall with rolls of expanded polystyrene which you can then wallpaper over or paint with emulsion. In severe cases this may not be completely successful and a painted wall, which can be treated with bleach from time to time, is preferable.

Penetrating damp

Patchy wall condensation is often confused with penetrating damp. Removal of a small area of plaster should tell you which it is. If it is condensation, the brick area behind will be perfectly dry; if it is damp, try to find the cause. At ground floor level it could be a faulty damp proof course; upstairs it may be a faulty gutter or down pipe or driving rain on porous solid brickwork might be the reason. Try to increase the circulation by warm, dry air in the affected area, but remedy the cause of the problem as soon as possible otherwise the trouble will recur.

Ceilings

Those with a high gloss finish are most susceptible to condensation and covering the area with expanded polystyrene, cork or fibre tiles will help solve the problem.

Damp floors

These are often caused by damp from the outside and not by condensation. You can make a simple test to see which condition is present with a piece of glass on a ring of Plasticine, as shown above.

Condensation on floors usually occurs with cold-surfaced materials on concrete, such as tiles in the kitchen. The most effective remedy is to substitute cork or a similar warm-surfaced flooring.

Home insulation

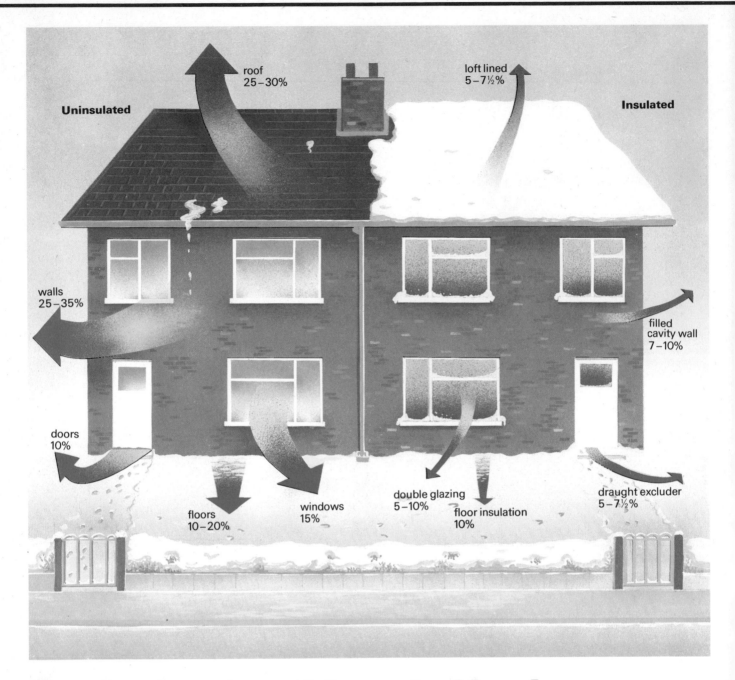

Uninsulated

roof
25–30%

loft lined
5–7½%

Insulated

walls
25–35%

filled
cavity wall
7–10%

doors
10%

floors
10–20%

windows
15%

double glazing
5–10%

floor insulation
10%

draught excluder
5–7½%

Reducing heat loss in the home

Many houses fall well below the minimum thermal insulation standards set under building regulations. Although some forms of insulation should be carried out by a professional, there is still much that can be done by the home handyman. Before you begin the process of keeping heat inside where it belongs, it is useful to understand the ways in which heat is lost from a house. The amount of heat lost does depend on the nature of the building, its aspect and exposure to winds – and figures vary from house to house.

In a typical uninsulated house approximately one-quarter is lost through the roof, one-third through the walls, one-tenth through the doors, one-fifth through the windows and one-sixth through the floors. After insulation these losses can be cut down to approximately one-twentieth, one-tenth, one-twentieth, one-ninth and one-tenth respectively. So although insulation does not prevent all the heat escaping, it substantially reduces the amount of loss and correspondingly diminishes the size of your heating bills. It shortens the time it takes to heat a room and enables you to keep down the number and size of radiators and the size of the boiler – or to install a less powerful and therefore less expensive central heating system around the home. Forms of insulation vary from the simple rubber strip draught excluder on your door to insulating boards lining the walls. What you decide to do will depend on the amount of time and money you have available; but the more thoroughly you carry out the job, the greater the rewards will be in terms of comfort and eventual savings, which will well repay the initial expense and effort.

The government, through its 'Save It' campaign, has for some time been encouraging both householders and industry to improve insulation standards in the interests of cutting the nation's horrific energy bill. If the rise in our own bills is depressing, the cost to the country as a whole is even worse, for much of our fuel is imported. Furthermore, future supplies cannot be guaranteed in a politically unstable world. Although the discovery of valuable oil and gas deposits in the North Sea has alleviated the problem, we must use this breathing space to good effect, and that means reducing energy needs where possible.

So keen is the government that we, as individuals, should reduce our energy requirements, that grants are now available to help pay for the installation of insulation material. Since these grants can represent a significant saving on the cost of basic insulation, from the laying of loft insulation to the provision of an insulating jacket around the hot water cylinder, anyone would be well advised to contact the local council for details of grant availability. The grants are available for both professionally installed and DIY schemes.

Perhaps the most beneficial insulation measure in terms of immediate savings for a low financial outlay is to invest in draught excluders. These can be remarkably inexpensive, installation is normally extremely simple, and draught excluders are very effective in raising the temperature of a room with ill-fitting doors and windows.

In time, most internal doors and windows will cease to fit snugly in their frames, and will benefit from attention. The problem can be at its most severe at the front door, where there is the extra weak point – the letter box, where wind can whistle through every time a newspaper or letter is

delivered. Luckily there are draught seals designed specifically to cope with the problem, sealing off the draughts without excluding the morning's post!

Similarly, there are special insulating jackets for hot water cylinders, which should be the next stage of the campaign against heat loss. None of these jackets should prove so effective it prevents enough heat escaping from the cylinder to keep an airing cupboard warm. Insulation of the plumbing system should not end at the hot water cylinder. All pipes require protection from freezing weather, particularly those exposed to the elements in the loft space. Time and money spent in insulating the pipes will be more than repaid by the time and money you save by avoiding the need to repair burst pipes and blockages in a severe winter.

When the loft is insulated, as it should be, remember not to lay insulation under the cold water cistern, to allow warm air rising from the room below to keep the water temperature above freezing point in the winter. The standard loft insulation material laid between the joists can be complemented by more complex measures, such as fixing felt between the rafters, screwing tempered hardboard panels over the rafters or laying chipboard panels over the joists.

None of the insulation techniques outlined above requires any special skill to achieve a satisfactory result. However, there are certain insulation jobs which many will prefer to leave to the professional. The major items are double glazing and cavity insulation. There are undoubtedly strong arguments in favour of leaving cavity wall insulation to a professional contractor. The main advantage is that the professional will guarantee the quality of the work, which can prove useful should you want to sell your house in the future. Of course, you must be assured that the written guarantee is sound, and it is therefore advisable to select only a contractor approved by the Agrement Board, whose work conforms with strict quality standards.

The arguments in favour of professionally installed double glazing are less overwhelming. This can be a very expensive item, and it could take many years before your investment begins to show a profit in terms of fuel bill savings. Obviously the cheaper the installation the quicker the return, as long as the double glazing is effective. The very cheapest form of double 'glazing' is provided by a sheet of plastic kitchen film fixed to the window frame with adhesive tape. This will pay for itself almost immediately, but some may feel that visually this is an unappealing proposition.

There is absolutely no reason why the DIY job should look inferior to a professional installation, as there is a growing number of attractive DIY systems on the market. Before you call in the professionals, study the various DIY options explained in the chapter on double glazing (see page 39). Fixing should not present insuperable problems, the most frequently heard complaint of the DIY double glazing practitioner being problems with condensation. The solution to this is to allow the circulation of air inside the cavity – which is explained on page 39.

Proper insulation measures will help protect your home, but the temptation to 'over-insulate' should be avoided. It is regrettably common to see airbricks blocked off by householders anxious to keep out the cold. Dry rot thrives in a damp, still atmosphere, and proper circulation of air is therefore crucial.

Insulating the loft

Heating costs rise with the warm air if heat is allowed to escape through the roof. By insulating the loft area you can keep down the bills and hold heat where it belongs – in the house. This is a job well within the scope of the handyman, requiring no special techniques. The materials are all readily available.

A loft that has no insulation will account for a heat loss of about 25 per cent in the average size house. Several forms of insulation are available and fall into two categories: loose-fill materials such as vermiculite granules, and the blanket type made from glass fibre or mineral wool. The materials we mention are all resistant to fire and you must check on the fire-resistance of any alternative product you consider buying. As a precaution, first treat all timber for woodworm.

joists in most houses, and can be cut quite easily with a large pair of scissors or a sharp knife. Even handled carefully, glass fibre can irritate the skin, so always wear gloves when working with it.

Mineral wool (Rocksil) Another blanket type, this is made from rock fibre and is handled in the same way as glass fibre.

Laying rolls Place the roll of material between the joists and tuck the end under the eaves. Working backwards, unroll the material until you reach the other end of the roof. Cut it and tuck the end under the eaves as before. Lay the strip flat between the joists or, if it is a little wider, turn the sides up against the sides of the joists. Continue in this way until the whole loft area has been covered. If you have to join two strips in the middle of the roof, overlap them by about 75mm (3in).

Below left To lay granules, pour them between joists and level them with T-shaped piece of timber
Below If your insulating roll is wider than space between joists, turn up each side against joists
Below centre Don't lay insulation under cold water cistern; leave area uncovered so warm air from below can stop water freezing
Bottom Use latex adhesive to glue piece of glass fibre on loft flap

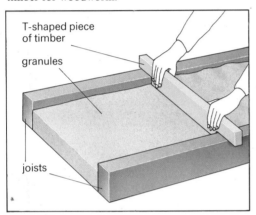

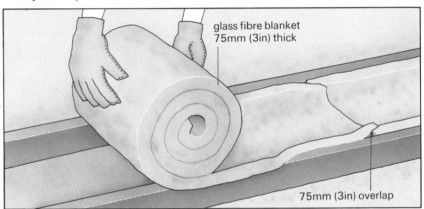

glass fibre blanket 75mm (3in) thick

75mm (3in) overlap

Granule insulation

One advantage of using granules to insulate your loft is that they flow easily and smoothly and will fill any awkward spaces. They are also safe to handle since they do not contain any splinters or loose fibres.

Vermiculite Expanded mica in granule form, this is supplied in easy-to-handle bags. The manufacturer's instructions will give you a guide to the number of bags needed for specific areas.

You should wear a mask and some form of eye protection when using vermiculite since it is a dusty material that easily gets into the atmosphere.

Laying granules Pour vermiculite between the joists to a depth of about 100mm (4in), which will bring it almost to the level of the joists. Level the granules to the required depth by dragging a T-shaped piece of timber along the top of the joists. This can be made from any piece of scrap wood at least 150mm (or 6in) wide and 500mm (or 20in) long. You must cut the base of the 'T' to fit the gaps between the joists. Use a broom or rake for awkward corners.

Blanket insulation

This form of insulation does not need to be laid as thickly as granules and should be used in lofts where there are gaps around the eaves, since wind might blow the granules about.

Glass fibre The most economical form of blanket insulation for loft spaces. It comes in 80 or 100mm (3 or 4in) thick rolls and is available in 400mm (16in) widths, equivalent to the space between roof

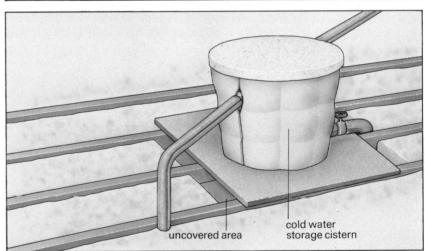

uncovered area

cold water storage cistern

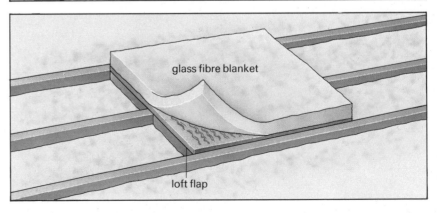

glass fibre blanket

loft flap

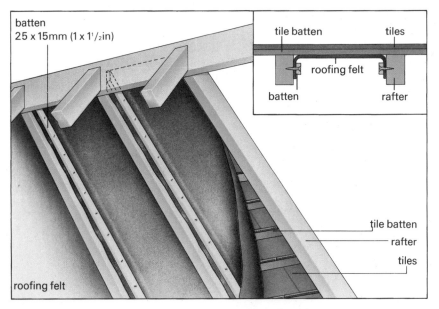

batten
25 x 15mm (1 x 1¹/₂in)

tile batten   tiles

roofing felt

batten   rafter

tile batten
rafter
tiles

roofing felt

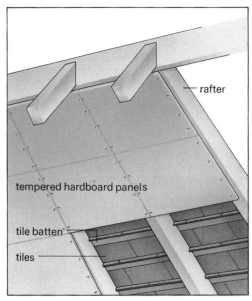

rafter

tempered hardboard panels

tile batten

tiles

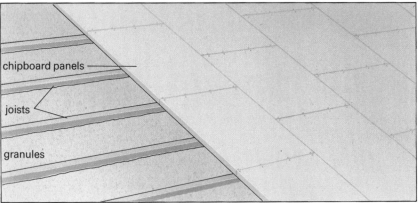

chipboard panels

joists

granules

Top When fixing felt between rafters, allow enough width to turn onto rafters and hold felt in place by screwing through battens and felt into rafters. **Inset** Cross-section of felt and batten fixing

Top right When insulating with tempered hardboard, butt-join panels and fix to rafters with countersunk screws

Above Improve insulation by laying floor using chipboard panels, staggering joins and screwing through sides of each panel into joists. Cut panels so they butt-join each other in middle of each joist

Insulating awkward areas You will find it easier to cover awkwardly shaped or inaccessible areas with granules. A 100mm (4in) thickness of granules is equivalent to 80mm (3in) of blanket materials in terms of effective insulation.

Warning Whichever method of insulation you use, don't insulate under the cold water tank. You must allow a warm air current to flow from below to prevent the tank from freezing in cold weather. But don't forget to insulate the loft flap or cover. Cut a piece of blanket material to the size of the cover and stick it down with a latex adhesive. And when working in the loft, remember to tread only on the joists or on a board placed across them.

Other forms of insulation

Even more insulation can be provided if you make a floor to the loft by fixing panels of chipboard or planks of timber to the joists above the insulating material. This will also give you extra storage space, but you may have to strengthen the joists by spanning the load-bearing walls with large timbers before laying the floor if you want to put heavy items on it. Seek advice from a builder or your local authority.

Heat loss through the roof space can be further reduced by lining the ceilings immediately below the loft with an insulating-type material such as expanded polystyrene or acoustic tiles. It should be emphasized, however, that this is not a substitute for loft insulation.

Effective insulation of the floor will make the loft colder, so it is vitally important to ensure the

cold water tank (except beneath it) and all pipes are thoroughly protected, otherwise they will be susceptible to frost damage.

Protection from frost

The type of loft most likely to suffer from frost damage is one with an unboarded tile-hung roof. If your roof has no close-boarding or roofing felt – as is the case with many older houses – it is worth insulating it.

Cut lengths of roofing felt about 200mm (8in) wider than the distance between the rafters. Lay one long edge onto the inside edge of one rafter, lay a 25 × 15mm (1 × ½in) batten onto the felt and screw through the batten and felt into the rafter. Use No 8 countersunk screws 25mm long, spacing them at 300–380mm (12–15in) intervals. Don't use nails as the vibration from hammering could dislodge and break the roof tiles. Stretch the roof felt across to the next rafter and fix the other edge onto the edge of that rafter, again screwing through a batten. Leave a space between the roof and the felt to allow air to circulate, otherwise you may find rot will form on the rafters.

An alternative to roofing felt is tempered hardboard: butt-joint each panel of hardboard to the next by screwing it to the centre of each rafter with No 8 countersunk screws 25mm long. You may have to trim your cut panels so they fit neatly in the middle of each rafter.

All this work can be done in easy stages; when you have finished, the roof space will certainly remain warmer in winter and will also be much cleaner – an important consideration if you are using the loft for storage.

Cutting sheets to size

Boards are available in 2440 × 1830mm (8 × 6ft) and 1830 × 1220mm (6 × 4ft) sheets. You need 25mm (1in) thick flooring grade chipboard or 6mm (¼in) thick hardboard. Cut the larger sheet into six convenient 1830 × 407mm (6ft × 1ft 4in) panels, or the smaller one into three panels of the same size. If the loft opening space allows, cut the larger sheet into three 1830 × 813mm (6ft × 2ft 8in) panels, or the smaller sheet into one similar size panel and one 1830 × 407mm (6ft × 1ft 4in) panel.

Door, floor and window insulation

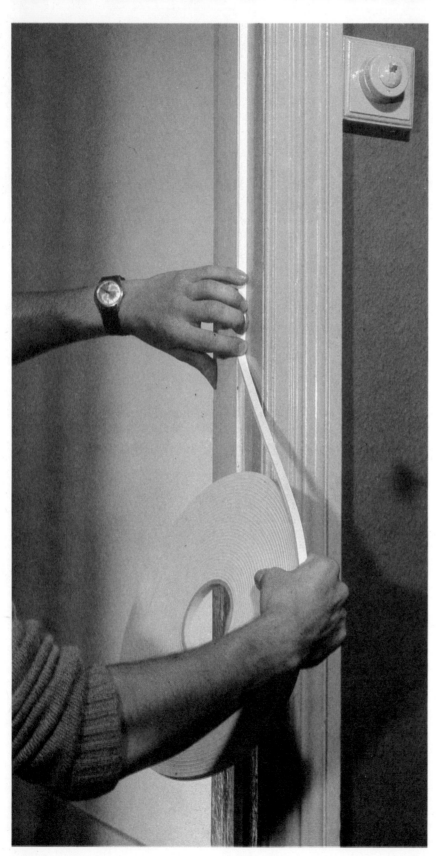

Cold air leaking in through gaps around doors and windows or through floorboards can account for up to ten per cent of the heat lost from a house. Eliminating the worst effects of draughts through doors, floors and windows is quite a simple task for the handyman, giving immediate financial returns which quickly pay for the inexpensive materials. Your winters will also be considerably more comfortable in a draught-free home. One solution to prevent draughts and help keep up the inside heat is to fit an excluder.

Draught excluders
One of the cheapest draught excluders is the plastic foam strip with an adhesive backing which you peel off as you apply the strip to a clean surface and cut to length with scissors. Although this is simple to use, it is less durable than other types and has to be replaced each year. It is effective if the gaps are not too wide and two strips can be used, for instance, on doors and door jambs or windows and frames so they come together when the door or window is closed.

Two more permanent draught excluders are the plastic (polypropylene) strip and the sprung metal strip. Both of these have ready-punched clearance holes, usually at about 25mm (1in) intervals, are tacked round the door or window rebate and are not visible when the door is closed. Because closing the door puts the strip under tension, however, it can cause the door to stick.

When using aluminium or phosphor bronze strips, position them with care and make sure there are no kinks when nailing them into place. For metal windows you should use an aluminium strip with a special groove to fit the window frame. Clean the frame with a stiff wire brush to remove rust and dirt and fill pit holes with plastic filler before applying the strip. If you clean right down to the bare metal you will have to apply a coat of metal primer after filling holes and leave it to dry before fixing the strip. With wire cutters or scissors, cut the strip in sections to the size of the frame sides and mitre across the width at the ends of each section. Fitting the top piece first and then the sides and bottom, push the groove of the strip over the outside lip of the frame. Push the corner clip tongues over the strip junctions and then turn the tongues of the clips over the flanges to secure the strip.

Under-door draughts
To eliminate draughts under doors, you can nail or screw a piece of 6mm ($\frac{1}{4}$in) thick timber batten at regular intervals, say two nails or screws per floorboard, across the threshold to form an effective seal. A carpet of the same thickness placed either side of the batten will stop people tripping

Foam tape seal, impregnated with adhesive, comes in 5 or 20m (16 or 65ft) long rolls. Easy to apply, it can be painted; and because it is very flexible you do not have to mitre the corners

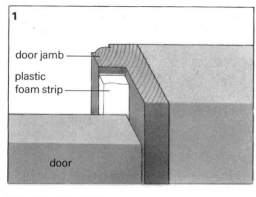

1

door jamb
plastic foam strip
door

2

door jamb
plastic or spring metal strip
door

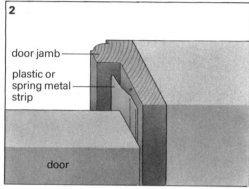

3

glass
fixed frame
corner clip tongue
putty
flange
groove
opening frame
aluminium strip

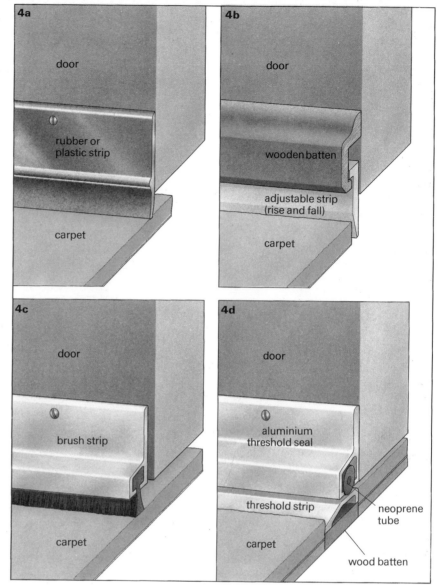

4a

door
rubber or plastic strip
carpet

4b

door
wooden batten
adjustable strip (rise and fall)
carpet

4c

door
brush strip
carpet

4d

door
aluminium threshold seal
threshold strip
neoprene tube
wood batten
carpet

For doors and windows
excluder (of type required)
tacks, nails, screws, adhesive (as needed)
wire-cutters or tin snips
scissors
hammer
hacksaw (for aluminium)
panel saw (for wood)
screwdriver
plane (as needed)
wire brush (as needed)
plastic filler (as needed)
metal primer (as needed)

For floors
papier mâché or wood filler
22mm ($\frac{7}{8}$in) quadrant or scotia moulding
32mm ($1\frac{1}{4}$in) oval wire nails
paper-faced glass fibre flanged
    building roll
knife
staple gun
staples
hammer
filling knife

equipment

over it. Alternatively, bevel the edges of the batten with a plane to make a less sharp rise from the floor.

Other excluders are made of rubber mouldings, aluminium sections or a combination of metal and plastic, so you must choose the most effective for the job in hand.

Warning You may have to take the door off its hinges and trim the bottom so the door opens and shuts freely. Otherwise, fix excluders when the door is in place.

A simple type of excluder for interior doors is a flexible plastic or rubber strip which you screw or stick to the bottom of the door so it brushes over the floor covering. Measure carefully so you do not fix this too high to be effective or too low so as to put too much wear on the floor covering. If the door has to clear a mat, a rise and fall type excluder is available. Here a flexible strip is forced, by moving over the floor covering, to ride up into a hollow wood moulding fitted to the bottom of the door and drops back into place when the door is shut. A brush strip excluder and aluminium threshold seal are also designed to ride over carpets. For exterior doors some draught excluder threshold strips come in two halves – one is fixed to the threshold and the other to the door. The two halves interlock when the door is closed.

1 Plastic foam strip attached to door jamb
2 Plastic or sprung metal strip fixed to door jamb
3 Aluminium strip around window frame
4a Flexible rubber or plastic strip on bottom of door
4b Rise and fall strip
4c Brush strip attached to metal plate at bottom of door to ride over carpet
4d Aluminium threshold seal with threshold strip raised to clear carpet

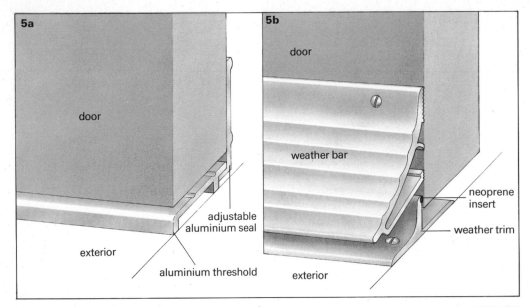

5a Aluminium door strip in two halves which interlock

5b Weatherproof threshold excluder

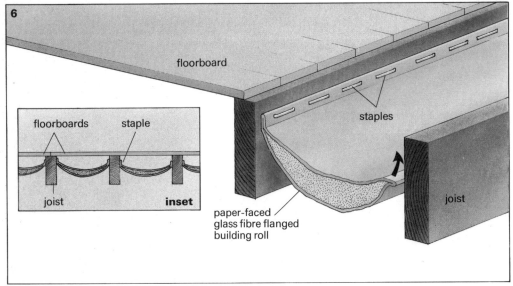

6 Paper-faced glass fibre flanged building roll stapled between joists. **Inset** Staple to each joist in turn to insulate complete floor

A badly-fitting letter-box can be very draughty. Inexpensive draught excluders are made specifically to overcome this problem.

Floor draughts

Having prevented draughts around doors and windows, the problem may still not have been entirely solved. Floorboards may have gaps which you should plug with papier-mâché or wood filler. You can also nail down strips of quadrant or scotia moulding to the floor to cover gaps between the floor and the skirting. Covering the floor with either vinyl or carpet afterwards makes an even better job.

If the boards are badly worn and damaged, and there are a lot of gaps between them, it is best to relay the floor. If it is a ground-floor room this is a good opportunity to install underfloor insulation. **Underfloor insulation** A very simple method is to staple paper-faced, glass-fibre, flanged building roll under the floorboards. Rolls are available in a range of widths to fit exactly between the joists.

Using a staple gun or hammer and staples, fix one flange of the roll to a joist. The staples should be about 100mm (4in) apart. Then staple the flange on the other side of the roll to the next joist and repeat the process for the other joists to complete the insulation.

Checking for draughts

It is best to work systematically around the house so no likely areas are missed. Eliminate the worst draughts first. To find out where door and window draughts are coming from, check paintwork which has not been washed down for some time. Draughts bring with them a considerable amount of dirt, so a build-up of dirt around the edges of doors and windows and their frames indicates some form of excluder is needed. Another way is to hold a lighted candle a safe distance away from the edges of doors and windows and move it gently along the line of the edge. Any sudden flickering of the flame indicates a draught. Don't get too close to any soft furnishings when using this method.

Double-glazing

Undoubtedly, this is the best answer to a draughty window and double-glazing will be covered in detail later on in the book. A well-fitting system will completely seal off the sources of entry of cold air. Although this is certainly an expensive undertaking solely to overcome draughts, remember that not only will sound insulation be substantially increased, but additionally a quite considerable saving on fuel bills will result after the initial outlay.

Wall insulation

Heat loss through walls can be reduced in a number of ways. Apart from one specialist method, there are three simple jobs you can tackle yourself – lining walls with plasterboard laminate, expanded polystyrene or foil.

Heat produced in a house eventually escapes to the outside via draughts and through the roof, walls and windows. The nature of the building affects the rate of loss and the path it takes. A bungalow loses more heat through the roof, while a two-storey detached house loses more through the walls. After thermal insulation there will still be heat losses, but the warmth will be dissipated at a much slower rate and heat can therefore be replaced at an equally slower rate. If your heating system is inadequate, insulation can at least ensure more effective use of the heat before it escapes.

Besides comfort from warmth, another reason for insulation is to reduce condensation. The warmer the air in a heated room, the more water vapour it can contain. When the air cools, as it does when it meets a colder wall or window, the water turns into droplets known as condensation. Insulating the walls results in these internal surfaces being kept warmer and the heat in the room being retained longer, so there is not such a dramatic contrast between the temperature of the air and the surfaces on which condensation forms. So condensation is eliminated or at least reduced. Also, insulation means that heating levels can be kept lower and, when desirable, temperatures can be boosted more effectively.

Cavity walls

Insulation of cavity walls is not a job for the home handyman – it should be carried out only by an approved contractor. The material generally used for cavity filling is urea formaldehyde foam which is injected into the cavity under pressure through holes drilled in the outer wall. There it sets, trapping millions of tiny air pockets which act as a barrier against escaping heat.

Other materials used are mineral wool fibre blown into the cavity in a similar way to urea

To insulate cavity walls, small holes are drilled in the mortar courses (below), the foam is pumped into the cavity (top) and the holes made good (above)

formaldehyde foam, and glass fibre panels placed in the cavity at the time the wall is built.

Warning A reliable contractor will survey your property to see whether cavity wall insulation is suitable. Check the guarantee which is offered to see whether any damp which may arise from this method of insulation will be rectified free of charge.

Solid walls

There are a number of ways to insulate solid walls. The method you choose will depend on the lengths you wish to go to and the time and money you have available.

Lining with boards

see next page

One of the most common and effective methods of insulating solid walls is to line the inside of exterior walls with insulating board. Good results can be obtained with ordinary fibre insulating panels, but greater savings in heat loss can be gained by using plasterboard laminate, which is an extremely bad conductor of heat. This material consists of rigid urethane foam (polyurethane having a very low level of thermal conductivity) with a tough waterproof backing, a vapour barrier and a layer of plasterboard with a paper backing. When used on ceilings in particular, this board not only reduces heat losses and gives a surface which warms up rapidly but, when bonded to the ceiling with adhesive and finished with gypsum plaster or texturing compound, it minimises the risk of condensation and is especially valuable in combating persistent condensation. For use on walls, the total thickness of board should be 21mm (or $\frac{7}{8}$in). It is

most effective when fixed to a timber batten framework and used with other insulating material such as mineral wool quilting.

Fixing First remove all electrical fittings (after isolating the supply at the mains), cove, window and door surrounds and skirting. Cut the boards to shape by slicing through the waterproof backing and foam with a sharp knife or fine tooth saw, before snapping the board and cutting through the facing paper. It is important to cut away the foam at the joins so plasterboard edges will butt together to give a continuous surface. With screws and wall plugs, fix a timber batten framework (treated with wood preservative) to the wall. The main framework is made of 50×25mm (2×1in) timber and the inside supporting pieces of 38×25mm ($1\frac{1}{2} \times 1$in) timber. Ensure the timber framework is 25mm (1in) thick overall. Apply impact adhesive to the wall and loosely fix strips of mineral wool quilting between the battens. Then apply impact adhesive to the battens in strips and in a corresponding position on the boards so the strips match up when the two surfaces are joined. Fix the boards in place, taking care to position them accurately since they cannot easily be moved once contact has been made. For a smooth finish, fill any gaps between the boards with cellulose filler reinforced with plasterboard joint tape.

You will have to remount electrical fittings and refix ceiling cover door and window surrounds and skirting to bring these to the new level. If desirable, window sills can be tiled to raise their level using an RE (rounded edge) tile to project slightly in front of the plasterboard face. This will ensure a really neat finish.

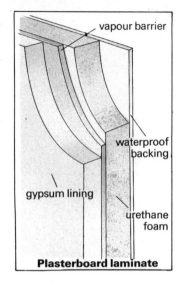

Plasterboard laminate

vapour barrier

waterproof backing

gypsum lining

urethane foam

Above The composition of plasterboard laminate – an extremely effective insulating material
Below left To fix the boards, screw a timber framework to the walls and apply mineral wool quilting between the battens
Below Spread impact adhesive on the boards and the battens and position the boards accurately on the framework

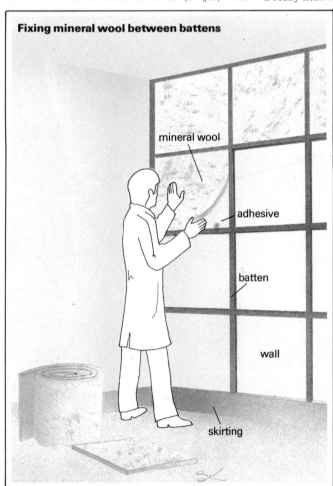

Fixing mineral wool between battens

mineral wool

adhesive

batten

wall

skirting

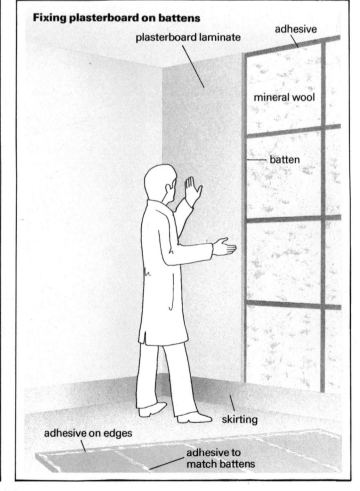

Fixing plasterboard on battens

plasterboard laminate

adhesive

mineral wool

batten

skirting

adhesive on edges

adhesive to match battens

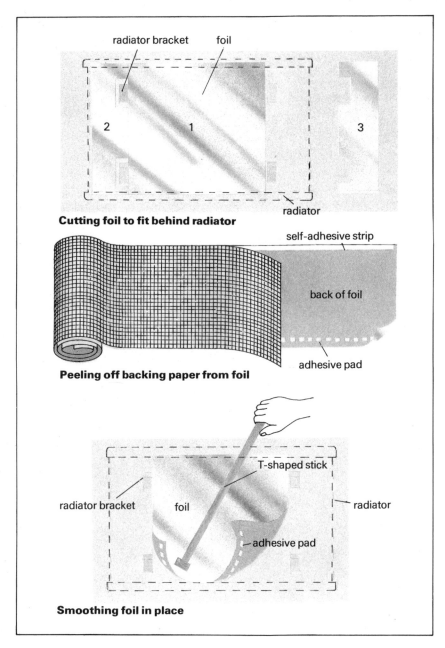

Cutting foil to fit behind radiator

radiator bracket | foil
2   1   3
radiator

Peeling off backing paper from foil

self-adhesive strip
back of foil
adhesive pad

Smoothing foil in place

T-shaped stick
radiator bracket   foil   radiator
adhesive pad

Above Use heat-reflecting foil behind radiators. Cut the foil into three, trimming it to fit round the radiator brackets. Peel off the paper backing, position the foil behind the radiator and smooth it into place

Most Builders Merchants knew nothing of this board as described on page 34. Finally at Aspins Blackburn I was told they had once ordered for a customer, a product known as STYLO LINER which they said was similar to the description. It is very expensive, in March 1984 it was about £23 a sheet 8'x4' including VAT. They dont stock but would order it on request (£353 for 15 sheets)

Lining behind radiators
It is also worthwhile lining the wall behind radiators with self-adhesive heat reflecting foil. This is reinforced with glass fibre and plastic-coated (to prevent tarnishing for several years).

Turn off the radiators and make sure the wall behind them is cool and clean before applying the foil. Cut the foil to a size slightly smaller than the radiator so it will not protrude when in position. For easy application, cut it into three pieces with slots in the end sections cut to fit round the radiator brackets. Remove the backing of the centre piece, place it in position against the wall and smooth it down with the applicator which is supplied with the foil. Repeat for the end pieces.

Another type of foil is available which allows more flexibility when positioning, where there is very limited space between the radiator and wall. It is fixed by an adhesive tape at the top and self-adhesive pads at the bottom. Hang the foil behind the radiator and, when it is in the correct position, press along the top to seal the tape to the wall. Then press the pads at the bottom into place to complete this very simple process for reducing heat wastage.

Both types of foil are easier to fix than the frequently-used aluminium kitchen foil, which tears easily during fixing. Applying any foil is obviously considerably simplified if access to the wall is improved by removal of the radiator from its wall brackets. If the radiators are positioned below a window, make sure no damp is penetrating the wall around the window frame before fixing foil, as the drying effect will be reduced.

Lining with expanded polystyrene
A simple, inexpensive way of reducing heat loss through walls is to line them with expanded polystyrene veneer before papering or decorating, although this makes a rather fragile surface which is vulnerable to denting.

This lining is available in 2–5mm (or $\frac{1}{12}-\frac{3}{16}$ in) thicknesses and is supplied in rolls. Apply it in the same way as wallpaper. Make sure walls are clean and dry then spread a heavy duty fungicidal wallpaper adhesive or polystyrene adhesive onto the wall and apply the lining. At joins allow 13mm ($\frac{1}{2}$in) overlap, cut the overlap with a sharp knife, remove the waste edges, apply more adhesive and lightly roll the edges. If you intend to decorate with a heavy wallpaper, it is advisable to apply a lining paper over the polystyrene lining before fixing the wallpaper.

Expanded polystyrene panels or tiles can be used instead. Use the tile-fixing adhesive recommended by the manufacturer. If you decide to paint the tiles or panels, remember to use a fire-retardant paint. Check with your supplier which paint is suitable.

Warning Never paint expanded polystyrene with gloss paint as this causes a chemical change in the material and makes it highly inflammable.

Lining with plasterboard laminate
21mm (or $\frac{7}{8}$in) thick plasterboard
   laminate insulating boards
50×25mm (2×1in) timber batten
38×25mm ($1\frac{1}{2} \times 1$in) timber batten
wood preservative
No 10 countersunk screws 63mm ($2\frac{1}{2}$in)
   long, wall plugs 38mm ($1\frac{1}{2}$in) long
mineral wool quilting
RE (rounded edge) tiles (if needed)
trimming knife or fine tooth saw
hand or electric drill, 5mm ($\frac{3}{16}$in) twist
   drill and masonry bits,
   countersink bit
impact adhesive
hammer, screwdriver
cellulose filler, plasterboard joint tape

Lining with expanded polystyrene
expanded polystyrene veneer
heavy duty fungicidal wallpaper
   adhesive or polystyrene adhesive
brush, knife, boxwood roller
lining paper (if needed)
expanded polystyrene panels or tiles,
   tile adhesive (for ceiling)

Lining behind radiators
self-adhesive heat reflecting radiator
   foil with applicator, or foil with
   self-adhesive pads and tape
scissors   **equipment**

Insulating with boards

Hardboards and insulating boards are made from wood: the natural timber is reduced to fibres which are then reassembled to form large sheets. There is no grain, there are no knots and the surface is smooth and even every time. Wood fibre boards provide insulation where it's needed – on the warm side – to reduce heat loss through walls, ceilings and floors.

Types of board
The range of special types for a great variety of commercial uses is considerable, but for the home handyman the ones most readily available – apart from insulating board – are standard, tempered, medium and decorated hardboard.

Insulating board is non-compressed, lightweight and porous and is used for heat insulation, particularly on ceilings and walls. It is available in 13, 19 and 25mm ($\frac{1}{2}$, $\frac{3}{4}$ and 1in) thicknesses and also comes in the form of planks or tiles. Decorated insulating board is most commonly found in the form of ceiling tiles.

Conditioning Wood fibre boards may take up moisture from the surrounding air, causing them to expand, so it is always best to condition the boards before fixing. The treatment varies with the type of board so always check first with your supplier.

All these materials are relatively easy to handle and will cover large areas quickly. The following suggestions will give you ideas for using boards, planks and tiles.

Insulating walls
Hardboard and insulating boards can provide effective insulation if used on the inside of external walls. In houses with solid walls – as is the case with more than half of Britain's homes – this is almost the only way of providing insulation.

Where the board is unlikely to suffer rough treatment (in bedrooms, for example) and the walls are sound and flat, decorated insulating board may be stuck direct with impact adhesive. Denser standard or medium hardboards should be used if walls are likely to suffer at the hands of children. These provide heat insulation when mounted on a batten framework by creating an air gap. Lining the cavity with aluminium foil will also help.

Direct gluing Prepare painted walls by washing with household detergent or a solution of water and sugar soap. Glasspaper down to remove any flaking paint and to provide a key for the adhesive. Wallpapered areas must be completely stripped and glasspapered down.

Above Boards finished with hessian provide an attractive wall covering as well as insulation against heat loss. Fix the boards quickly by gluing them direct to the wall with impact adhesive **(inset)**

Fixing to battens (wall)

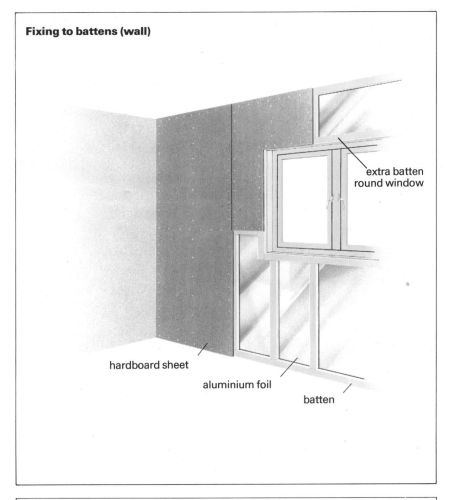

extra batten round window

hardboard sheet

aluminium foil

batten

Order of tiling unsquare ceiling

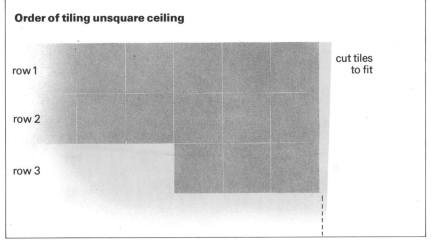

row 1

row 2

row 3

cut tiles to fit

Spread impact adhesive in strips on both the wall and the insulating boards. Start fixing at the corner of the wall, as far as possible pressing each board onto the wall from the centre, upwards and downwards, to prevent bulging. Butt-join the boards, taking care not to damage the edges.

Fixing to battens Construct the framework from 50 × 25mm (2 × 1in) timber battens. Drill holes in the horizontal battens at about 400mm (16in) intervals for standard hardboards and 610mm (24in) intervals for thicker ones. Drill holes in the vertical battens at 1200mm (48in) intervals. Now drill corresponding holes in the wall, insert wall fixings and screw the battens into position. Make sure the battens are level, packing low areas with hardboard offcuts if necessary.

Fixing the boards If desired, tape sheets of aluminium foil into place between the battens. Fix decorated boards to the framework with impact adhesive to avoid damaging the finish and work from the centre of the board, upwards and downwards, to prevent the board bulging in the middle.

Other types of board should be fixed with rust-resistant round head nails or hardboard pins. Fix the top of the board to the battens about 13mm ($\frac{1}{2}$in) in from the edge at 100mm (4in) intervals, working outwards from the centre. Then fix the board to the vertical battens at 150mm (6in) intervals, working upwards and downwards from the centre. Finally secure the other edges at 100mm (4in) intervals, 12mm ($\frac{1}{2}$in) in from the edge.

Finishing off For an attractive finish you can use either emulsion paint or wallpaper. Before painting, use glasspaper to round off the board edges and key the surface for the paint. Prime the boards with special hardboard primer or diluted emulsion paint (one part water to four parts paint) before giving the finishing coats. If using wallpaper, first seal the boards with a coat of hardboard primer.

Insulating ceilings

In the average house most heat is lost through the roof and it has been estimated that more than a quarter of the homes in Britain have either no lofts or no access to loft space. In such cases insulating the underside of the upstairs ceiling is the only effective answer. Fixing 13mm ($\frac{1}{2}$in) fibre insulating board tiles to the ceiling will reduce the heat loss from the house in winter by about ten per cent; the time it takes to heat up a room is also reduced. Using decorated tiles ensures an attractive finish. from the house in winter by about ten per cent; the

Planning and fixing

First decide on the method of fixing. If the ceiling can be easily cleaned and is reasonably flat, fixing the tiles direct to the ceiling with acoustic tile adhesive is the easiest and most economical way. If the ceiling is loose, badly cracked or very uneven, it will be necessary to screw wood battens through the ceiling to the timbers above.

Measure the ceiling and other surfaces to be tiled. For a symmetrical job, with equal margins of cut tiles at opposite sides of the room, it is worthwhile drawing the areas to be tiled on a planning grid. This will not only act as a guide to the number of tiles required but will also help in determining the positions, lengths and number of battens, if these are to be used, and amount of adhesive needed.

Insulating board tiles usually come in 305 × 305mm (12 × 12in) sizes in cartons of 30, 60 or 100. Adhesive manufacturers also normally state the covering capacity of their products – for example, 1 litre for 2sq m (or 2pt for 22sq ft) of tile area.

Direct gluing First wash down the ceiling with household detergent or a solution of water and sugar soap and scrape away any stubborn flaking paint. Check the corners are square by drawing a line at right-angles to the longer wall. Plan to start fixing in a corner with the first row of tiles against the longer wall.

With a putty knife apply 25mm (1in) diameter blobs of acoustic tile adhesive to the back of the tiles at each corner. Press the tiles into place on the ceiling, ensuring each tile lines up with the one before. Adhesive can be applied to a number of tiles at a time and the tiles fixed one after the other.

Tiles which fit together with tongues and grooves

Fixing tongued and grooved tiles

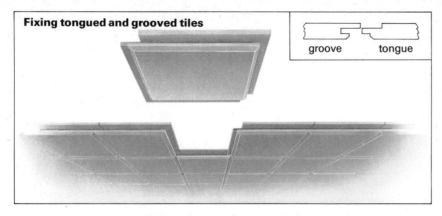

groove   tongue

Concealed fixing method

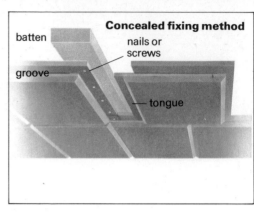

batten
nails or screws
groove
tongue

Fixing to battens (ceiling)

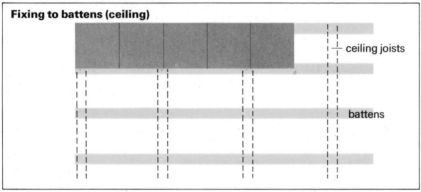

ceiling joists

battens

Section of finished surface

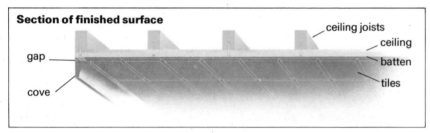

ceiling joists
ceiling
gap
batten
cove
tiles

Order of nailing hardboard to floorboards

row 2

row 1

Fixing hardboard to panelled door

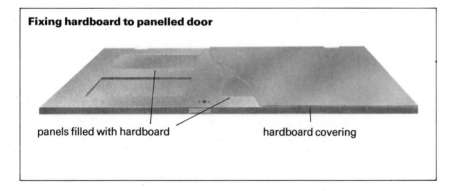

panels filled with hardboard   hardboard covering

are easier to use and give a more level finish. For the first row, however, remember to cut off one of the tongues on each tile so the plain edges go next to the wall, allowing a small gap for expansion.

Fixing to battens First establish by trial and error the position and direction of the roof timbers by knocking nails through the ceiling. Once you have located one or two timbers the rest will be easy to locate since they run parallel to, and are equidistant from, each other. Since the ceiling will later be covered, a few holes will not matter.

Cut 50×25mm (2×1in) timber battens to run across the line of the timbers and screw them to the timbers at 305mm (12in) intervals. Make sure the undersides of the battens are level with one another, packing them if necessary with offcuts of hardboard.

Fix the tiles to the battens with staples or round head nails. With tongued and grooved tiles the fixings are concealed by the tongue of the next tile.

Finishing For the best finish fix cove to cover the join between the tiles and the walls.

Insulating floors

Standard hardboards are used to improve both timber and concrete floors. On suspended timber floors you can eliminate draughts and so reduce heat loss by nailing hardboard to the floor, making sure the joins in the hardboard and the floor do not coincide. Hardboard applied to plain-edged floorboards above lath and plaster ceilings provides the minimum fire resistance required by current building regulations. Again, the joins in the hardboard and the floor must not coincide.

Heat insulation on concrete floors is improved by bonding sheets of insulation board in place with bituminous adhesive. Cover this with carpeting or, if you intend to place heavy items on the floor, use a harder-surfaced insulating board.

Never put down hardboard or insulating board on a concrete floor where damp is suspected. Treatment for this situation has already been described – see Chapter 1.

Insulating doors

You can improve the fire resistance of old panelled doors by fixing on hardboard. To do this you will have to remove the door and take off the fitments. Glue medium board into the existing panels and cover the whole door with 3mm ($\frac{1}{8}$in) standard hardboard, nailed into place. The extra thickness of hardboard on the door may mean you have to re-hang the door further away from the closure bead (by extending the hinge recesses in the door frame) or move the closure bead further away.

Double glazing

While heat losses vary depending on the nature of a building and its aspect, in a typical uninsulated house about 15 percent of house heat is lost through the windows. If all the windows in such a house are double-glazed, this heat loss will be halved to give a seven and a half percent saving on fuel bills. There are many factors which can affect this figure – for example, the type of system used and how well it is fitted. Installing double glazing in an old cottage with just a few small windows would not obtain this saving, whereas there will be higher savings in a modern 'goldfish bowl' type of property.

Double glazing is not a money saver on the scale of other forms of insulation such as glass fibre laid in the loft or cavity wall infill; however, there are a number of reasons why you will find the necessary expenditure worthwhile to add to the comfort of your home. An efficient system will eliminate cold, draughty areas round windows, making the whole floor area of a room usable on cold days, and rooms will seem larger without the need for occupants to cluster round the fire or radiators.

Preventing condensation

When rooms are properly heated and ventilated, condensation will be reduced and possibly eliminated by double-glazed windows, since the inner panes of glass will be warmer and less susceptible to misting. With some double glazing systems, interpane misting may occur; this is usually slight and can be wiped away provided the new window is hinged or sliding. Alternatively you can place silica gel crystals between the panes of glass; these absorb moisture and, when saturated, should be temporarily removed and dried in a warm oven.

Misting on the room side of the window indicates the temperature of the glass is too low, given the water content of the room's atmosphere; by a process of trial and error, you should carry out adjustment until there is a proper balance between heat and ventilation in the room.

Condensation on the cavity surface of the outer glass is usually a sign that moist air is leaking into the cavity from the room. Make the seal round the new double glazing as airtight as possible, using a

1 Sachets of silica gel crystals placed between the two panes of glass can help reduce interpane misting; when saturated, the sachets should be removed, dried in a warm oven and replaced
2 To cure condensation on the cavity surface of the outer glass, drill ventilation holes right through the primary frame
3 Drill the ventilation holes 10mm deep and pack them with glass fibre to act as a filter

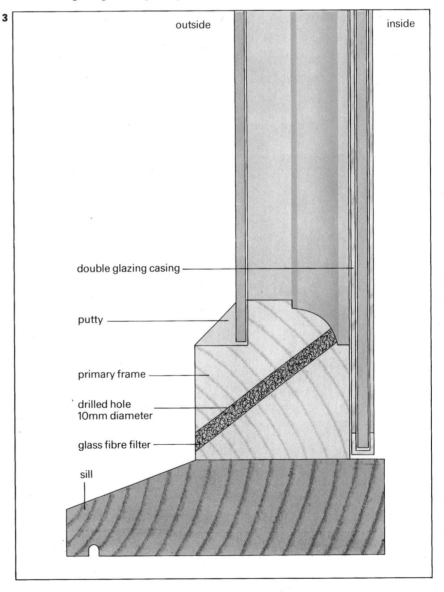

outside   inside

double glazing casing

putty

primary frame

drilled hole 10mm diameter

glass fibre filter

sill

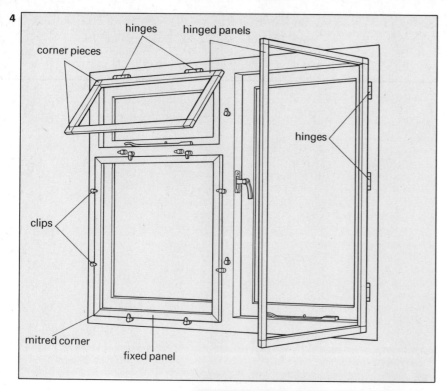

4 hinges   hinged panels   corner pieces   hinges   clips   mitred corner   fixed panel

4 Installing fixed or hinged double glazing. The new panes are fitted in aluminium or plastic U-shaped channel, joined at the corners by mitring or by using special corner pieces; use hinges to fix the panels to opening windows and clips for fixed windows

5 Using plastic film as double glazing; cut the film to size and fix it to the frame with double-sided adhesive tape

noise permeating through windows from typical town traffic or a local playground. However, if your noise problem is more acute, noise prevention is a more extensive technical matter – the actual source of the noise, the location of the house, the type of glass thickness needed, the distance the two panes are set apart and any additional insulation around windows or between the double glazing should all be considered before you buy any expensive system to solve the problem.

Remember Government grants to install double glazing can be given to people living in certain heavy traffic areas or where there is an airport nearby. Your local authority will be able to supply details and advice.

In normal noise level situations the two sheets of glass in a double glazing system should be at least 100mm (or 4in) apart to provide adequate sound insulation. To provide effective thermal insulation, the optimum gap should be of 19mm ($\frac{3}{4}$in). If you want both sound and thermal insulation, you should select a wider gap of up to 200mm (or 8in); you will find thermal insulation is not greatly reduced in this case.

Buying double glazing

Certain double glazing firms do not cater for the DIY market, others cater for both professional and DIY work and some solely for the DIY market. If you choose a professional installation, a representative from the company will call on you, discuss your requirements, measure up and arrange for the work to be carried out by company operatives. If you choose to install double glazing yourself, you will find local retail outlets stock at least one kind of kit for the framework. Measure up your requirements and buy the correct size; then read the instructions carefully to find out the thickness of glass required – 3 or 4mm (or $\frac{1}{8}$ or $\frac{1}{6}$ in) – and the height and width of glass. Glass can vary in price, so it is well worth shopping around.

One or two companies offer a mail order service whereby you measure up, send the firm the dimensions and they return a kit – in one case at least the glass also is supplied. At least one company offers the best of both worlds – a company representative will call and measure up and you will then receive a tailor-made kit complete with glass. The advantage of this method of buying double glazing is the company takes responsibility for any errors in measuring and making the framework; also, since you are dealing directly with a company and not through a middle man, this system is often less expensive than other systems.

Costs Depending on the house style and the system chosen, to double glaze all the windows in a house could be a costly business. You could reduce the amount by completing only selected windows – perhaps those in the living room, hall and landing or a particularly draughty bedroom. A little-used dining room or spare bedroom might not be worth the expense; it would probably be better to keep the doors of these rooms closed and well sealed in cold weather to prevent the house heat drifting into them. When they are in use, heavy curtains pulled across would be as effective as double glazing, as long as the windows have been effectively draught-proofed.

Factors which can drastically affect the price of double glazing one window, let alone all the windows in the house, are obviously the cost of the

tape form of draught excluder, and seal any gaps in the joints of a timber framework with a matching wood filler, making sure the filler penetrates through to the full depth of the joint.

If this fails to cure the problem, drill ventilation holes through the primary frame to the drier air outside. In a 1m (39in) wide window, two 10mm (or $\frac{3}{8}$in) diameter holes set 500mm (or 20in) apart should be sufficient. More will be needed for larger windows; you can decide the exact number by a process of trial and error – drilling an extra hole and waiting to see if this cures the problem. Pack the holes with glass fibre to act as an air filter.

With hermetically sealed units (see below) the air in the cavity is dried, so condensation between the panes is not possible as long as the seals remain sound; failure of the seals is a rare occurrence, but reputable manufacturers give long-term guarantees to cover the possibility.

Sound insulation

Installing a good quality double glazing system will give a substantial reduction in the decibel level of

glass and the retail price of the kit you choose, which again can differ from shop to shop.

Types of double glazing

There are four types of double glazing in common use: insulating glass, secondary sashes, coupled windows and plastic film.

Insulating (hermetically sealed) glass These units look like a single pane of glass and consist of two pieces of glass joined together and hermetically sealed in the factory – a process in which the air space between the panes is dried to prevent misting when installed. The pieces of glass are sealed with edge spacers of metal, alloy or plastic. The units are tailor-made and replace a single pane, enabling a window to open and close normally.

There are two types – standard and stepped. The stepped units are ideal where there are shallow rebates since installation can be carried out without having to alter the existing frame to accept the new units. The existing frame must be well fitting and sound enough to take the extra weight which will be imposed by the units.

Secondary sashes This is the most popular DIY method of installing double glazing. A second pane of glass in its own frame is secured to the existing frame or to the inner or outer sill and reveal; in some circumstances it is possible to fit the new window outside the existing frame. The existing window remains unaltered to form the other half of the double glazing. Manufacturers supply frames of aluminium or plastic; other types consist of plastic extrusions which are cut to length and joined with corner fittings to enable a frame for the glass to be made up. Hinges or clips are then used to secure the secondary sash to the existing window. The secondary sash is movable for cleaning, ventilation or summer storage and can be fixed, hinged or sliding.

Coupled windows These are usually specified only for new buildings or where entire frames are being replaced during conversion. One single-glazed window has an auxiliary window coupled to it, allowing both to move together. They are fitted with hinges and fasteners so the frames can be separated for cleaning purposes.

Plastic film This is not double glazing in the traditional sense, although at least one proprietary system is available. Plastic film is cut to size and applied to the window frame with double-sided adhesive tape. If you use this method, make sure that where windows are to be opened they are double-glazed separately from fixed panes; if a complete film was stretched across the entire window it would not be possible to open the window without first removing the film.

If you are restricted to a very small budget, you can use kitchen self-clinging plastic to make a form of double glazing for small panes. For larger panes, you will have to break up the pane space with a thin timber framework to create the effect of smaller panes and fix the film inside these smaller areas.

Installing double glazing

If you are going to install your own double glazing, it is likely you will choose a secondary sash type since kits for these are widely available and are relatively easy to install.

There are, however, a number of problems you may come across when fitting them. For example,

they can be fitted to existing timber or metal window frames; but if metal frames are fixed directly into masonry, you will have to drill and tap the frame to provide screw-fixing points or fit a secondary timber frame to accept the double glazing, particularly if the frame is too narrow. However, most metal windows are set in a timber surround and this can be treated as the window.

If you want to fix the double glazing frame to the reveal, you may come across the problem of an out-of-square reveal; to deal with this you will have to pack the out-of-square area with timber wedges or choose a system which fits directly to the window. Again, certain types of kit require the channels in which the new glazing is fitted to be mitred at the corners and joined. If you think you will find this too much of a problem, choose a type which is supplied with corner pieces. Remember to cut the channel lengths squarely at the ends or you will find it difficult to fit on the corner pieces and the final appearance of the glazing will be marred. Also, don't expect the glass to be a push-fit into the channel; it might slide in, but often you will need to encourage this by tapping gently with a mallet or with a hammer and a block of wood placed to protect the glass.

Warning If you are going to double glaze bay windows, remember to treat each window as a separate unit.

There are many makes of secondary sash double glazing available and the manufacturers supply

6 Fitting sliding secondary sashes; this type may be fixed to the face of the window or to the reveal

7 Fitting shatterproof panels into self-adhesive plastic track; mark the sill trim where it reaches the edge of the frame

8 Cut the side channel to length, remove the adhesive backing and press the strip onto the wall

9 Fit the top channel along the top of the frame

10 To shape the panels, score with a sharp knife and break over the edge of a firm surface

11 Fit the first panel, slit the top channel at the end of the panel and clip in place

12 Fix a panel divider and continue fitting the panels

13 Fit the final panel, ensuring the side channel is pressed firmly along its length

14 The finished installation; separate panels can be removed by opening the channel at the top and side

6

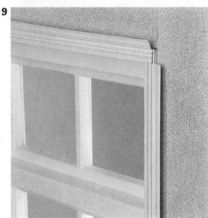

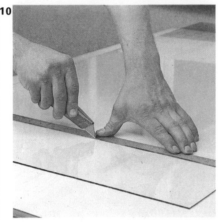

detailed instructions for installation. There are, however, three basic types of system: plastic channel, fixed or hinged, and sliding secondary sashes.

Plastic channel With this type, each pane of glass is fitted into a frame made by cutting lengths of U-shaped plastic channel to size; remove any sharp edges from the glass with a carborundum stone. The corners of the channel have to be mitred. Using a sharp knife and a mitre guide, cut the first mitre corner and then fit the channel to the glass to determine the position of the second corner. Remove the channel and mitre-cut at this position; repeat this process until all four corners have been cut. Secure the channel to the glass; some kits require the use of adhesive to form a rigid frame. Hold this assembly up to the window and fix it in place on the frame with the plastic clips supplied with the kit.

With this type of double glazing, out-of-square reveals will not cause problems since the channel is always fixed to the frame.

Fixed or hinged Usually this type consists of plastic or aluminium channel cut to shape and joined at the corners by mitring or by using special corner pieces. Fixing is either by clips to non-opening windows or by hinges to opening windows (the new windows can be hinged to open sideways or upwards). You could, of course, use hinges with fixed windows to make them easier to clean. This type of double glazing will, if correctly assembled, eliminate draughts and the new windows can be removed for summer storage.

Before you buy this type of system, read the manufacturer's instructions carefully to check the frame around your window is wide enough to take the double glazing and that it is made of the right material to take this particular system. With some systems the manufacturer recommends fixing only to wood rather than metal frames. Again, your existing window catches or handles may protrude in such a way they will interfere with the installation of the new system. You can usually solve these problems by fitting a secondary timber frame to take the double glazing; butt-join the corners of the frame, fill in any gaps with wood filler and apply a wood primer followed by two coats of paint, allowing the first coat to dry before applying the second.

There is one system which uses PVC shatterproof panels instead of glass. These are fitted into self-adhesive plastic tracks which are cut and pressed into place to the wall outside the reveal. The panels can be easily removed, but you may consider this too much trouble with opening windows.

Sliding Usually this type is fitted in the reveal. An outer frame is fixed in the reveal to square up the opening; use pieces of wood as packing if necessary. The glass is fixed in a separate frame which is fitted inside the outer frame to enable the glass and its separate frame to slide. The framed glass is removable and horizontal and vertical sliders are available. Depending on the size of the window, two or more sliding panels will be needed.

One system can be fixed to the face of the window frame so you will avoid the problems of squaring up a reveal, although it can be reveal-fixed as well. In this case the company offers a kit specially designed to suit your windows; it comprises plastic channelling cut to size and ready to be joined on site so no cutting or mitring is required. The glass comes complete in its tailor-made frame ready to be installed in the channelling.

Roof repairs

slate

gable end

creasing slate

bedding mortar

tile-and-a-half slate

creasing slate

slate

soakers

batten

felt

slates

shaped slates

Repairing a tiled roof

While most roof repair jobs are easy and straight-forward, difficulties arise because the work has to be done at height; this may well deter some people from tackling them. Make safety the number one priority: whenever possible use a scaffold tower to reach the roof and to give a working platform at gutter level; always use roof crawling boards to enable you to climb on the roof.

Double lap (plain) tiles Any remaining parts of broken or crumbling plain tiles must be removed before new tiles can be fitted. To release the tile-holding nibs from the roofing battens, use small pieces of timber to lift up the tiles in the course above the tiles to be replaced; then lift the broken tile over the batten with a bricklayer's trowel. If the tile is held by nails, it may be possible to work it loose by moving the tile from side to side while prising up the tile with the tip of a trowel. Should this method fail, use a slate ripper to cut the heads off the nails; hook the blade of the ripper round the nail and pull to cut through it. Normally only the tiles in every fourth course are nailed, but in particularly exposed positions all the tiles may be nailed to prevent them being lifted by the wind.

Fit the replacement tile under the tiles in the row above, pushing it upwards until the nibs hook over the batten. Again, a trowel under the tile will help you to position it accurately. A tile without nibs can be held in place with a gap-filling adhesive applied from a special gun.

Single lap tiles These are fairly easily displaced, so where possible fix each tile with one or two 32mm (1¼in) aluminium alloy nails into the roofing batten or secure the tile with a clip nailed onto the batten, where this system is used on your roof.

Clay pantiles This type is often simply hung on battens. If they become dislodged, it is best to drill holes at the top of the tiles, using a masonry drill bit, and refix them with aluminium alloy nails.

Ridge tiles If the joints between ridge tiles have cracked but the tiles themselves are still firmly bedded, you can repair the joints with beads of non-hardening mastic applied with a mastic gun, or with thick bitumen mastic trowelled into the joints.

Loose ridge tiles must be lifted and rebedded on a mortar mix of one part Portland cement to four parts sharp, washed sand. Soak the tiles in water and place the mortar along the edges of the tiles

Above Replacing ridge tiles on a roof: always handle the tiles with care and remember they are much heavier than they look

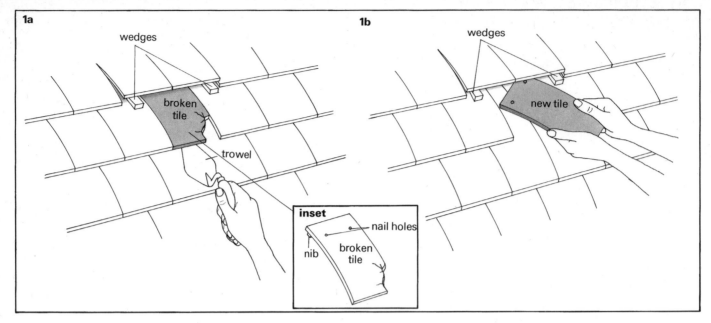

1a To remove a damaged tile, use timber wedges to raise the tiles in the row above and lift the tile with a trowel until the holding nibs are clear of the roofing batten

1b Fit the replacement tile under the tiles in the row above, pushing it up until the nibs hook over the roofing batten

2 Some single lap interlocking tiles are held in place with clips; the clip hooks over the tile and is nailed to the batten (**inset**)

3 To repair cracked joints between ridge tiles, rake out the old mortar and replace it with beads of non-hardening mastic applied from a mastic gun

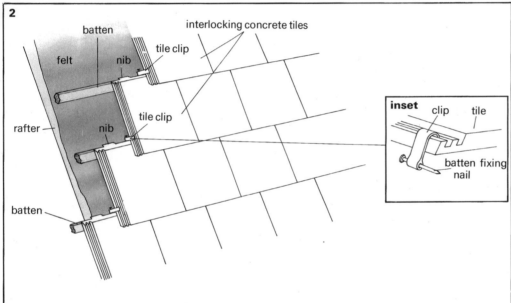

and at the joints. It is important not to fill the tiles completely with mortar because the cavity allows air to circulate under the tiles, helping them to dry out quickly after rainfall and reducing cracking.

To close the cavity at each end of the ridge, use flat pieces of tile (called tile slips) set in mortar – any pieces of scrap tile will serve this purpose.

Hip tiles These are usually bedded on mortar in the same way as ridge tiles; repairs are the same as for ridge tiles except hips are usually prevented from slipping down the roof by a hip iron. If this has corroded, it should be replaced; new galvanized hip irons are obtainable from builders' merchants. Carefully lift the hip tile adjacent to the hip iron, remove the old bedding mortar and the remains of the hip iron. Screw the new iron to the foot of the hip rafter using rustproof screws and rebed the hip tiles on cement mortar, filling the open end with small pieces of tile set in mortar.

Bonnet hip tiles are fixed at the top with aluminium alloy nails, while the tail (exposed part) is bedded on cement mortar. If only one bonnet hip tile has to be replaced, it may be possible to fix it without disturbing the other hip tiles by using a

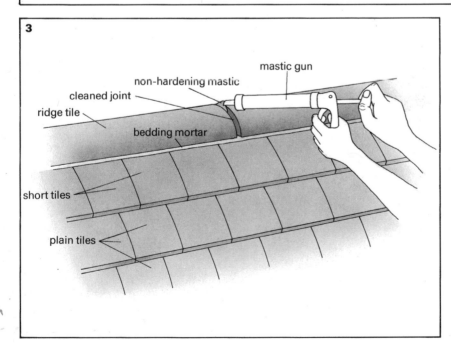

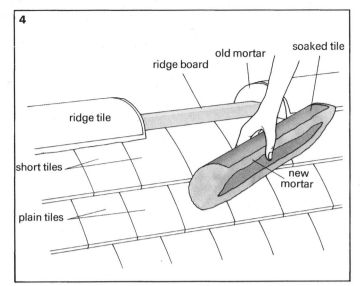

4

ridge board — old mortar — soaked tile

ridge tile

short tiles

plain tiles

new mortar

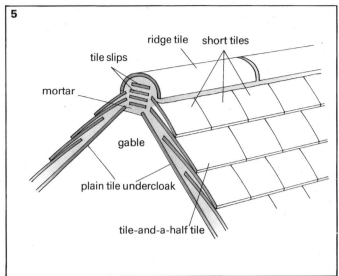

5

ridge tile   short tiles

tile slips

mortar

gable

plain tile undercloak

tile-and-a-half tile

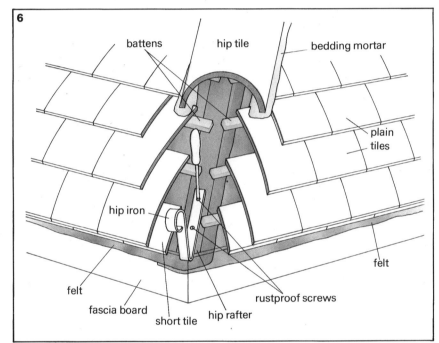

6

battens   hip tile   bedding mortar

plain tiles

hip iron

felt

felt

fascia board   short tile   hip rafter   rustproof screws

mortar mix of one part fine sand to one part cement. If you cannot do this, you will have to strip off all the tiles and renail them, working from the eaves towards the ridge.

Verge and eaves tiles The tiles on a verge are usually nailed and bedded on mortar; eaves tiles are sometimes similarly bedded, but modern practice is simply to nail them. Cracks can usually be filled with mastic, as described for ridge tiles; where damage is more severe, the tiles can be repointed with a mix of one part cement and four parts sand.

4 When replacing a ridge tile, soak it with water and apply mortar along the edges and at the joints. **5** Set tile slips in mortar to close the cavity at the end of a ridge. **6** You will have to lift the first hip tile to gain access to the hip iron. **7** You should be able to replace a single bonnet hip tile by bedding it in mortar. **8** Repair crumbled joints between verge tiles by repointing them with fresh mortar mix

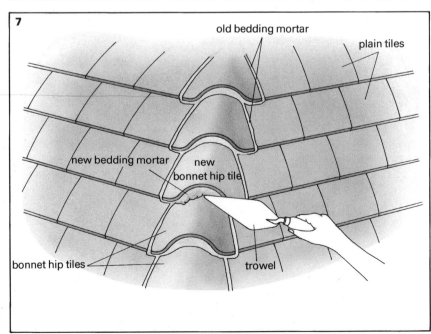

7

old bedding mortar

plain tiles

new bedding mortar   new bonnet hip tile

bonnet hip tiles   trowel

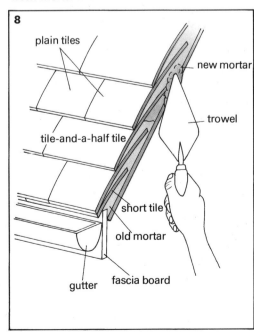

8

plain tiles

new mortar

trowel

tile-and-a-half tile

short tile

old mortar

gutter   fascia board

Types of roof tile

Before attempting repairs to a tiled roof, you need to know what sort of tiles have been used and how they are laid out on the roof. Tiles are made of either clay or concrete, with a variety of designs to choose from.

Types of concrete tile: **1** Bonnet hip; **2** Valley; **3** 90 degree angle – right; **4** 90 degree angle – left; **5** Baby ridge; **6** Ridge; **7** Tile-and-a-half tiles; **8** Plain tiles; **9 & 10** Plain tiles with arrowhead and bullnose; **11** Modern interlocking; **12** Bold roll interlocking; **13** Wessex interlocking; **14** Plastic rooflight; **15** Ludlow Major interlocking; **16** Mendip interlocking
Opposite page 1 English pantiles. **2** Single Roman. **3** Double Roman. **4** Spanish. **5** Italian. **6** Interlocking Somerset. **7** Interlocking concrete. **8** Interlocking vertical joint concrete. **9** Monopitch ridge. **10** Rooflight

There are specially shaped tiles designed for use on specific areas of the roof, but there are basically two types of roofing tile – double lap (or plain), and single lap.

Double lap tiles
Double lap, or plain, tiles are slightly curved with two holes for fixing nails and usually two nibs, or projections, on the underside at the top edge; some tiles, however, are continuously nibbed along the top edge. The tiles are normally fixed to battens with aluminium alloy nails and the nibs hook over the battens for extra security. The camber, or curve, to each tile provides air spaces between tiles and battens for ventilation and to prevent water ingress by capillary action.

Once made by hand, plain tiles are now mainly machine-made from clay or concrete. Many clay tiles are smooth-faced, although they are also available with a sand face. Concrete tiles are becoming increasingly popular because they are slightly cheaper than many clay tiles; they are also not so likely to laminate (or flake) and are available in a wide range of colours, including brown, red, grey, green and buff. In some cases the colour is confined to the granule facing, although often the tiles are coloured throughout. Because there are many types, sizes and colours of plain tiles, take a sample as a pattern when ordering replacements to make sure you get the right ones.

In plain tiling, the tiles hook over roofing battens so each course overlaps the tiles in the course-but-one below it; this amount of overlap (called the lap) should not be less than 65mm (2½in). Tiles in each course are butted together side by side and do not overlap. In this way there are at least two thicknesses of tile in every part of the roof – and three thicknesses in most places.

The usual size of plain tiles is 265 × 165mm (10½ × 6½in), although some hand-made tiles are 280 × 178mm (11 × 7in). In addition there are special tiles to maintain the lap and weatherproof the roof at the verge (the side of the roof), eaves (gutter level) and ridge (the apex of the roof).

Verge tiles At the verges special tile-and-a-half tiles, usually 265 × 248mm (10½ × 9¾in), are used in alternate courses. These tiles are normally bedded on an undercloak of plain tiles, laid face downwards and projecting 38–50mm (1½–2in) over the gable walls or bargeboards. Sometimes the verge is finished with a clip-on plastic verge channel which holds the end tiles firmly and stops water penetration.

Eaves tiles These usually measure 190 × 165mm (7½ × 6½in) and are used as an undercourse at the eaves and as a top course just below the ridge tiles.

Ridge tiles Half-round ridge tiles, bedded with mortar along their edges and at the joints between tiles, are used to weatherproof the ridge. Hog back, segmental (or third-round) and angle ridge tiles are also used. It is most important the bedding mortar is placed only along the edges and joints between the ridge tiles, since cracking can occur if the ridge tiles are filled with bedding mortar.

Hip tiles There are several ways in which hips (the junction of two sides of the roof) may be finished. It is common to use third-round ridge tiles bedded on mortar in a similar fashion to the way a ridge is formed. Because third-round tiles are not secured by nailing, a galvanized hip iron is screwed to the foot of the hip rafter before the hip tiles are laid to give them support.

Hip irons are not necessary when bonnet hip or angular hip tiles are used. These are nailed to the hip rafter and are bedded on mortar at the tail; they should be fitted so they lie snugly against the plain tiling at each side.

Valley tiles In plain tiling, valleys are often formed with purpose-made valley tiles of similar colour and texture to the main roof tiles. Valley tiles butt against plain tiles on each side and are usually fixed by nailing or bedding in mortar.

Single lap tiles
Single lap tiles are designed to overlap, or be overlapped by, adjacent tiles in the same course and in the course above and below. In most parts of the roof there is only a single thickness of tile – except at overlaps, when there is a double thickness.

Clay single lap tiles have been in use for many years, but are being replaced by interlocking concrete tiles which are cheaper. Although some clay patterns are still made, it may be difficult to buy replacements; if they are not stocked by your local builders' merchant, try specialist roofing contractors or local demolition firms – but ensure second hand tiles are not flaking or cracking.

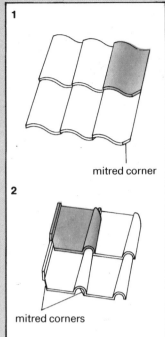

1
mitred corner

2
mitred corners

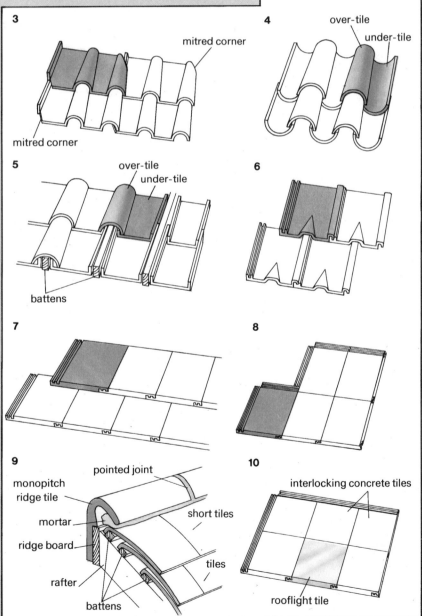

3
mitred corner
mitred corner

4
over-tile
under-tile

5
over-tile
under-tile
battens

6

7

8

9
monopitch ridge tile
pointed joint
mortar
ridge board
rafter
battens
short tiles
tiles

10
interlocking concrete tiles
rooflight tile

49

Layout for a tiled roof with details for both single and double
lap (or plain) tiling. For single lap tiling: at the ridge
(**inset A**), the valley junction (**inset B**), the verge
(**inset C**), the eaves (**inset D**) and the hip (**inset E**)

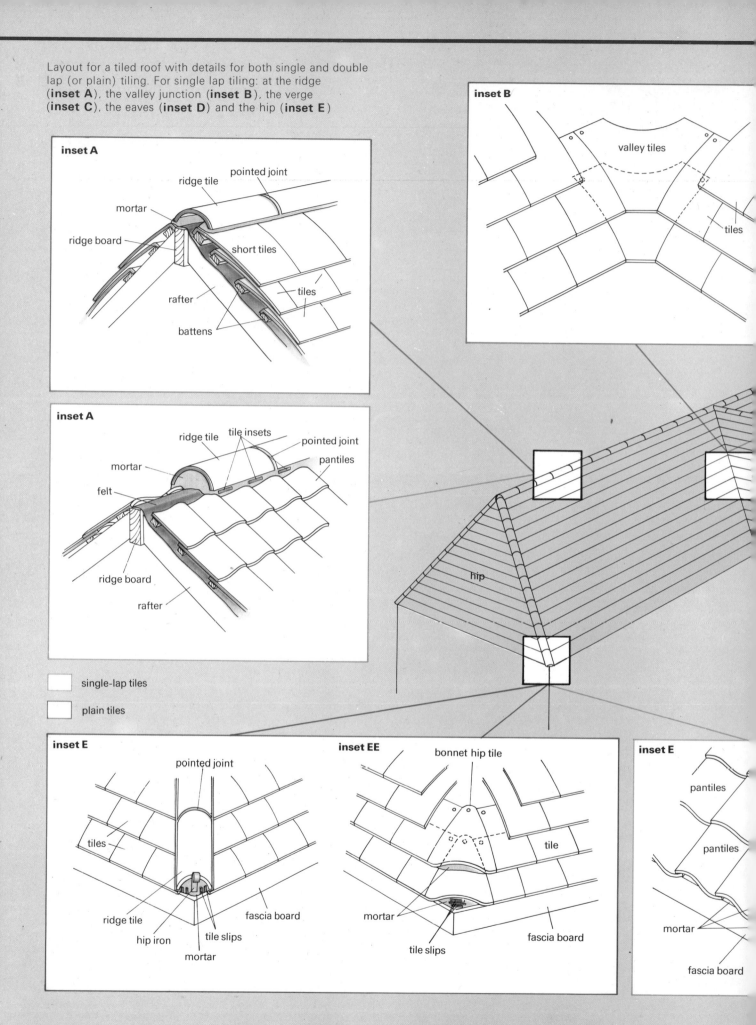

inset A

pointed joint
ridge tile
mortar
ridge board
short tiles
rafter
tiles
battens

inset A

ridge tile
tile insets
pointed joint
mortar
pantiles
felt
ridge board
rafter

inset B

valley tiles
tiles

single-lap tiles

plain tiles

hip

inset E

pointed joint
tiles
ridge tile
hip iron
tile slips
mortar
fascia board

inset EE

bonnet hip tile
tile
mortar
tile slips
fascia board

inset E

pantiles
pantiles
mortar
fascia board

50

For plain tiling: at the ridge (**inset A**), the valley junction (**inset B**), at the verge (**insets C and CC**), at the eaves (**inset D**) and at the hip (**insets E and EE**)

inset B

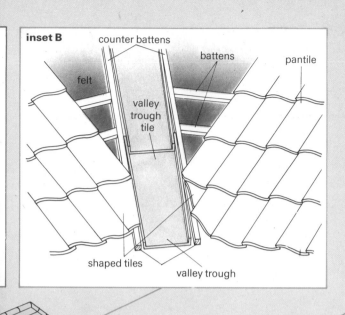

counter battens

battens

pantile

felt

valley trough tile

shaped tiles

valley trough

inset C

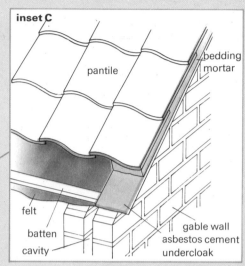

pantile

bedding mortar

felt

batten

cavity

gable wall asbestos cement undercloak

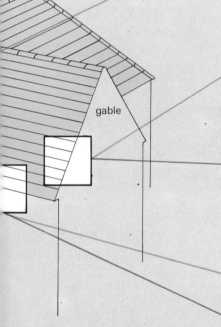

gable

inset CC

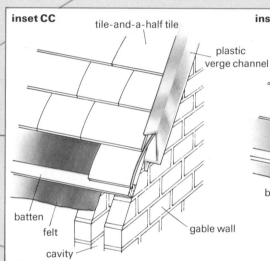

tile-and-a-half tile

plastic verge channel

batten

felt

cavity

gable wall

inset C

tile-and-a-half tile

tile

bedding mortar

batten

felt

rafter

cavity

undercloak

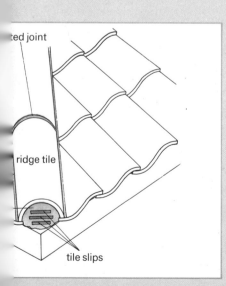

ted joint

ridge tile

tile slips

inset D

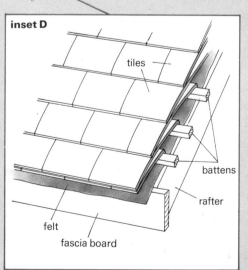

tiles

battens

rafter

felt

fascia board

inset D

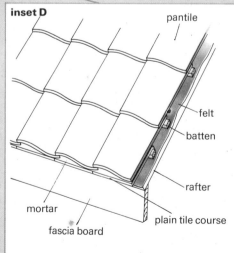

pantile

felt

batten

rafter

mortar

fascia board

plain tile course

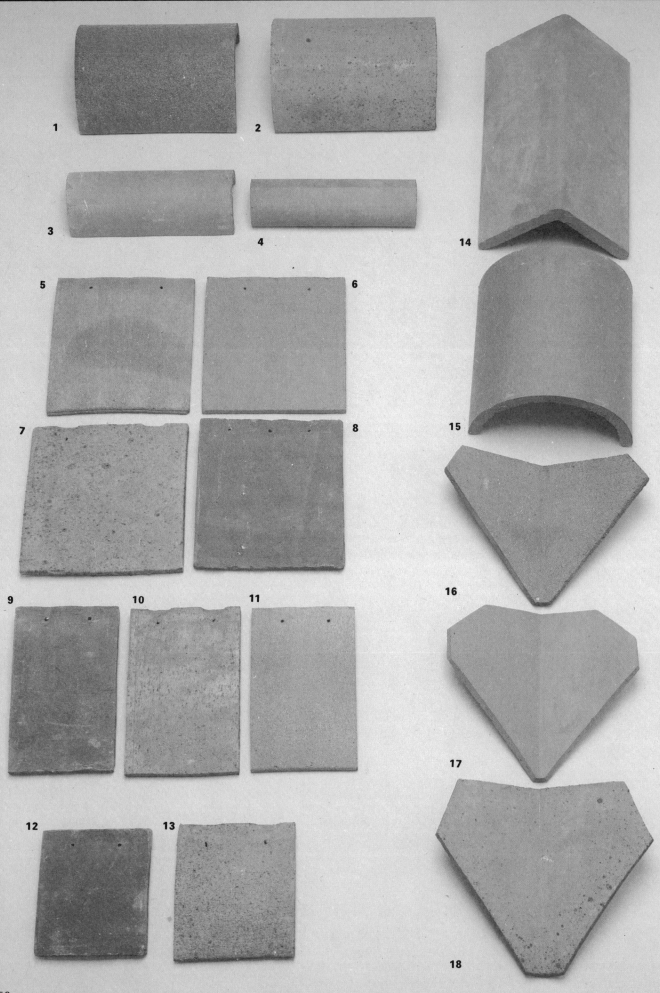

A selection of some of the many types of clay tile available; it should help you to recognize the tiles on your roof. Try builders' merchants for replacements; they should be able to order tiles for you if they do not have them in stock

1 Hawkins half-round ridge
2 Dreadnought half-round ridge
3 Half-round baby ridge
4 Pascall roll ridge
5 Hawkins machine-made tile-and-a-half
6 Rosemary machine-made tile-and-a-half
7 Dreadnought hand-made tile-and-a-half
8 Keymer hand-made tile-and-a-half
9 Keymer 265 × 165mm hand-made and sand-faced
10 Dreadnought 280 × 178mm hand-made
11 Hawkins 265 × 165mm machine-made, sand-faced
12 Keymer hand-made eaves
13 Dreadnought hand-made eaves
14 Angle ridge
15 Round ridge
16 Hawkins machine-made valley
17 Rosemary machine-made valley
18 Dreadnought hand-made valley
19 Six patterns of interlocking tiles, glazed and unglazed
20 Dreadnought machine-made bonnet hip
21 Rosemary machine-made bonnet hip
22 Rosemary machine-made arris hip
23 Rosemary machine-made 90 degree angle

A commonly found single lap tile is the English pantile; you can also buy interlocking clay pantiles which are available in a range of colours and with a glazed or matt finish. In some situations only alternate pantiles are nailed to the roofing battens but, if you have to replace this type of tile, it is a good idea to fix each one with rustless aluminium alloy nails (you may have to drill fixing holes at the top of the tiles using a masonry drill bit).

Other common single lap clay tiles are double and single Roman tiles, interlocking Somerset tiles, Spanish tiles which have concave under-tiles, and Italian tiles which have flat under-tiles.

Interlocking concrete tiles are available in a wide range of designs and colours and in smooth and granule finishes. Some have an acrylic finish which gives the roof a lustre as well as promoting rainflow off the roof and inhibiting the growth of fungi and moss. Concrete tiles imitate many of the clay tile designs and some are patterned to look like roofing slates.

Some single lap tiles have interlocking head and tail joints as well as interlocking side joints; this enables them to be used on roofs with very low pitches (or slopes) – down to 15 degrees in some cases. (Compare this with the minimum pitch for a plain roof tile which is 35 degrees.)

Fittings Fittings for use with interlocking concrete tiles include angle, half-round and third-round ridge tiles, as well as monopitch ridge tiles for monopitch roofs.

Rooflight tiles To give light in the roof space, rooflight tiles made from translucent reinforced plastic are available in the contours of the single lap roof tile patterns.

Valley trough tiles Valleys can be formed with special valley trough tiles, with adjacent tiles neatly cut and bedded on mortar.

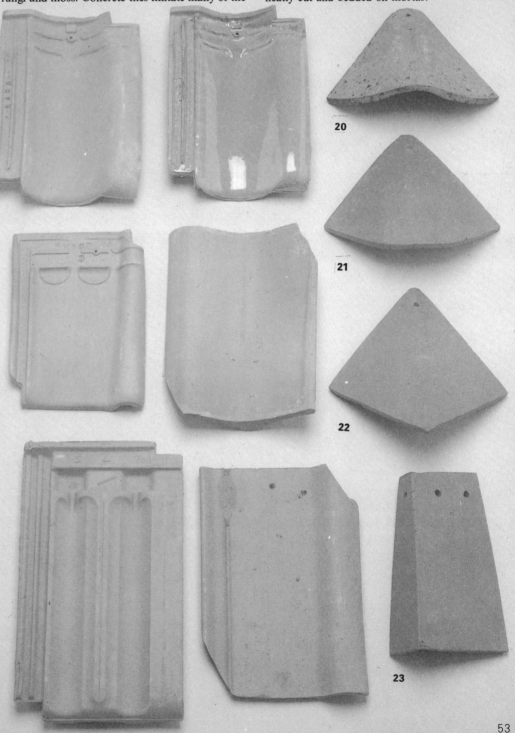

Repairing a slate roof

A sound roof keeps out water – and thus helps prevent problems caused by damp.
In this section on roof repairs, we describe how to deal with the most common
types of roof damage and look first at slate roofs.

Roof slates deteriorate over a period of time as a result of weathering and movement of the roof structure. If you have slates, check the roof regularly so you can make repairs before the damage lets in water. The first sign of wear may be a hairline crack, or flaking may occur along the edges or round the fixing holes. You should also check for loose slates.

Slates vary in size, shape, thickness and colour, so note your requirements carefully before ordering new slates. It is a good idea to take one of your slates to a builders' merchant to match it up. You can buy second-hand slates from a builders' yard or demolition site, but examine them carefully to make sure they are undamaged. If you cannot get a replacement of the exact size, choose a larger one of the same thickness and cut it to size.

Roof layout Slates are laid from the eaves upwards and each row, known as a course, is overlapped by the one above. The vertical joints of the slates are staggered, so each slate partially covers the two below. The slates are nailed to battens, spaced according to the pitch (or slope) of the roof.

The slates on the first row, at the eaves, and those on the last row, at the ridge, are shorter than those used on the rest of the roof. At the end of every alternate row a wider slate, called a tile-and-a-half, is used to fill the gap left on a straight edge. If the roof is angled at the edge, slates have to be cut to fit. On the edge of a gable roof there may be a narrow slate, known as a verge or creasing slate, which is laid under the slates at the end of each row; these slates give the roof a slight tilt and prevent rainwater running down the wall. V-shaped slates are used for the ridge of the roof.

Drilling and cutting slates

Roof slates may be nailed in the centre or at the top. When replacing slates, use the same nailing position as that of existing slates; to make nail holes, place the old slate over a new one and mark the position of the holes with a nail. Lay the new slate on a piece of wood and make the holes by hammering a nail through or by drilling, using a bit to match the size of the nail to be used.

Above Make regular checks on the condition of your roof. Here not only the slates, but also the roofing battens, have deteriorated badly; both will have to be replaced
1 Layout of a slate roof with details of the ridge (**inset A**), valley (**inset B**), gable end (**inset C**), eaves (**inset D**) and hip (**inset E**)

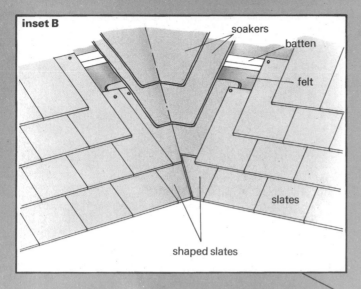

inset B

soakers

batten

felt

slates

shaped slates

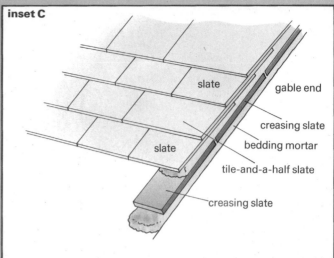

inset C

slate

gable end

creasing slate

bedding mortar

tile-and-a-half slate

slate

creasing slate

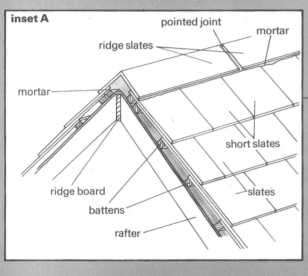

inset A

pointed joint

mortar

ridge slates

mortar

short slates

ridge board

battens

rafter

slates

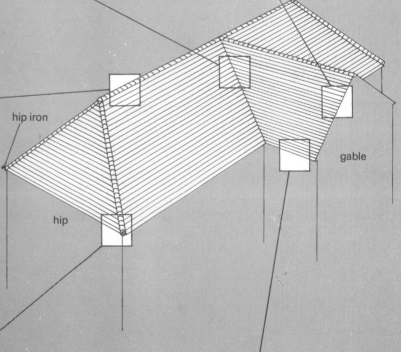

hip iron

hip

gable

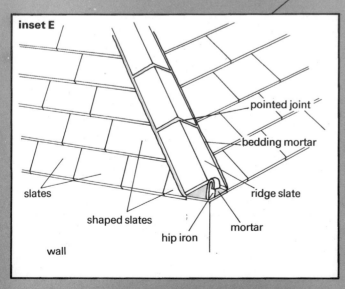

inset E

pointed joint

bedding mortar

slates

ridge slate

shaped slates

hip iron

mortar

wall

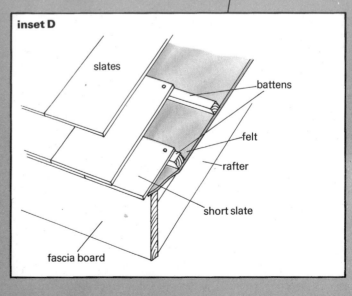

inset D

slates

battens

felt

rafter

short slate

fascia board

If you need to cut a slate, score the cutting line on both sides with the point of a trowel. If you are cutting a large slate down to a smaller size, use an old slate as a guide. To mark out a shape – for example, to fit the angled edge of a roof – use the old slate as a guide (if it is not too badly damaged) or make a template. Place the marked slate on a firm, flat surface with the waste section overhanging. Chop halfway along the cutting line with the sharp edge of a trowel, then turn the slate over and work in from the other end so the cuts meet in the middle. Never try to snap the slate along the cutting line.

Replacing a damaged slate

When removing a single slate, take care not to damage surrounding slates. If the fixing nails have corroded through, you will be able to pull the slate away quite easily. To remove a securely nailed slate, use a slate ripper. Slide the claw of the ripper under the damaged slate and hook it round the nails. Pull the ripper to break the nails and carefully take out the old slate, making sure you do not dislodge adjacent slates.

You cannot nail down a single replacement slate, since the fixing holes will be overlapped by the slates above. To fix it you need a strip of lead about 250mm (10in) wide; nail one end of the strip to the batten between the nails of the two exposed slates. You will need to lift the edge of the slate above; be careful not to crack it. Slide the new slate into position under the overlapping ones, lining up the edge with adjacent slates, and bend up the free end of the lead strip to hold the slate in place.

Ridge slates These are bedded down in mortar. Remove any loose ridge slates for refitting and take away any damaged ones. If you need access to the top batten for fixing the top row of replacement slates, remove the relevant ridge slates. To remove securely fixed ridge slates, loosen the mortar under the slates with a sharp brick bolster. Hold the bolster parallel to the slate and tap it with a club hammer. Clean away old mortar from the top course of slates in the same way and chip away mortar from any ridge slates which are to be relaid.

For relaying ridge slates, mix a mortar of one part cement to three or four parts sand. Lay the fresh mortar along the ridge with a trowel and roughen the surface. Place the ridge slates on the mortar and tap them level with adjacent slates. Fill the joints between the slates with mortar and also press mortar along the bottom of the slates; then smooth off with a trowel. If you have to fit a whole new ridge, you may find it cheaper to use clay ridge tiles rather than slate ones.

Repairing large areas

Rotten battens may cause damage to a large area of slates. If you have to carry out major repairs, erect scaffolding and secure crawling boards to the working area to ensure safety and avoid damage.

2a Use a hammer and a nail to make fixing holes in a new slate

2b Alternatively use an electric drill

3a When cutting a large slate to size, use an old slate as a guide

3b To shape slates, make a card or hardboard template; again use an old slate (**inset**) as a guide

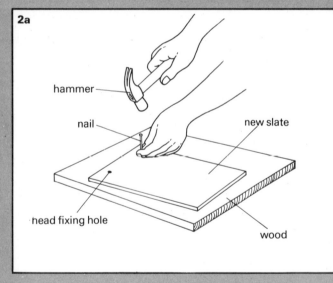

2a

hammer

nail

new slate

head fixing hole

wood

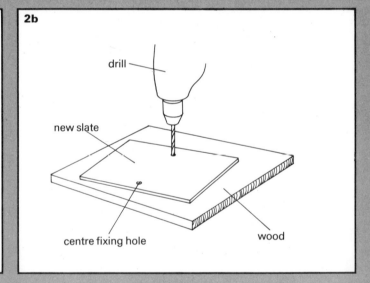

2b

drill

new slate

centre fixing hole

wood

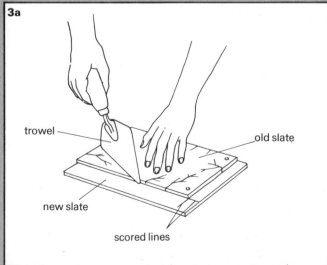

3a

trowel

old slate

new slate

scored lines

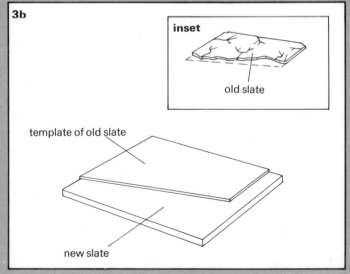

3b

inset

old slate

template of old slate

new slate

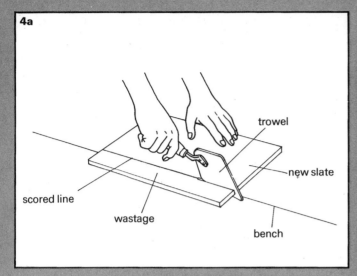

4a

trowel

scored line

wastage

new slate

bench

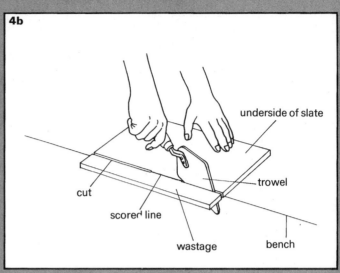

4b

underside of slate

cut

scored line

wastage

trowel

bench

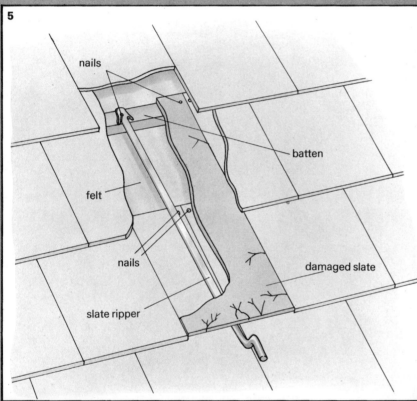

5

nails

felt

nails

slate ripper

batten

damaged slate

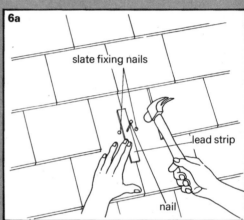

6a

slate fixing nails

lead strip

nail

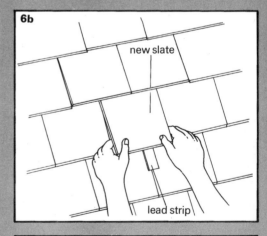

6b

new slate

lead strip

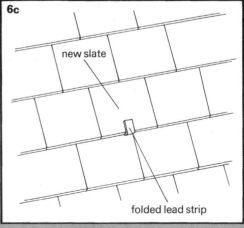

6c

new slate

folded lead strip

4a Cut slates with a trowel; work from one end to the centre; **4b** Turn the slate over and work from the other end to finish the cut. **5** Remove slates with a slate ripper. **6a** To replace a single slate, first fix a lead strip to the batten between the nails of the two exposed slates; **6b** Lift the slates immediately above and slide the new slate into position; **6c** Bend the end of the lead strip over the slate to hold it in place. **7** Loosen the bedding mortar of ridge slates with a bolster. **8** Saw through rotten battens where they cross the rafters

Remove all the slates from the damaged area and stack the undamaged ones carefully. Remove any unsound battens by sawing through them diagonally where they cross the rafters.

Cut new lengths of the same size softwood as the existing battens – usually 50 × 25mm (2 × 1in) – at a matching angle to provide a tight fit; fix the new battens with a 50mm (2in) nail at each end. If there is any bituminous felt which is damaged, repair it before you fit the battens in place. Cut the torn piece to a neat rectangle, fit a larger rectangle of new felt over it and stick it down with bitumen adhesive. Coat all new timber and the surrounding old structure with a wood preservative before replacing the slates.

Fixing slates Start at the eaves with a row of short slates. If you are making the repair in the middle of an existing row, slide the first new slate under the last overlapping slate, placing the holes over the centre of the batten. Secure the exposed part

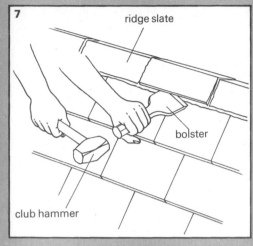

7

ridge slate

bolster

club hammer

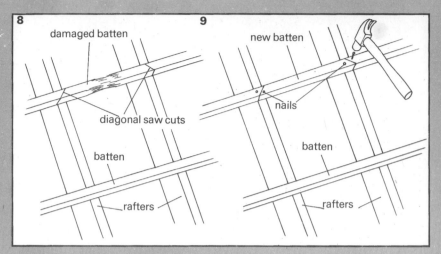

8 **9**

damaged batten

new batten

nails

diagonal saw cuts

batten

batten

rafters

rafters

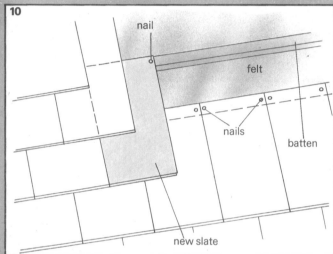

10

nail

felt

nails

batten

new slate

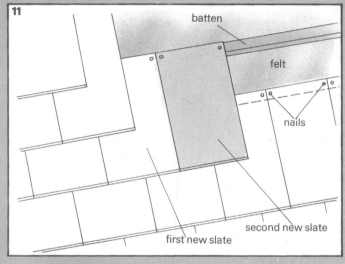

11

batten

felt

nails

second new slate

first new slate

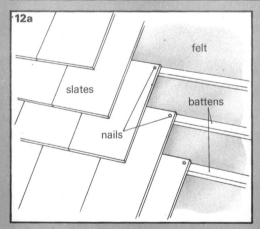

12a

felt

slates

battens

nails

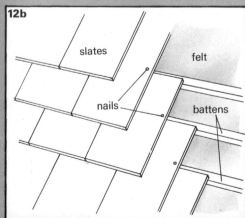

12b

slates

felt

nails

battens

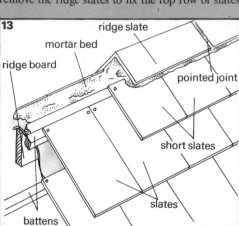

13

ridge slate

mortar bed

ridge board

pointed joint

short slates

slates

battens

of the slate with a nail driven into the batten. Butt-join the remaining slates in the row and fix each one with two nails, lining up the upper edges.

The second row will completely cover the row of short slates (this gives extra protection against damp). Fix the slates as for the first row, covering the vertical joins of the slates below. Continue fixing the slates, moving up the roof one course at a time. All vertical joins should be covered and each course should overlap the one below.

Unless you are reslating to the ridge of the roof, the nail holes of the last few slates will be covered by the overlapping slates above, so use lead strips to fix these in position, as described earlier. If you are working right up to the ridge, you will have to remove the ridge slates to fix the top row of slates.

9 Fix replacement battens with a nail at each end
10 To replace slates in the middle of an existing row, slide the first new slate under the last overlapping one; place the holes over the centre of the batten and secure with a nail
11 Butt-join the second slate and secure it with two nails; fix the remaining slates in the course in the same way
12a When replacing head-nailed slates, line up the top of the slates with the top of the battens
12b For centre-nailed slates, position the top edge of the slates in the centre of the batten above
13 Ridge slates will have to be removed when replacing the top row

Repairing flashings and valleys

If flashings (weatherproofing where the roof joins walls, chimney stacks or roof windows) or valley linings (weatherproofing at the junction of two sloping roof surfaces) become defective, the first signs of trouble may be spoiled ceiling decoration or damp patches on chimney-breast walls due to rainwater penetration. Check these areas of the roof regularly, making any repairs as soon as possible, and you should be able to stop the trouble before it gets too bad. Many repairs are simple and ones you can do yourself.

Flashings

Traditionally flashings are made from sheets of lead or zinc; but other corrosion-resistant materials, such as aluminium alloy, copper, bituminous felt and rigid bitumen-asbestos, are also used. A fairly recent development is the self-adhesive flashing strip; this is available in various widths and is cheaper and easier to fit than most traditional materials. These flashing strips usually consist of heavy duty reflective aluminium foil, coated on one side with a thick layer of specially formulated pressure-sensitive bitumen adhesive. The adhesive surface is protected with a siliconized release paper which you peel off just before applying the flashing. In some cases the aluminium foil is coated with a grey vinyl lacquer, so it looks like lead.

Making repairs

If flashings are torn or cracked, clean the damaged area thoroughly with a wire brush and go over it with emery paper. You can then cover the crack or tear with a patch of self-adhesive flashing strip: simply peel off the paper backing and smooth the strip firmly into place. Alternatively press thick bitumen mastic into each crack so there is about 1.5mm ($\frac{1}{16}$in) of mastic over the crack and overlapping it by about 1.5mm ($\frac{1}{16}$in) all round. Lay a piece of aluminium foil or thin roofing felt over each repair and press the edges into the mastic. Apply another layer of mastic and brush liquid bitumen proofing over the entire flashings.

Repointing Along its top edge, metal flashing is tucked into the mortar joints of the brickwork; if the joints are defective and the flashing comes away from them, rainwater will trickle behind and eventually seep through the roof. To repoint the joints, first rake out the old mortar with a cold chisel and club hammer, then tuck the flashing back in place, wedging it at intervals with scraps of lead or small pieces of timber. Dampen the joint with water and fill it with a mix of four parts sand to one part cement.

Replacing flashings

Flashings which are badly corroded are best replaced with new material; the method of replacement varies with the type of flashing and the material used.

Stepped flashing With a single lap tiled roof (and some slate roofs) the flashing at the side of the chimney is usually stepped and dressed (pressed down) over the tiles. Stepped flashing is inserted in the mortar joints all the way down the side of the chimney and it is difficult to replace in the same way. However, you can apply a self-adhesive flashing

1a Rainwater will seep through your roof if flashings are damaged; having cleaned the area, press mastic into the damaged area and push on a piece of foil or roofing felt
1b Apply another layer of mastic over the patch and brush liquid bitumen over the whole flashing
2 If flashings come away from the brickwork, rake out the old mortar and wedge the flashing back into the wall with timber pegs; refill with fresh mortar

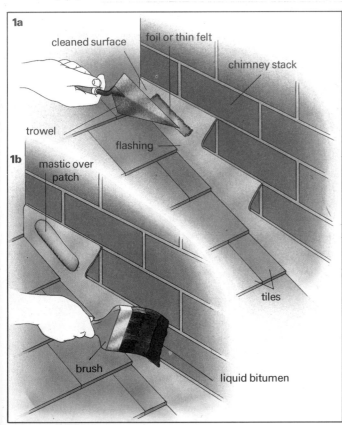

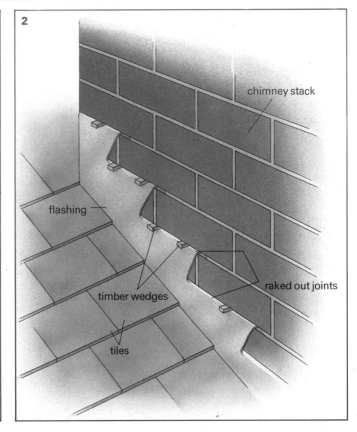

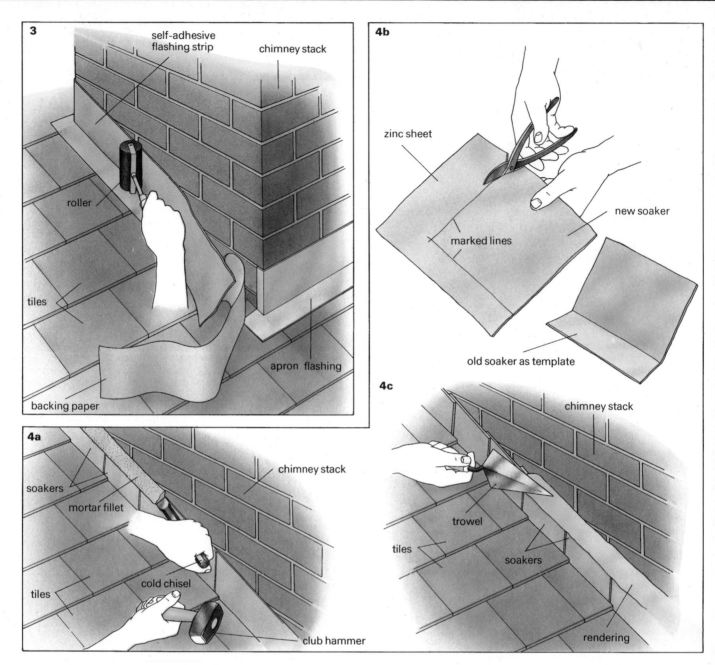

3
self-adhesive
flashing strip
chimney stack
roller
tiles
apron flashing
backing paper

4a
soakers
mortar fillet
chimney stack
tiles
cold chisel
club hammer

4b
zinc sheet
marked lines
new soaker
old soaker as template

4c
chimney stack
trowel
tiles
soakers
rendering

strip which does not need stepping or inserting in the mortar joints. Carefully lever out the old flashing and thoroughly clean the area with a wire brush; you can then apply a primer as recommended by the manufacturer – this is not essential, but it does ensure the strip adheres firmly to the brickwork. Cut the strip to length with a pair of scissors and carefully peel off the backing paper; press the strip into place and smooth it down with a cloth pad or a wood seam roller as used for wallpapering, making sure there are no gaps between the strip and the surface.

Soakers On a double lap (or plain) tiled roof – and again on some slate roofs – the flashing at the side of the chimney and against parapet walls usually consists of separate pieces of metal, called soakers, interleaved with the tiles. The soakers are turned up against the wall or side of the chimney and a stepped flashing or mortar fillet covers their up-turned edges. To replace faulty soakers, chip away the old mortar fillet, or lever out the flashing, and rake out the joints between the bricks to about 19mm ($\frac{3}{4}$in). Remove adjacent tiles, numbering

them as you work to enable you to replace them in the correct order, and remove the damaged soakers – again numbering them as you do so. Cut pieces of zinc to the shape of the soakers, using the old ones as templates. If you intend to use self-adhesive flashing dampen the raked out joints with water, repoint, and replace the soakers, interleaving them with the tiles in the same way as they were originally fitted. You can now apply the flashing over the soakers, as described above. If you intend to apply rendering over the soakers and to the wall above, leave the mortar joints open to provide a key for the rendering. Use a mix of four parts sand to one part cement and trowel on the mortar to a thickness of 13mm ($\frac{1}{2}$in). Score the surface to ensure good adhesion, leave the render to dry and apply a second coat, again 13mm ($\frac{1}{2}$in) thick.

Straight flashings When replacing straight, horizontal flashings of traditional materials, such as lead or zinc, lever out the damaged flashing and rake out the mortar joints to about 25mm (1in). Cut the lead or zinc sheet to the required length, lay it over a batten and bend over a 20mm (or $\frac{3}{4}$in) strip

3 Replace stepped flashing with self-adhesive strip; peel off the backing paper and roll down the strip
4a When replacing faulty soakers, chip off mortar fillet
4b Cut the new soakers, with old ones as templates
4c Apply render over the soakers and the mortar joints
5a When replacing straight flashing, bend the edge of the new strip over a batten
5b Use a sliding bevel to check the required angle
5c Shape the metal to the correct angle
5d Fit the new flashing strip into the dampened mortar joint, hammering the lower half to match the roof slope
6 Seal cracks in cement fillet with non-hardening mastic

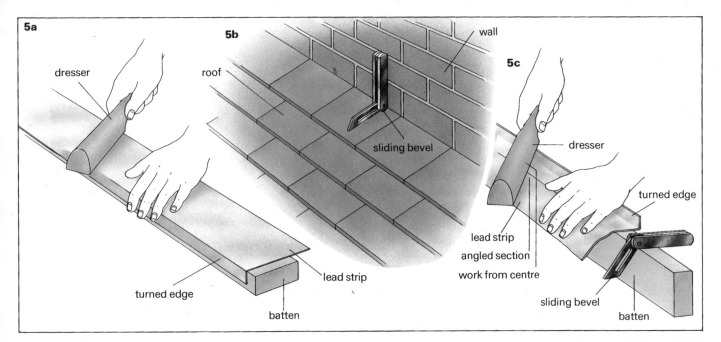

5a dresser

5b roof · wall · sliding bevel

5c dresser · turned edge · lead strip · angled section · work from centre · sliding bevel · batten

turned edge · lead strip · batten

at right-angles down one long edge. Use a sliding bevel to determine the angle between the roof and the wall; turn the sheet over and shape it to match the angle on the bevel, working from the centre of the sheet outwards. Dampen the mortar joints with water and insert the angled section of the new flashing in the joint, packing with small wedges of zinc or lead at both ends and overlapping joins in the flashing by about 150mm (6in). Gently hammer the lower half of the flashing to match the slope of the roof then fill the joint with fresh mortar. Finally remove surplus mortar with the point of a trowel.

Alternatively you can replace this type of flashing with a self-adhesive strip, as described for stepped flashing.

Cement fillets Occasionally the flashing round the base of a chimney or against a parapet wall is made from a triangular fillet of cement mortar; it is quite common for this type of flashing to crack where it joins the wall. If the damage is not severe, seal the gap with a non-hardening mastic; if the fillet is in bad condition, it is best to chip the fillet away and replace it with a self-adhesive flashing strip.

Valley linings

Lead, zinc and aluminium are all commonly used for valley linings. Small cracks and holes can be repaired in the same way as for metal flashings; but after making such repairs, it is important to seal the entire valley with liquid bitumen proofing or liquid plastic coating.

Replacing valley linings

If the valley lining is severely corroded or wrinkled, it must be replaced; this involves lifting several tiles at each side of the valley, so have a tarpaulin or heavy duty polythene sheeting ready to cover the roof in case of rain. You can replace the lining with zinc or lead sheet or use roofing felt; but the simplest method is to apply a wide self-adhesive flashing strip.

Zinc or lead lining Remove the tiles covering the valley edge at each side, numbering them so you can replace them in the correct order. Lever up the old lining and lower it carefully to the ground, then remove the fixing nails with pincers. Check the

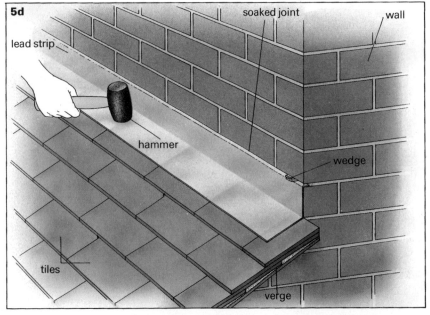

5d lead strip · soaked joint · wall · hammer · wedge · tiles · verge

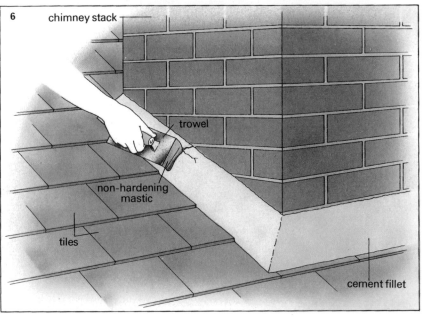

6 chimney stack · trowel · non-hardening mastic · tiles · cement fillet

timber underlining is securely fixed and coat it with creosote for protection. Cut the replacement zinc or lead to length, allowing for a 50mm (2in) overlap at the eaves, and place it over the underlining; press the lining down firmly to fit the angle of the valley and hold it in place with galvanized nails. If you have to use more than one sheet of metal, make sure the sheets overlap by about 225mm (9in). Where the lining meets the junction of the roof and wall, shape the end to match the junction, allowing a 75mm (3in) turning against the wall. Fix the sheet to the battens at both sides using galvanized nails, then relay the tiles; work from the eaves upwards and make sure you replace the tiles in the correct order. Finally apply self-adhesive flashing strip at the junction of the roof and wall to guard against rainwater penetration.

Felt lining You can replace an old metal lining with three layers of roofing felt. Remove the tiles and old lining as before and cut the felt to length. Fix the first layer of felt to the valley underlining, using galvanized nails, and fix the second and third layers with felt adhesive. Then replace the tiles in their original positions.

Valley tiles The major concrete roof tile manufacturers now produce special valley tiles which can be used as a cheaper alternative to the traditional lining materials. However, the method of fixing these tiles involves modifying the tile battening on each side of the valley, and the financial saving on materials may therefore be more than offset by the loss of time involved in carrying out the necessary modifications to the structure before the tiles can be positioned.

7a When replacing valley linings, remove the tiles on each side and fit felt onto the battens
7b Cover the felt with lead sheet nailed to alternate battens
7c Shape the lead sheet to fit the corner of the walls
7d Replace tiles from the eaves upwards
7e Apply self-adhesive flashing at the wall joins
8 Three layers of felt can be used instead of lead; nail the first layer and glue the other two

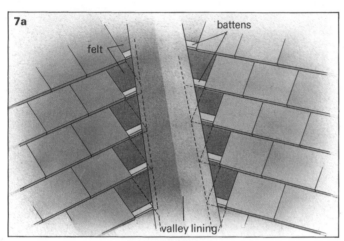

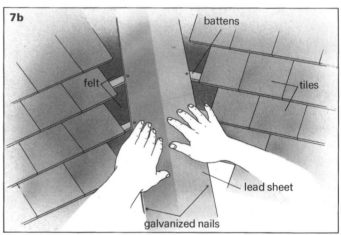

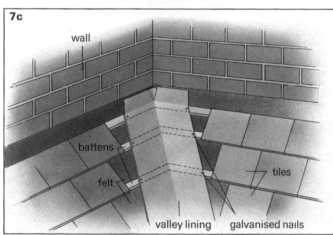

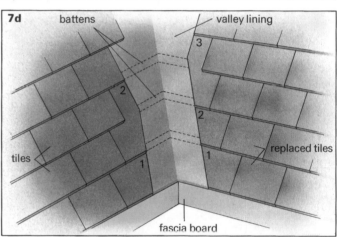

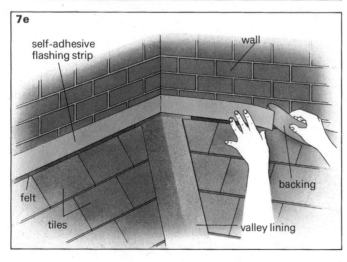

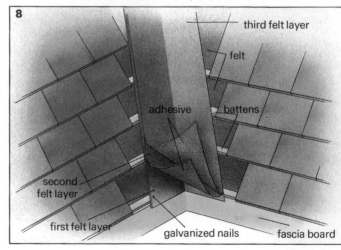

Repairing gutters

Plastic or cast iron guttering
comes in three shapes
1 Half-round, to rest in
brackets fixed to fascia
board, rafters or brickwork
2 Square, fixed as above
3 Ogee, to be screwed direct
to fascia, or rest on brackets
as shown here

1

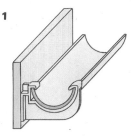

2

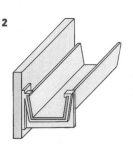

3

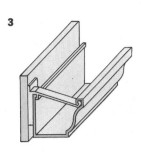

Defective rainwater systems cause all sorts of damp problems in the house structure. Water constantly pouring down an outside wall will eventually penetrate inside, ruining the decoration and causing mould growth. So it is important to keep your guttering in good repair. If you are prompted now to check your guttering for the first time, you may have a fair amount of work on hand to get it into shape. But once the repair work has been done, maintenance is a simple yearly task.

If you need an extra incentive to start immediately, remember if you allow things to deteriorate you may have to call in a professional to repair the guttering or even to replace the complete system and this would prove expensive. The best time to check the gutters is in the late autumn, once all the leaves have fallen. If you have already noticed leaks or damp patches, make the job a priority.

Working at height is not to everyone's liking. Use a secure ladder or make the job easier with a scaffolding system (available from hire shops). When working on metal gutters, wear an old pair of gloves to guard against cuts from sharp edges.

Types of gutter
In the past cast iron was the most common material for guttering, but plastic is now widely used. Today you cannot easily obtain a complete cast iron system, although you can buy replacement parts. Cast iron guttering comes in three shapes: half-round, square and ogee (a cross between half-round and square section). Half-round and square types rest in brackets fixed to the fascia board, rafters or brickwork. Ogee section can either be screwed direct to the fascia or be supported on brackets. The joints are sealed together with red lead, putty or other suitable jointing mastic and secured with bolts.

Plastic rainwater systems have a distinct advantage over cast iron ones since plastic is light, durable and needs little or no decoration. Plastic guttering is made in half-round, ogee and square sections which fit into special brackets. The lengths are joined together with clips housing rubber seals, or gaskets, to make them waterproof; a jointing cement is sometimes used instead of, or in addition to, the gasket.

Gutter blockages
Scoop out the rubbish with a trowel or a piece of card shaped to the profile of the gutter. Don't use the downpipe as a rubbish chute as it may become blocked or the rubbish sink into the drain.

Flush out the gutter with water; it should flow steadily towards the downpipe. If it overflows at the entrance then the downpipe is blocked and needs to be cleared.

If the downpipe gets blocked tie a small bundle of rags to the end of a pole and use this as a plunger to push away any obstruction. Place a bowl at the outlet on the ground to prevent rubbish sinking into the drain. If there is a 'swan neck' between the gutter and the downpipe, use a length of stiff wire to clear it of debris. To prevent further blockages, fit a cage into the entrance of the downpipe. You

Basic items
drill, hammer and screwdriver

For clearing blockages
trowel or piece of card
pole or stiff wire, rags and bowl
wire or plastic netting (to prevent blockages)

For realigning
string line, spirit level (if used)
nails 150mm (6in) long
No 8 chrome-plated round head screws 37mm (1½in) long
wall plugs

For treating rust
wire brush or electric drill with wire cup brush
rust killer, rust-resistant primer

epoxy repair material
fine glasspaper

For repairing joints
epoxy repair material
medium glasspaper
mastic sealer or replacement gasket

For replacing a section
nails (to locate bolt holes)
rust killer
penetrating oil or hacksaw (to remove bolts)
old chisel (to scrape off)
metal putty
rust-resistant primer
aluminium primer (over bituminous coatings)
undercoat and top coat paint

equipment

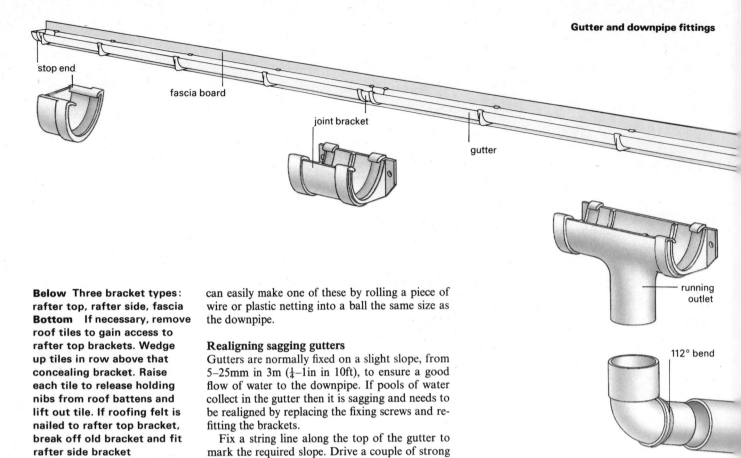

stop end

fascia board

joint bracket

gutter

running outlet

112° bend

Below Three bracket types: rafter top, rafter side, fascia
Bottom If necessary, remove roof tiles to gain access to rafter top brackets. Wedge up tiles in row above that concealing bracket. Raise each tile to release holding nibs from roof battens and lift out tile. If roofing felt is nailed to rafter top bracket, break off old bracket and fit rafter side bracket

can easily make one of these by rolling a piece of wire or plastic netting into a ball the same size as the downpipe.

Realigning sagging gutters

Gutters are normally fixed on a slight slope, from 5–25mm in 3m ($\frac{1}{4}$–1in in 10ft), to ensure a good flow of water to the downpipe. If pools of water collect in the gutter then it is sagging and needs to be realigned by replacing the fixing screws and re-fitting the brackets.

Fix a string line along the top of the gutter to mark the required slope. Drive a couple of strong

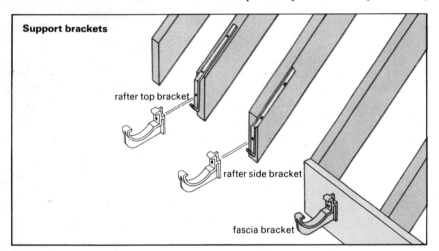

Support brackets

rafter top bracket

rafter side bracket

fascia bracket

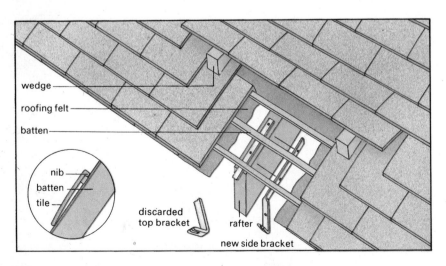

wedge

roofing felt

batten

nib

batten

tile

discarded top bracket

rafter

new side bracket

nails into the fascia about 25mm (1in) below the gutter for support while it is being refitted. Take out the old fixing screws (if these are in the edges of the rafters you may have to remove a tile from the roof to gain access to them). Now release the brackets so the gutter rests on the support nails; tap wall plugs into the old screw holes and refix the brackets using new screws. Pack the gutter up to the required height with bits of timber placed between it and the support nails. Finally remove nails and string line.

Rust and cracks

Inspect metal systems for any signs of rust and clean back with a wire brush or, if you have an extension lead, with an electric drill fitted with a wire cup brush – this saves a lot of hard work. Now treat the cleaned areas with a rust killer.

Fill hairline cracks with two coats of rust-resistant primer. Fill definite cracks or holes with an epoxy (water-resistant) repair material. Rub down with fine glasspaper.

Corrosion is always worst at the back edge of the gutter and to repair this you will have to dismantle the system and treat each section separately.

Leaking joints

Seal leaking joints in metal gutters with an epoxy repair material and rub down. If a leak develops at the joints of a plastic system, release the affected section by squeezing it at one end and lifting it clear of the adjoining length. If the gasket in the joint is sound, simply replace the section making sure the spigot end butts tightly against the socket of the adjoining piece. If the gasket is worn, scrape away all the old material and insert a replacement gasket or apply three good strips of mastic sealer in its place. Then press the two sections together again.

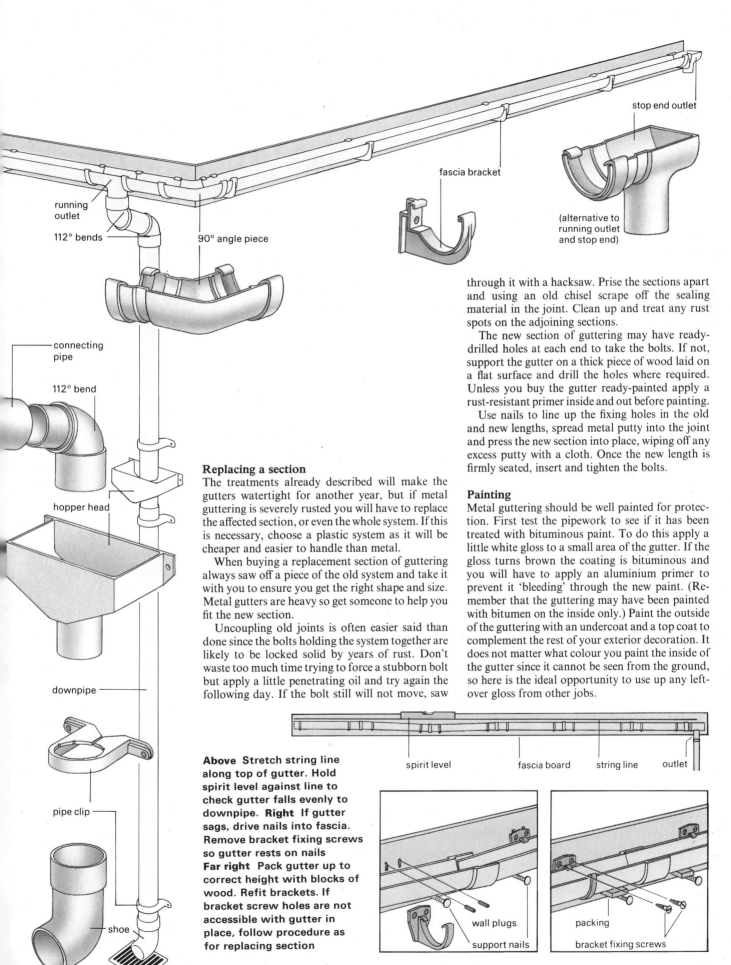

stop end outlet

fascia bracket

(alternative to running outlet and stop end)

running outlet

112° bends

90° angle piece

connecting pipe

112° bend

hopper head

downpipe

pipe clip

shoe

Replacing a section

The treatments already described will make the gutters watertight for another year, but if metal guttering is severely rusted you will have to replace the affected section, or even the whole system. If this is necessary, choose a plastic system as it will be cheaper and easier to handle than metal.

When buying a replacement section of guttering always saw off a piece of the old system and take it with you to ensure you get the right shape and size. Metal gutters are heavy so get someone to help you fit the new section.

Uncoupling old joints is often easier said than done since the bolts holding the system together are likely to be locked solid by years of rust. Don't waste too much time trying to force a stubborn bolt but apply a little penetrating oil and try again the following day. If the bolt still will not move, saw through it with a hacksaw. Prise the sections apart and using an old chisel scrape off the sealing material in the joint. Clean up and treat any rust spots on the adjoining sections.

The new section of guttering may have ready-drilled holes at each end to take the bolts. If not, support the gutter on a thick piece of wood laid on a flat surface and drill the holes where required. Unless you buy the gutter ready-painted apply a rust-resistant primer inside and out before painting.

Use nails to line up the fixing holes in the old and new lengths, spread metal putty into the joint and press the new section into place, wiping off any excess putty with a cloth. Once the new length is firmly seated, insert and tighten the bolts.

Painting

Metal guttering should be well painted for protection. First test the pipework to see if it has been treated with bituminous paint. To do this apply a little white gloss to a small area of the gutter. If the gloss turns brown the coating is bituminous and you will have to apply an aluminium primer to prevent it 'bleeding' through the new paint. (Remember that the guttering may have been painted with bitumen on the inside only.) Paint the outside of the guttering with an undercoat and a top coat to complement the rest of your exterior decoration. It does not matter what colour you paint the inside of the gutter since it cannot be seen from the ground, so here is the ideal opportunity to use up any left-over gloss from other jobs.

Above Stretch string line along top of gutter. Hold spirit level against line to check gutter falls evenly to downpipe. **Right** If gutter sags, drive nails into fascia. Remove bracket fixing screws so gutter rests on nails **Far right** Pack gutter up to correct height with blocks of wood. Refit brackets. If bracket screw holes are not accessible with gutter in place, follow procedure as for replacing section

spirit level   fascia board   string line   outlet

wall plugs

support nails

packing

bracket fixing screws

Repairing chimneys

When making repairs to the roof, it is always a good idea to check the condition of the chimney as well. Loose pots, cracked flaunching and crumbling mortar joints in the chimney stack are not only unsightly; they can also lead to damp inside and, if left to deteriorate, can become dangerous.

Repairing flaunching

Flaunching is the sloping cement mortar which holds the chimney pots in place and seals the top of the chimney stack. It is quite common for the flaunching to develop cracks, especially round the base of the pots. You can repair narrow cracks with a bead of non-hardening mastic applied from a cartridge with a mastic gun or with thick bitumen mastic pressed into cracks with a flat filling knife.

Wider cracks can be repaired temporarily with a cement filler paste; for a lasting repair the flaunching should be renewed. Use a club hammer and cold chisel to remove the old flaunching, taking care not to let large lumps of debris fall from the roof; collect the pieces in a bucket and lower them carefully to the ground. (It is also a good idea to cover fireplaces inside the house to prevent dust and dirt filtering into the rooms.) **Warning** Chimney pots are larger and heavier than you might expect, so handle them carefully and, if the pots are sound, take care not to crack them as the flaunching is chipped away. In old houses it is not unknown for the chimney pots to drop into the flue when the flaunching is removed; rope them to the chimney stack in case they become dislodged.

Rake out and brush all loose material from the bricks at the top of the stack; if there are any loose bricks, refix them with new mortar. Thoroughly wet the base of the pot and the surface of the bricks with water, then place the pot centrally over the flue. The base of the pot should fit the flue exactly; if there are any gaps which would allow the flaunching mortar to fall into the flue, cover them with pieces of roofing slate or asbestos cement.

Spread the flaunching mortar (a mix of one part Portland cement and three or four parts sharp, washed sand) over the top of the chimney so it is about 60mm (or 2½in) thick against the base of the pots and slopes down to about 20mm (or ¾in) thick round the edge of the stack; form a gentle curve all round to throw water away from the pots.

Replacing pots

Cracked or broken pots must be replaced since they may be displaced in a gale and cause damage to the roof or injure people below. To find the size of the pot required, remove part of the bedding mortar and measure from top to bottom and the internal diameter at the top; if possible, the replacement pot should have a square base so it fits exactly over the flue opening in the stack. To replace a pot, remove all the flaunching as previously described, place the new pot over the

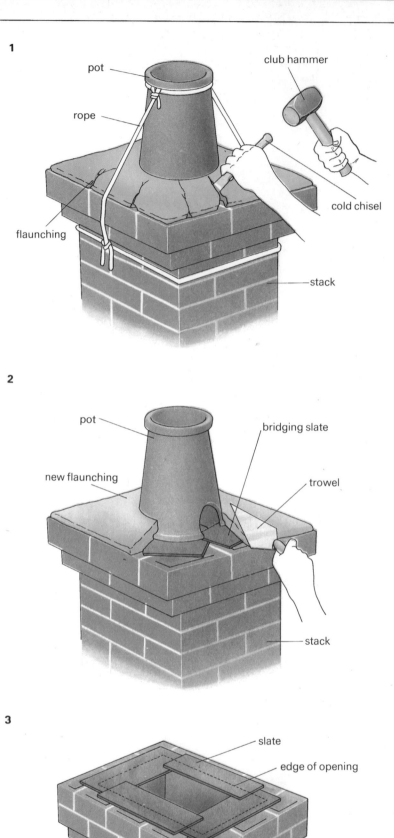

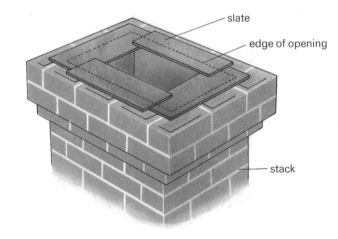

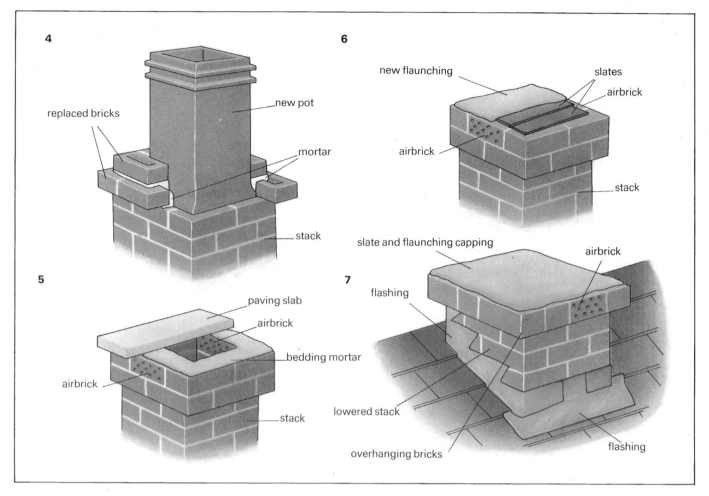

4
- replaced bricks
- new pot
- mortar
- stack

5
- paving slab
- airbrick
- bedding mortar
- airbrick
- stack

6
- new flaunching
- slates
- airbrick
- airbrick
- stack

7
- slate and flaunching capping
- airbrick
- flashing
- lowered stack
- overhanging bricks
- flashing

1 Remove cracked flaunching with a club hammer and cold chisel; before starting work, rope the pot to the stack
2 Set the pot centrally over the flue, covering any gaps with slate or asbestos cement; apply flaunching to the top of the stack and around the base of the pot
3 If a new pot is too narrow to rest over the flue, bridge the edges of the opening with pieces of slate and place the pot on these
4 Where a pot is built into the brickwork of the flue, release the pot by removing the bricks around its base; fit the new pot and replace the bricks so they overhang
5 To seal a disused flue, replace two of the bricks in the top row with airbricks and cover the opening with paving slabs bedded on mortar
6 Alternatively lay slates instead of paving slabs and cover with flaunching
7 You can reduce the height of the stack if the chimney will never be used again; lay a course of bricks on top of the lowered stack and cap with slate and flaunching

flue opening and apply new flaunching mortar.

If you are working on an old house, you may find the base of the new pot is too narrow to rest over the flue opening. In this case straddle the edges of the opening with pieces of roofing slate to restrict its size to a suitable width and support the pot on these. Where the base of the pot is built into the brickwork of the flue, you will have to remove bricks to release the pot; fit the new pot by replacing the bricks around it.

Sealing the stack
If the chimney is no longer used, you can cap the flue to make it weatherproof, but it should not be tightly sealed or the flue will become damp and spoil wall decorations in rooms through which it passes. Metal and clay capping cowls are available. The metal type simply clips into the top of the chimney pot; the clay ones, which are longer lasting and less obtrusive, are secured with cement mortar between the cowl and the inside of the pot.

When a disused flue has cracked pots or flaunching, it is best to remove the flaunching and pots and seal the flue with one or two paving slabs. Before fitting the slabs, knock out at least two bricks from the sides of the flue and replace them with airbricks. Bed the slabs on mortar so they are level and overhang the sides of the stack by at least 25mm (1in) all round. Alternatively you can lay slates over the flue after fitting the airbricks and cover the entire surface with new flaunching.

Lowering the stack
As long as you will never use the chimney again you can reduce the height of a chimney stack if you

feel this will improve the appearance of the house or if the stack is dangerous and in need of repair. It is essential to erect scaffolding round the chimney or to work from a scaffold tower when possible.

Use a club hammer and bolster chisel to remove the bricks course by course from the top down to the required height, taking care to prevent rubble falling down the flue. It is a good idea to tie a long length of stout string to the handles of the tools and tie the string firmly round the base of the stack; if you drop the tools down the flue, you can then retrieve them easily. Place the bricks in a bucket and lower them to the ground as work proceeds. At the top of the lowered stack, relay one or two courses of bricks to overhang the general brickwork surface slightly; this will help to throw water clear of the stack. Finally cap the flue.

Repairing brickwork
If the mortar joints between the bricks of a chimney are crumbling, they must be repointed using the same technique as for repointing walls. After repointing or sealing a stack, it is a good idea to paint the brickwork with a clear silicone water repellant to prevent rainwater penetration.
Cracked bricks These can often indicate serious faults and you should seek the advice of a builder or roofing specialist. Bulging brickwork or cement rendering should also be referred to a specialist.

Repairing roof boards and snowguards

Where you are repairing a roof covering you should check the structure around it is in sound condition; damage in this area will shorten the life of the covering. Sometimes it may be sufficient to patch the damaged areas. Barge boards, fascias and soffits, for example, which have only slightly rotted can be temporarily repaired by scraping away the rotten timber, filling the cavity with an exterior grade filler and painting thoroughly with a waterproof paint. In slightly more serious cases the affected section should be cut out and replaced with a new piece of timber. For a lasting repair and where the damage is too bad for patching, the boards should be replaced.

Replacing boards

Before you begin, remember these boards are heavier than they look from the ground and you should attempt replacement only if you can work from a scaffold.

Fascias and soffits Fascia boards, to which the gutters are fixed, cover the ends of rafters and a soffit board seals the gap underneath, between the wall and the fascia. To replace fascias and soffits, take off the gutters and gutter brackets and remove

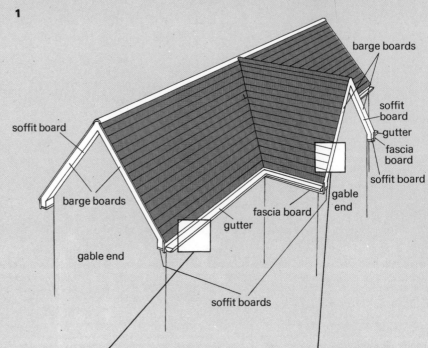

1

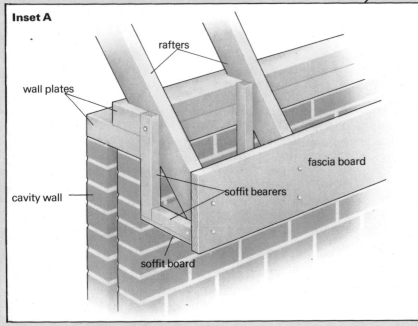

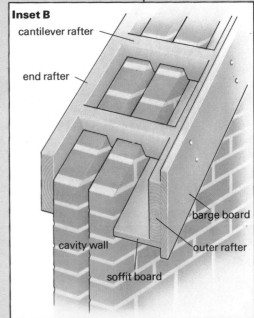

the fascia by prising it away from the rafter ends with a cold chisel or wrecking bar. The soffit is nailed to the rafter ends and supported by a batten plugged and screwed to the wall or by bearers nailed to the rafters. If the soffit supports are sound, simply prise away the soffit; where the soffit is fixed to bearers you will have to remove the fixing nails partially to release the soffit. If the soffit supports are rotten, these too should be removed and replaced; where the fixings which hold these in place are too difficult to remove, you can cut out the rotten sections with a panel saw and replace them with pieces of new timber.

Where rafter ends are rotten you may be able to form new ends by bolting pieces of new timber alongside the decayed rafters. If this is impossible,

the ends should be removed and replaced.

Treat all the roof timbers with wood preservative before fixing the new boards. Cut the soffits and fascias to length; if you have to join several lengths to make up a long run, check the joints coincide with the centre lines of the rafters and make the saw cuts at an angle of 45 degrees to ensure neat joints. Hold the soffit in position; if there is a definite gap between the wall and the soffit, you will have to cut the soffit to the shape of the wall so make sure the board is wide enough. To mark the cutting line on the soffit, hold a pencil against a scrap of wood and move this along the wall, tracing the contour of the wall onto the soffit. Trim the edge of the soffit to match, making an allowance for the width of the block of wood.

1 Locating the position of soffit boards, fascias and barge boards
Inset A Detail of the fascia fixing at the eaves
Inset B Detail of the barge board fixing at the verge

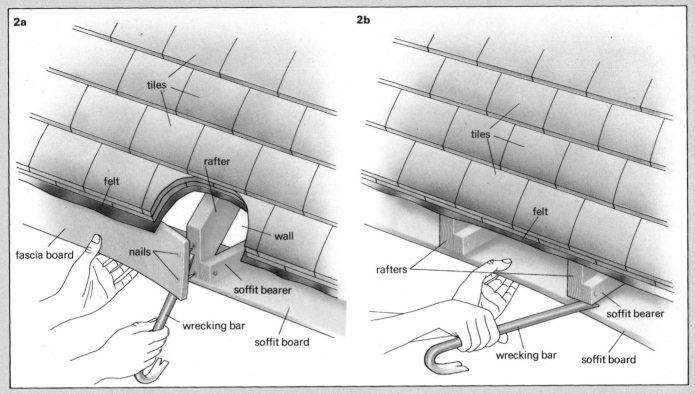

2a Removing the fascia
2b Levering the soffit
away from its bearers
3 Tracing the wall outline
onto the new soffit
4 Fitting the new soffit
and fascia

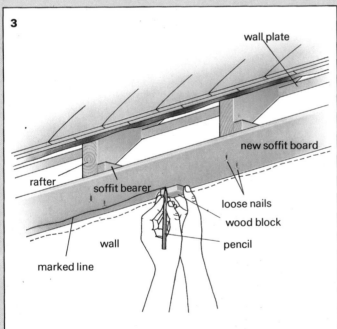

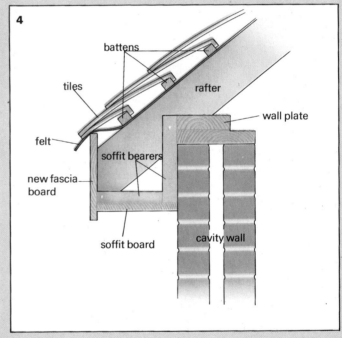

Treat the new boards with wood preservative and apply a wood primer. Replace the soffit by fixing it to the underside of the rafter ends and supports with galvanized nails. Fix the new fascia by nailing it to the rafter ends and through the edge of the soffit. The top edge of the fascia should tuck under the overhang of the roof slates or tiles and any underfelt should overhang the front of the fascia so it can be tucked into the gutters later. The lower edge of the fascia should protrude below the face of the soffit to protect the soffit and the walls.
Barge boards These are fitted at the gable end of the roof. They are screwed to the roof timbers and, like the fascia board, incorporate a soffit which seals the gap underneath. Lever out the old boards with a crowbar or wrecking bar, starting at the

eaves and working upwards. Use the old boards as a guide to cut the new ones to the correct angle at the ridge; alternatively make a card template of the angle before removing the boards and transfer the shape to the new boards, trimming as necessary. Treat the boards with clear wood preservative and allow this to dry, then prime all surfaces. Fix the soffit to the underside of the roof timbers, using rustproof screws, then fit the barge board over the soffit and screw it to the roof timbers. After fixing, you may find you have to seal the verge by re-pointing the tiles.

Repairing snowguards
Usually these consist of a strip of galvanized steel mesh fixed to support brackets which are screwed

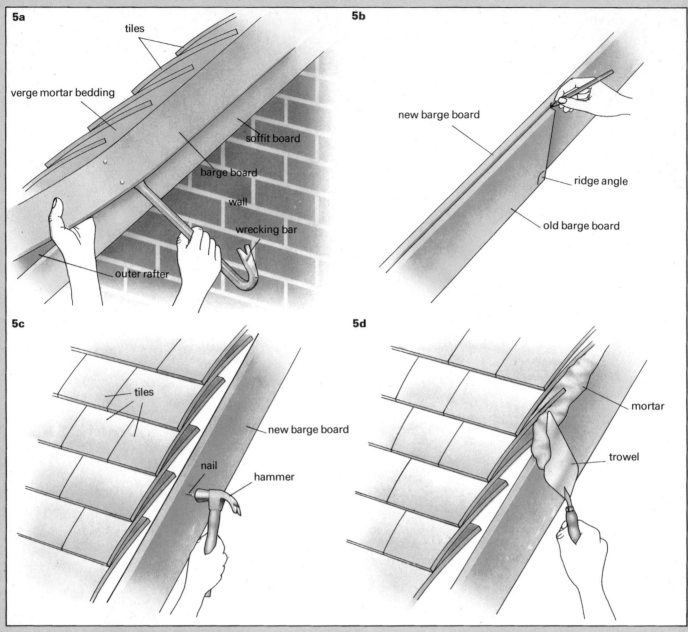

5a
tiles
verge mortar bedding
soffit board
barge board
wall
wrecking bar
outer rafter

5b
new barge board
ridge angle
old barge board

5c
tiles
nail
hammer
new barge board

5d
mortar
trowel

to the sides of the rafters or to the fascia board. Where the mesh has come loose, refix it to the supports with twists of copper or galvanized steel wire. If the mesh has corroded, remove the fixings which hold it in place and, after lifting away the mesh, replace it with galvanized steel mesh fixed to the roof side of the support brackets with wire twists. Remove any loose brackets and refix them in a slightly different position so the fixing screws can bite into new wood. If brackets are bent, you can straighten them by using a length of strong tube as a lever, slipping it over the bracket.

Warning For safety reasons, you should always work from a secure foothold, such as a scaffold tower cantilevered over the roof or a ladder which is securely tied at the top.

5a Removing an old barge board with a wrecking bar
5b Using the old board as a guide to mark the shape of the new board
5c Nailing the new board in place
5d Repointing the tiles at the verge
6 Repositioning loose snowguard brackets

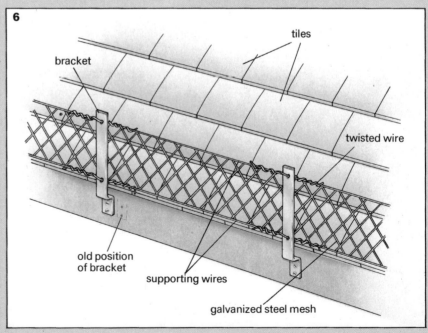

6
tiles
bracket
twisted wire
old position of bracket
supporting wires
galvanized steel mesh

Repairing glass roofs and skylights

If you have a glass roof on your property, you can successfully carry out repairs yourself. There is a range of products available which make some types of repair work relatively straightforward. For example, cracks in the glass and leaks along the glazing bars, the usual faults in a glass roof, can be sealed with a self-adhesive flashing strip. Alternatively you can use mastic waterproofing tape – it is best to buy a foil-covered type since this lasts longer and is less messy to handle than plain mastic tape. Where you want the repair to be unobtrusive, you can buy a clear glass-sealing tape; this is applied in the same way as the other tapes.

Sealing roofs

Clean the glazing bars with a wire brush and use soap and water or a detergent to clean the glass, rinsing with clean water. Allow both to dry before applying the tape or strip. The sealing material should be wide enough to overlap the glass and glazing bar by at least 13mm ($\frac{1}{2}$in). In the case of a glazing bar, start at the highest point of the bar and lay the tape or strip over the bar, pressing it down on each side. When dealing with a crack, start at the glazing bar immediately above the crack. At glass overlaps, double the tape on itself since this helps to form a watertight joint. If you are joining two pieces of tape, place the upper piece over the lower piece to prevent water seeping in.

Making permanent repairs

For long-lasting repair on a leaking glass roof it is best to remove and renew the glass; you can replace cracked sheets of glass at the same time. Check with your supplier for the most suitable type of glass. After you have lifted the glass, clean and repaint the glazing bars with a waterproof paint and bed the glass back on mastic glazing strips. These are preferable to putty since they never completely harden and allow for expansion.

Some metal glazing bars have special clips to hold the glass on the glazing strips; with timber glazing bars, the glass is held down with small glazing sprigs which you drive into the bars, using the flat edge of a wide chisel.

Cracked glass in a skylight should be removed and replaced with wired glass bedded all round on a mastic glazing strip. Check the flashings around the skylight and, if necessary, repair or replace them. Remove any flaking paint from the skylight area and treat the timber with clear wood preservative; when dry, paint with primer, undercoat and at least two top coats.

Glass roofs are not reserved for the greenhouse. Conservatories, for example, normally have glass roofs, while many more houses have some form of skylight. Repairs will be needed if decay and penetration by damp are to be avoided.

1 To stop leaks along a glazing bar, fix sealing tape so it overlaps the glass
2 Double the tape where the glass overlaps
3 Bed replacement glass on mastic glazing strips and secure to metal glazing bars with glazing clips
4 Bed glass on mastic glazing strips and secure to timber glazing bars with glazing sprigs

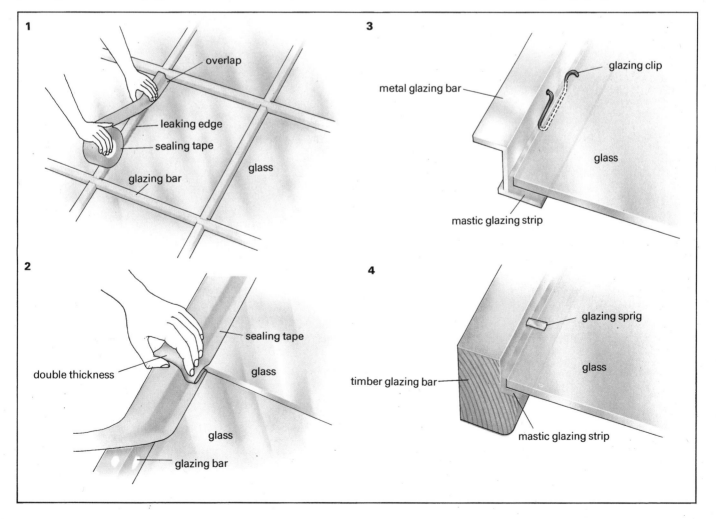

Repairing flat, shed and corrugated roofs

While the most common type of house roof is pitched and covered with tiles or slates, there are other kinds of covering and you may have one on your property. The main roof can be flat rather than pitched or there may be a flat roof on a room extension, garage or other small-scale construction; some roofs are corrugated and you may have a shed with a roof covered in roofing felt. Whatever the type of roof, it is worth checking for signs of deterioration – where repairs are needed, it may be possible for you to carry them out yourself.

Flat roofs

A faulty roof may be indicated by a damp patch on a ceiling. Tracing the source of a leak in a flat roof can be difficult since water may have travelled some distance before it shows as a damp patch. Therefore looking at a roof directly above a damp patch will not necessarily show where the problem lies and you should examine the entire roof for damage.

If the roof looks in reasonable condition, it should be sufficient to apply two coats of heavy duty liquid bitumen coating to waterproof it. Alternatively you can apply an overall plastic membrane to the roof surface. Both treatments can be carried out on roofing felt, asphalt, zinc, lead or concrete.

Bitumen proofing Before applying this waterproofing liquid, remove dirt and dust with a wire brush and a knife or wallpaper scraper and sweep the roof to remove debris. If there is any moss and lichen, scrape it off and treat the roof surface with a proprietary fungicide solution, allowing this to dry before carrying out the waterproofing treatment. Bitumen proofing can be applied by brush to damp as well as dry surfaces; you will find dipping the brush in water from time to time makes it easier to spread the bitumen. Make sure the first coat is thoroughly dry before applying the second.

Where there is more serious damage to the roof

1a Before laying new felt, remove the old felt by cutting round the edges and tearing it off; trim round fixing nails as necessary
1b Nail battens to the top of the fascia boards to form drip rails. If the fascia board projects upwards at the verge, also nail an angled timber fillet to the inside of the board
1c Use nails to fix the first layer of felt, working from the centre outwards
1d Fix the second layer of felt using adhesive; make sure the joints do not coincide with the joints of the first layer

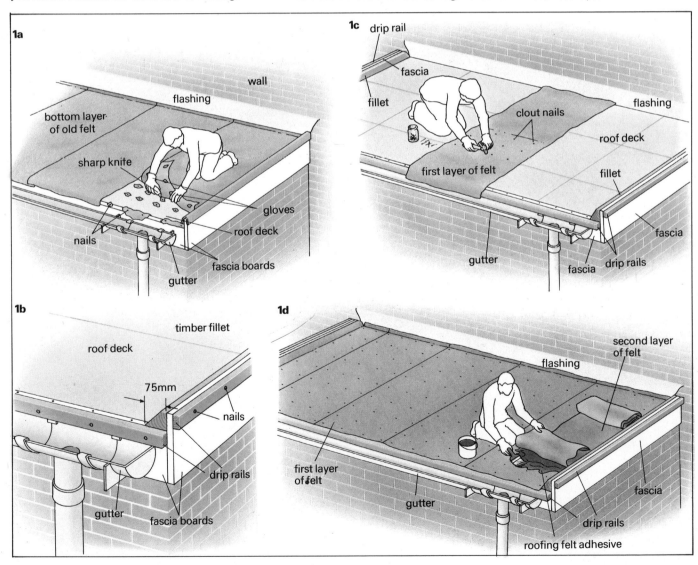

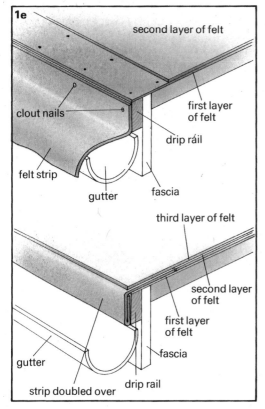

1e

second layer of felt

clout nails

first layer of felt

drip rail

felt strip

gutter

fascia

third layer of felt

second layer of felt

first layer of felt

gutter

fascia

strip doubled over

drip rail

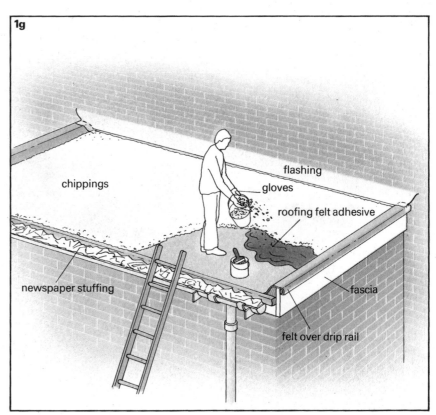

1g

chippings

flashing

gloves

roofing felt adhesive

newspaper stuffing

fascia

felt over drip rail

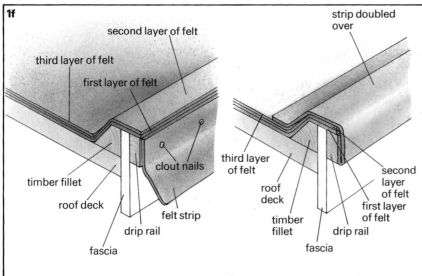

1f

second layer of felt

third layer of felt

first layer of felt

strip doubled over

clout nails

third layer of felt

roof deck

second layer of felt

first layer of felt

timber fillet

roof deck

drip rail

fascia

timber fillet

drip rail

fascia

felt strip

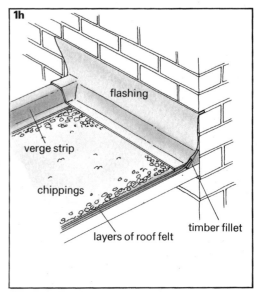

1h

flashing

verge strip

chippings

layers of roof felt

timber fillet

covering, such as severe cracks, loose areas and bad wrinkles, the roof should be stripped and the covering replaced. In the case of an asphalt roof, this work should be left to a professional. Where a concrete roof has cracked, trowel on a mortar mix to fill the cracks before treating with bitumen proofing. Where the roof has a timber base, check the timber is sound and remove and replace any unsound boards before carrying out further repairs.

Roofing felt Flat roofs covered with bituminous roofing felt are quite easy to strip and replace. On house extension or garage roofs there are usually three layers of felt fixed down over a roof deck of timber boards or chipboard sheets. Tear off the old felt, using a sharp knife to cut round the nails. It is best to wear tough gloves when doing this job since the felt is rough and may cut or scratch your hands. Remove the old fixing nails with a claw hammer or hammer them as flush with the

surface as possible. Sweep the surface clean and check it is smooth – high points can be taken off with an abrasive disc fitted to an electric drill and depressions levelled with an exterior grade filler. Nail a 50×38mm ($2 \times 1\frac{1}{2}$in) batten along the outside edge or verge of the roof to serve as a drip rail over which felt will later be fixed to form an apron; this weatherproofs the edge of the roof and throws water clear of the walls of the building or into a gutter, if one is fitted. If the fascia board projects upwards at the verge, you should also nail a 75mm (3in) wide angled timber fillet behind the fascia.

Before you buy felt, consult your local building inspector to check that the type you have in mind complies with the current Building Regulations. Felt manufacturers make recommendations regarding the kind of felt to be fitted to suit the type of roof and will supply comprehensive fixing instructions. Where possible, cut the felt roughly to length and

1e At the eaves, nail a strip of felt to the drip rail and then double it back over to lie flush with the second layer of felt

1f At the verge, nail a strip of felt to the drip rail and then double it back to lap over the third layer of felt

1g Apply adhesive and chippings to the top layer of felt after stuffing the gutter with newspaper

1h At the parapet wall, fit a felt flashing with the end cut at 45 degrees and the top tucked into the raked-out mortar joint

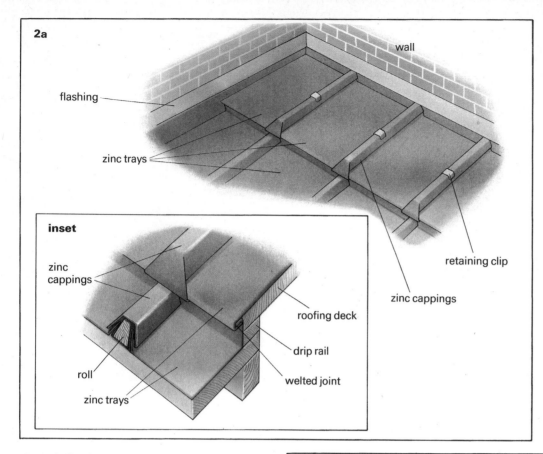

2a

wall

flashing

zinc trays

retaining clip

zinc cappings

inset

zinc
cappings

roofing deck

drip rail

roll

welted joint

zinc trays

2a A zinc roof is made up of zinc trays, which are separated by timber battens or rolls (**inset**); these are covered with zinc cappings
2b To remove a tray, lever up the flashing and use a claw hammer to remove the nails from the zinc cappings over the rolls
2c Open the welted joint at the bottom edge of the tray and release the retaining clips to enable the tray to be pulled out

leave it flat for at least 24 hours before fixing to minimize the effects of subsequent curling and stretching. Usually, you will have to fix the first layer of felt to the roof boards with galvanized clout nails at 150mm (6in) intervals. Fix from the centre of the sheet outwards to prevent wrinkles and bubbles forming and secure subsequent layers of felt by brushing on roofing felt adhesive. Also apply roofing felt adhesive over the surface of the top layer of felt and sprinkle on small stone chippings to protect the felt and give a non-slip surface – or you can spread on a special chipping compound. Protect the gutter from the chippings by blocking it with newspaper or rags while you are carrying out this operation. To form the weatherproofing apron at the eaves, the middle layer of felt should be cut a little shorter than the other layers; cut a separate strip, nail it to the drip rail with galvanized clout nails and double the edge over to lie flush with, and butting against, the second layer. At the verge, a similar piece of felt is nailed to the drip rail and doubled over to form the apron and then taken over the roof to overlap the top layer of felt.

Zinc roofing Normally a zinc roof is constructed in tiers called drips and each drip is subdivided into sections or zinc trays; the trays are separated by timber battens or rolls which are also covered with zinc. While extensive repairs are probably best left to a roofing specialist, you can replace a damaged tray yourself. Where the tray meets a retaining wall there will be a flashing overlapping the tray. Lever this up and use a claw hammer or pincers to remove the nails from the zinc capping covering the rolls. Open the welted joint at the bottom edge of the tray, release the retaining clips which hold the tray in place and slide the tray free. Use the old tray as a pattern to cut the new one to size with tin snips. Repeat for the cappings, remembering to make sure

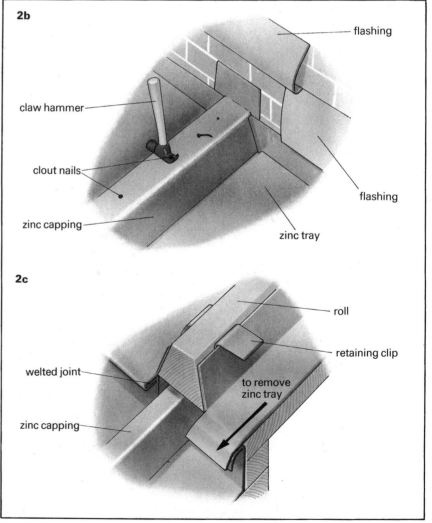

2b

flashing

claw hammer

clout nails

flashing

zinc capping

zinc tray

2c

roll

retaining clip

welted joint

to remove
zinc tray

zinc capping

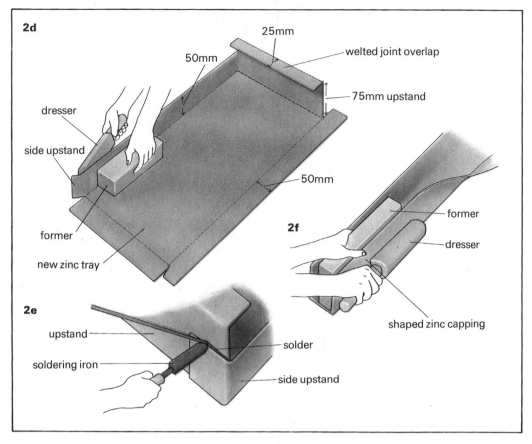

2d To shape the new tray, use a batten as a former and press the zinc up round it with a wood dresser
2e Solder the tray corners
2f Fold the new capping with a former and dresser
2g Position the new tray, butting the upturned sides against the rolls and leaving the bottom end open to form the welted joint
2h Solder the edges of the capping to the tray at the roll end

on both occasions you fold out the welted joint to cut the new zinc to the right size.

Using a batten of suitable length as a former, bend up the sides and end of the new zinc to form the upstands of the tray, clean all round with wire wool, and solder the corners. Fold the capping in the same way as the old capping. Place the new tray in position, lap the flashing over it and butt the upturned sides hard up against the rolls, folding the retaining clips over the upstands. Secure the new capping in place with galvanized nails and solder the edges of the capping at the roll end where they butt against the zinc tray underneath.

Alternatively you can strip the zinc covering and replace it with roofing felt. You can replace the zinc with metal-faced glass fibre bitumen sheeting, but this type of work is best left to a specialist.

Lead roofing Normally a lead roof should last for a long time; but if there are small damaged patches in a roof, you can solder on small pieces of lead to cover the damage. Buying sheets of lead for more extensive repair work is expensive and it is cheaper and simpler to strip off the lead and apply three layers of bituminous felt.

Shed roofs

A single sheet of mineral-surfaced roofing felt is normally used to waterproof a shed roof, but sometimes it may be covered with bitumen strip slates which simulate a tiled roof. In both cases, you can patch small tears and cracks with new pieces of roofing felt stuck down with roofing felt adhesive. If the covering is in very bad condition, it should be removed and replaced. Before carrying out replacement, remove any protruding nails with a claw hammer or drive them in flush with the roof.

Felt covering Lay new bituminous roofing felt in wide strips which run along the length of the roof. The strips should be cut and laid out for at least 24

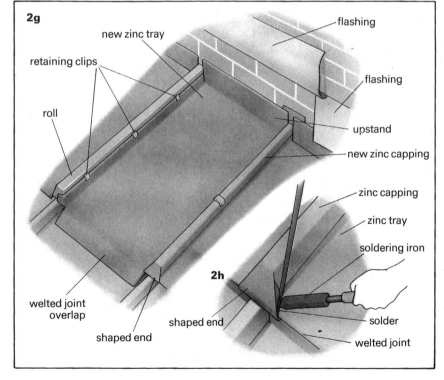

hours before fixing. Start fixing at eaves or gutter level and overlap adjacent strips by 75mm (3in), finishing off at the ridge or apex. Nail them down using 13mm ($\frac{1}{2}$in) galvanized clout nails at about 50mm (2in) intervals around the edges. Fold under exposed edges at the eaves and verges before nailing. For extra weather protection, secure the felt overlaps with roofing felt adhesive. Seal the ridge with a 300mm (or 12in) wide strip of felt fixed with adhesive and clout nails along the edges.

Bitumen strip slates These are fixed in place with galvanized clout nails. Start at the eaves and work up the roof to the ridge, making sure the strips are laid with staggered joints. With some types of strip slates, you should stick down the exposed part of each strip by melting the underside of the strip with a blowlamp: check the maker's instructions.

Corrugated roofs

Plastic, glass fibre, asbestos-cement, galvanized steel and aluminium are frequently used for corrugated roofing. In all cases, small cracks and holes can be repaired by patching with self-adhesive foil-backed flashing strip.

Patching Use a wire brush to clean the damaged area; cut the patch so it overlaps this area by at least 50mm (2in) all round and press it on. You should prime an asbestos-cement surface first with flashing strip primer to ensure the patch adheres firmly. As an alternative method, you can repair holes using the glass fibre matting repair kits sold for car bodywork repairs. When the repairs are complete, resurface the entire roof with two coats of heavy duty liquid bitumen proofing. This will seal pin-prick holes or porous areas on most surfaces, but cannot be used on thin plastic sheeting.

Replacing corrugated sheet Where there is extensive damage you should replace the damaged sheets. Use a claw hammer to remove the nails from an old sheet, then ease up the flashing and pull out the sheet. Cut the new sheet using the old sheet as a pattern. Put wood blocks under the third corrugation of a sheet next to the gap which the new sheet will fill and slide the new sheet under the raised sheet and over the sheet on the opposite side, checking it is properly in place. Remove the blocks and drill holes to take the fixing screws which should penetrate the high points of the corrugations, not the valleys. (Check with your supplier on the type of screw suitable for use with the material you are fixing.) If necessary, replace the flashing with self-adhesive flashing strip.

3a When covering a shed roof with felt, fix the first strip at the level of the eaves or gutter. Fold the felt at the corner and nail it in place (**inset**)

3b Make sure there is an overlap between adjacent strips of felt

3c Seal the ridge of the roof with a strip of felt. Where the felt laps over the edge of the ridge, fold and nail it (**inset**)

4a Use galvanized clout nails to fix trimmed bitumen strip slates at the eaves

4b Lay the rows of strips so the joints are staggered for weatherproofing

4c With some types of strip slates you will have to melt the underside of the slates with a blowtorch to stick them down

5a Use a self-adhesive flashing strip to patch small tears and cracks in corrugated roofing

5b To replace a damaged corrugated sheet, slide the new sheet under one sheet, which is raised up by a wood block, and over the sheet on the opposite side

5c Types of fixing for corrugated roofing

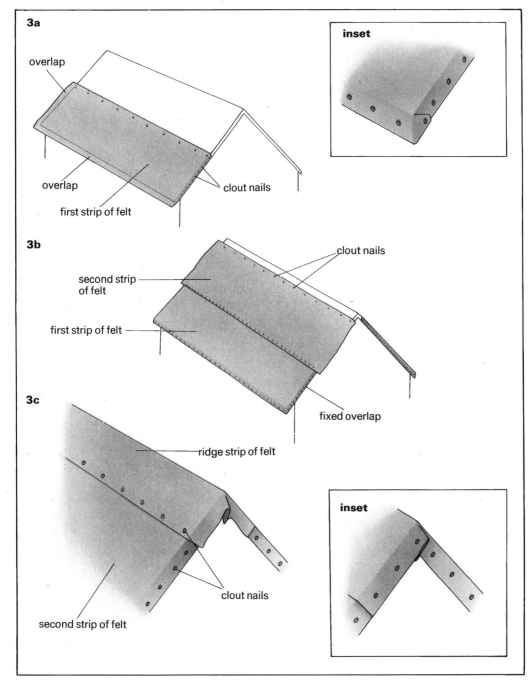

3a

overlap

overlap

first strip of felt

clout nails

inset

3b

clout nails

second strip of felt

first strip of felt

fixed overlap

3c

ridge strip of felt

clout nails

second strip of felt

inset

4a

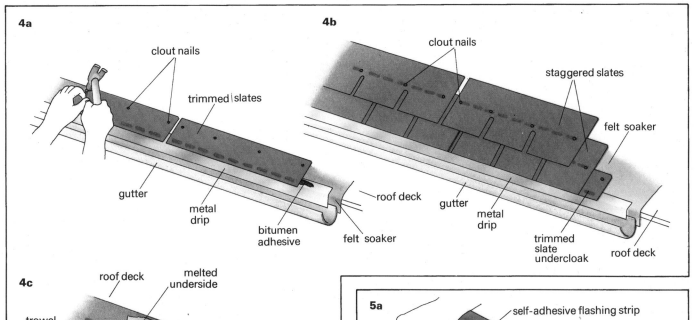

clout nails

trimmed slates

gutter

metal drip

bitumen adhesive

felt soaker

roof deck

4b

clout nails

staggered slates

felt soaker

roof deck

gutter

metal drip

trimmed slate undercloak

roof deck

4c

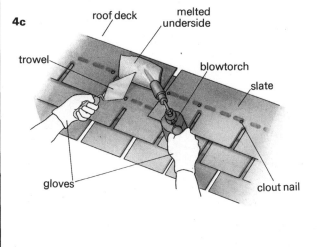

roof deck

melted underside

trowel

blowtorch

slate

gloves

clout nail

5a

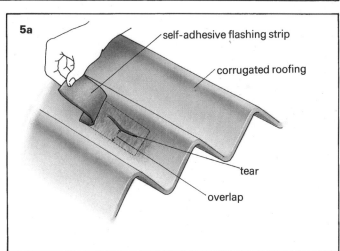

self-adhesive flashing strip

corrugated roofing

tear

overlap

5b

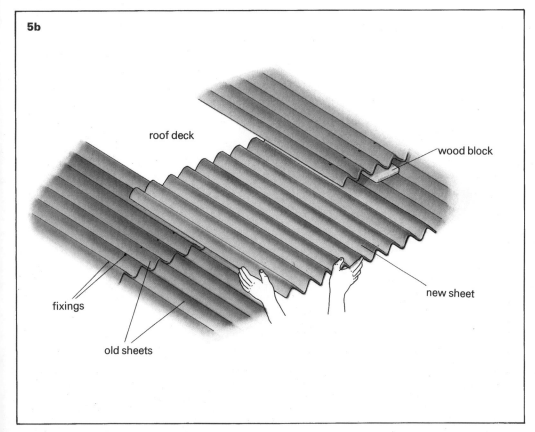

roof deck

wood block

new sheet

fixings

old sheets

5c

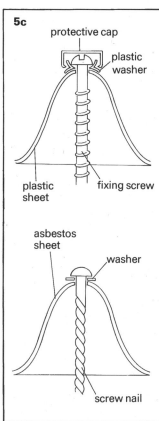

protective cap

plastic washer

plastic sheet

fixing screw

asbestos sheet

washer

screw nail

Window repairs

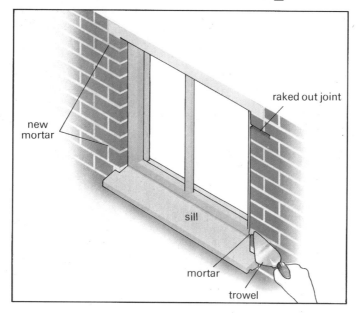

Replacing broken glass

Emergency repair

If you break a window and cannot get replacement glass immediately, as a temporary measure fix a sheet of polythene to the inside of the window.

With a wood frame either fix the polythene with adhesive tape or, for a stronger fixing, secure the top of the polythene to the window with drawing pins, nail a batten along the top and then secure each side and bottom edge with battens (**see 1**). Stretch the polythene to smooth out wrinkles as you work. You will not be able to nail through a metal frame, however, so use heavy duty polythene secured with strong adhesive tape.

Wood frames

Clear up the glass left on the ground and remove the fragments in the frame. These should pull away easily, but if the putty or wood beading keeping the glass in place is firmly fixed you may have to remove the holding material first.

Take out the glass from the top of the frame, then work down the sides and along the bottom edge. To remove stubborn pieces run a glass-cutter round the perimeter of the glass and close to the rebates (**see 2**). Tap out the pieces with the handle of a light hammer, holding each piece until it is free.

If the holding material is putty chop away with a hacking knife or old chisel (**see 3**). This will reveal a series of small headless nails (sprigs) which do the real job of holding the glass. Carefully remove the sprigs with pincers (**see 4**). If they are still straight, you can re-use them; if not, buy new ones 16mm ($\frac{5}{8}$in) long.

Sometimes the glass will have been secured by wood beading fixed with panel pins. Prise away the beading and remove the pins (**see 5**). Take care when removing since the beading will have mitred

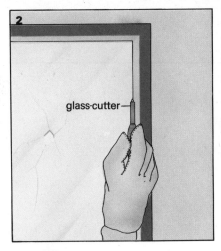
old putty
old chisel

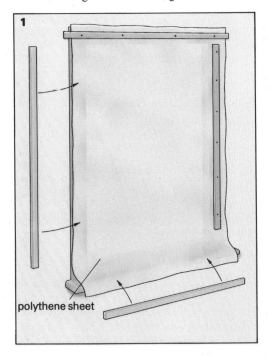
glass-cutter

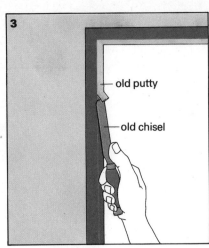
wood beading

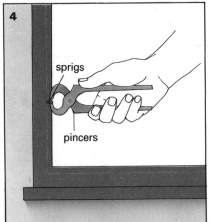
sprigs
pincers

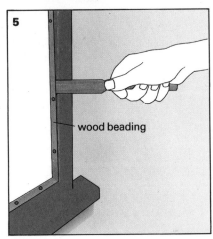
putty

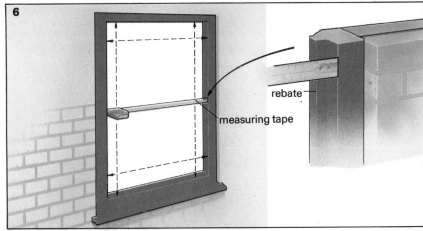
sprig

measuring tape
rebate

polythene sheet

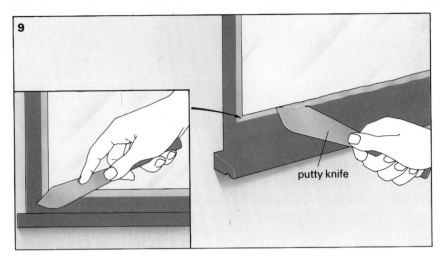

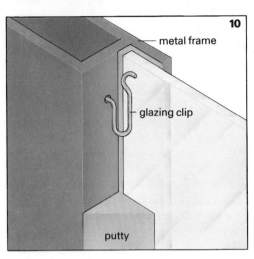

metal frame

glazing clip

putty knife

putty

1 Make a temporary repair to a broken window by covering it with polythene sheet
2 Use a glass-cutter close to the rebates to remove every piece of glass from the frame
3 Hack out all the old putty from the rebates
4 Remove the holding sprigs with pincers
5 If wood beading holds the glass in place, prise it away with an old chisel
6 To find the dimensions for the new glass always take three measurements across the width and over the length of the frame to ensure accuracy
7 Press soft putty in a continuous layer round the rebates
8 Refit the sprigs, tapping them in flush with the glass
9 Smooth out the final layer of putty shaping it to form mitres at the corners
10 When fitting glass in a metal frame use glazing clips and metal casement putty

ends to form neat corner joints and if you damage these you will have to buy more beading and shape the mitres yourself.

Brush out all the dust from the rebates and rub the timber smooth with medium coarse glasspaper. Apply a coat of wood primer and leave to dry.

Measuring up

Accurate measuring for the new sheet of glass is vital. Measure the full width of the opening between the side rebates at the top, centre and bottom of the frame (see 6). These should be the same, but if there is a slight difference work on the smallest measurement. Next measure between the other two rebates, top to bottom, again if necessary noting the smallest measurements. Deduct 3mm ($\frac{1}{8}$in) from these dimensions (this is to allow for the glass expanding and contracting in the frame). These are the dimensions to use when ordering your glass.

If your window frame is badly out of square or an awkward shape, such as curved, make a template (pattern) of the frame from card or stiff paper so the glass can be cut to the exact size.

For normal domestic use you will need 3mm ($\frac{1}{8}$in) sheet glass. Take some old newspapers to wrap round the glass or wear gloves to protect your hands from the edges when carrying it.

Fitting the glass

Hold the new glass up to the frame to check it is the right size. Knead some linseed oil putty into a ball in your hands to make it soft and pliable and if necessary add a little linseed oil to make the putty more workable. (Putty has an irritating habit of clinging to dry surfaces when you do not want it to, so keep both hands and the putty knife wet.)

Run a continuous layer of putty about 3mm ($\frac{1}{8}$in) thick round the rebates and press well in with your thumb (see 7). Carefully lift the glass into position, allowing for the 3mm expansion gap, and press it into the layer of putty pushing only on the edge of the glass, never in the middle.

Refit the sprigs, spacing them at intervals of about 150mm (6in) around the glass. They must be flat against the glass to hold it securely, so tap them in carefully. The flat edge of a wide chisel could be used for this (see 8). Run another layer of putty around the front of the glass, pressing it in with your thumb. With a putty knife smooth out the layer, shaping it to match the angle on your other windows, and form mitres at the corners (see 9). Use the edge of the knife to trim off surplus putty from the glass.

Run over the putty with a paint brush dampened with water to make sure it adheres firmly to the glass to give a tight, water-resistant seal. Leave the putty for one to two weeks to dry out before painting or the paint surface will crack.

Metal frames

To fit a new pane of glass into a metal frame adopt basically the same method as for a wood one except you must use metal casement putty, since linseed oil putty is not suitable for metal. The glass is held in place by special glazing clips rather than sprigs – one arm of the clip slots into a hole in the rebate, while the other arm of the clip clamps onto the face of the glass (see 10).

Hack away the old putty and note the positions of the glazing clips so you will know where to refit them. Remove the clips from the frame (if you do this carefully, you will be able to use them again). Brush the rebates clean, apply a coat of metal primer and leave to dry for a few hours.

Spread a layer of putty in the rebates and fit the new pane of glass into the frame on the putty. Replace the clips in their original positions and finish off as for a wood frame.

Basic items
protective spectacles and old leather gloves
glass-cutter, light hammer
hacking knife or old chisel
putty knife, small paint brush
measuring tape
card or stiff paper (for template)

For emergency repair
polythene sheet
adhesive tape or drawing pins
four 25 × 12mm (1 × $\frac{1}{2}$in) battens and round wire nails, 25mm (1in) long (for wood frames)

For wood frames
pincers
medium coarse glasspaper
wood primer
linseed oil putty
linseed oil (to soften hard putty)

For metal frames
metal primer
metal casement putty

equipment

Fixing faulty windows

Windows may crack or stick, the frames warp or let in water and sash cords break. These common faults in windows are relatively easy to correct and it is worth doing so at the earliest possible stage to avoid prolonged inconvenience or further damage. But make sure any repairs are done thoroughly or the problem is likely to reoccur.

Broken sash cords

Sash windows are commonly found in older houses and the sash cords on which the windows hang are likely to wear and break with age. When replacing sash cords there are several points which you should bear in mind. You will have to lever out the beads on either side of the window inside the room and it is important to keep the wood intact; start at the centre point of each bead to avoid damaging the mitre joints at the top and bottom.

You should replace all cords even if only one is broken. For replacement use terylene cord since this is much more durable than the old-fashioned wax type. You can prevent the cord fraying by heating the end with a lighted match to melt the fibres into a solid lump.

Sticking windows

There are various reasons why sliding sashes and hinged casement windows in both timber and metal start to stick. In some cases new paint may have gummed up the window. Cutting round the opening faces with a sharp trimming knife will usually alleviate the problem, but sometimes you may have to force the faces apart by inserting the blade of a broad filling knife between them. If the trouble is caused by a gradual build-up of paint over the years, use paint stripper to get back to the bare wood or metal; alternatively use a blowtorch to remove the paint from the wood. Make sure there is adequate clearance between the fixed and moving parts of the frame – in most cases 1.5mm ($\frac{1}{16}$in) clearance is sufficient – and repaint.

Poor paintwork and cracked glass can allow damp to get at the frame causing wood to swell and metal frames to rust. Use a wire brush to get rid of rust, treat the frame with rust killer and apply metal primer, undercoat and gloss paint. With a swollen timber frame it is best to strip off the paint with a blowtorch, taking care not to damage the glass, and gently play the blowtorch flame over the

1a When replacing sash cords use a chisel to remove the staff beads. Start at the centre of each bead to avoid damaging the mitre joints at top and bottom

1b With the bottom sash closed, cut any sound cord close to the top of the sash, after tying a length of string to the cord above where it is to be cut. (For a broken cord, tie string to the upper end of the cord.) Holding onto the strings, slowly lower the balance weights until they are at the bottom of the pockets and then remove the bottom sash. Leave the strings in position to pull the new cords through. Remove the parting beads in the same way as for the staff beads and the top sash in the same way as for removing the bottom sash. Use pincers to pull out the nails which attach the ends of the cords to the sashes

1c Remove the pockets and then the balance weights with the old cords attached. Mark which weights are for which sash – upper sash ones are heavier – and measure the old cord to get the new cord length

1d Where a cord is broken, rethread it using a small nail, or mouse, tied to a length of string. Feed the mouse over the pulley and retrieve it through the pocket. Replace the top sash first

1e Tie string to the new cord and draw it up over the pulley

1f Pull the cord through the pocket and attach the balance weight with a double knot. Heat the cut end with a match to melt the fibres into a lump to prevent fraying. Repeat for all the cords and replace the weights in the pockets

1g Measure the distance from the top of the sash to the bottom of the groove and mark on the frame this distance down from the top. Pull the cord so the weight is about 50mm from the bottom of the box and cut the free end level with the mark

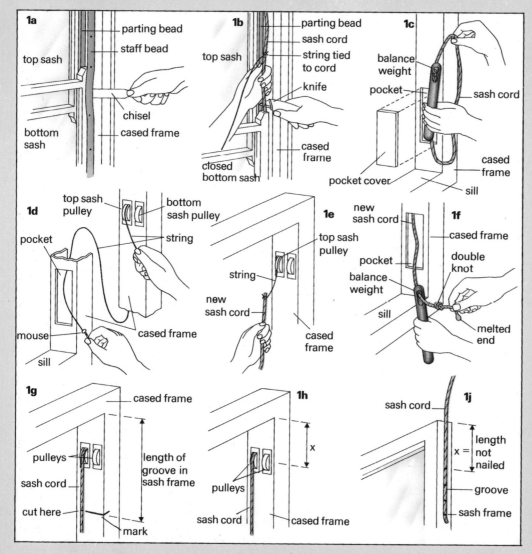

1a parting bead / staff bead / top sash / bottom sash / chisel / cased frame

1b parting bead / sash cord / string tied to cord / top sash / knife / cased frame / closed bottom sash

1c balance weight / pocket / sash cord / cased frame / pocket cover / sill

1d top sash pulley / bottom sash pulley / string / pocket / string / mouse / cased frame / sill

1e top sash pulley / string / new sash cord / cased frame

1f new sash cord / cased frame / pocket / double knot / balance weight / sill / melted end

1g cased frame / pulleys / sash cord / cut here / length of groove in sash frame / mark

1h x / pulleys / sash cord / cased frame

1j sash cord / length not nailed / x = / groove / sash frame

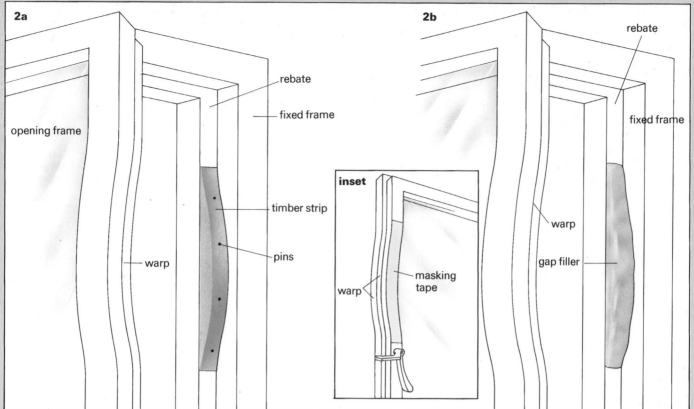

2a

opening frame

rebate

fixed frame

timber strip

pins

warp

2b

rebate

fixed frame

warp

gap filler

inset

warp

masking tape

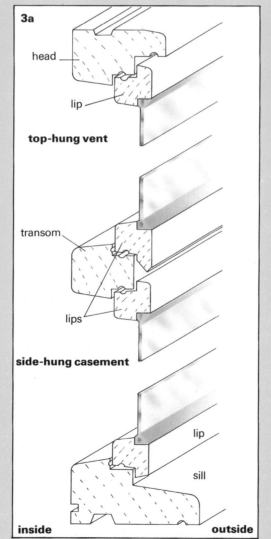

3a

head

lip

top-hung vent

transom

lips

side-hung casement

lip

sill

inside　　　　　　　　　**outside**

1h To decide the nailing position, measure the distance X from the mid-point of the pulley to the inside of the top of the frame
1j Pull the cord so the weight is at the top of the pulley, wedge a piece of wood between the frame and the pulley to prevent slipping and secure the new cord with galvanized 25mm broad head nails the distance X down from the top of the groove. Do not nail above this point or the window will not close. Replace the parting beads, fit the bottom sash in the same way and replace the staff beads
2a To seal the gap in a warped window, tack a shaped timber strip into the rebate of the fixed frame
2b Alternatively apply silicone rubber gap filler to the fixed frame. Fix masking tape on the inside face of the opening frame (**inset**) to protect this frame from the filler. Leave the filler to set with the window closed
3a Overhanging lips and drip grooves prevent rainwater ingress in a casement window
3b Where there is no overhanging lip, screw hardwood weatherstrips along the bottom of the opening casements or top vents

timber to dry it out. In hot weather you can leave the frame unpainted for a few days; this will help to get rid of damp. When the wood is dry, rub it down with glasspaper or use a plane to give a 1.5mm ($\frac{1}{16}$in) clearance round the frame. Make sure the putty is sound and, after priming any areas of bare wood, cover the frame with at least three coats of paint to ensure the timber is sealed against damp. Remember to take about 3mm ($\frac{1}{8}$in) of paint onto the glass to form a seal between the glass and the putty and prevent water seeping down into the frame.

Sash windows which stick may often be freed by opening the sash to its fullest extent and sanding the channel with coarse glasspaper wrapped round a block of wood. Where the trouble has been brought about by paint building up in the channel, you may find it necessary to strip the surface back to bare wood and repaint. If the wood has swollen, you should take the sash out of its channel and plane it on each side where the sash cord is fixed.

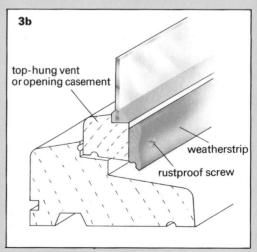

3b

top-hung vent or opening casement

weatherstrip

rustproof screw

With hinged timber windows, sticking may be caused by incorrectly fitted hinges. If the window is binding hard up against the side where the catch is fitted and there is a gap on the hinge side, the hinge flaps should be sunk deeper into the wood. On the other hand, if the window is binding hard up to the frame on the hinge side while there is a gap on the catch side, pack thin pieces of card under the hinge flaps to prevent the window sticking.

Warped windows

The opening frames of casement and vent windows often become warped and ill-fitting. It is usually possible to compensate for the warp and eliminate or minimize the gap by adjusting the position of the hinges. If the gap is not completely closed, you can seal a timber window with a suitably shaped timber strip; fix it with panel pins, at about 50mm (2in) intervals, into the rebate of the fixed frame. Alternatively, for both timber and metal windows use a flexible silicone rubber gap filler. Make sure the gap is thoroughly clean and dry; then apply self-adhesive masking tape to the inside face of the opening frame to prevent the filler adhering in this area. Squeeze the filler out of its tube into the gap and leave it to set overnight; the window can then be opened and the tape removed.

Warning Never try to force an ill-fitting frame back into the right position since the glass is likely to break under the strain.

Dampness around windows

Damp patches on a wall around a window may indicate an external gap between the brickwork and the frame. To seal the gap, use a bead of non-hardening flexible mastic, applying it with an applicator which injects the mastic through a plastic nozzle.

Check the frame has drip grooves incorporated to prevent rainwater being drawn between the opening and fixed parts of the frame and make sure the grooves have not been filled with layers of paint. If necessary, scrape them out and repaint. Modern casement windows are designed with overhanging lips as well as drip grooves to prevent water ingress. Old casements may not have this lip; if they are letting in water, it is a good idea to screw hardwood weatherstrips along the bottom of the opening casements and top vents. If French doors are letting in water, screw weatherboards to the bottom of the doors to throw water clear of the sill. In both cases use rustproof screws at approximately 100mm (4in) intervals.

Leaded lights

Leaded light windows are found in an ever-decreasing number of properties. They are only rarely used in new housing schemes, and over recent years large numbers of leaded lights have been replaced by modern picture windows. However, many people still find a period appeal in leaded windows, particularly when employed to create a design with panes of different colours, for example in the front door. Repairs will occasionally be necessary. Replacing glass pane in a leaded light window requires a technique rather different from that already described for standard windows. In leaded lights, the panes are secured in H-section strips of lead, called cames. To release a broken pane, cut the cames at each corner with a sharp knife and lever up the lead flanges at the sides and bottom with a wide chisel.

Either use the old pane as a template to cut a new pane or make a card template to fit in the cames and cut a new piece of glass about 1mm (or $\frac{1}{32}$ in) smaller than the template.

Traditionally gold size putty, obtainable from builders' merchants, is used to bed the glass in the cames; but you can bed the glass on a thin strip of grey mastic. Insert the new glass under the top flange and then carefully fit it at the sides and bottom; use a wood stick to press down the edges of the cames. Clean lead with medium glasspaper; resolder each corner with soft, resin-cored solder applied with a hot soldering iron.

Leaks If a leaded light leaks, scrape dirt away from the flanges of the cames and brush under the edges with clear polyurethane varnish. Make sure the flanges are well pressed down and use a razor blade to clear away varnish from the glass after it has set. If this does not stop the leaks, you should cut the came corners and use a chisel to fold back the lead in the affected areas so you can fit a thin strip of mastic or gold size putty under the flange.

4a The pane of a leaded light is held in H-section strips of lead, or cames
4b To remove a broken pane, use a sharp knife to cut the corners of the cames
4c Using a wide chisel, lever up the lead flanges at the sides and bottom to release the pane
4d Bed the new pane in gold size putty, fitting it at the top first and then the sides and bottom

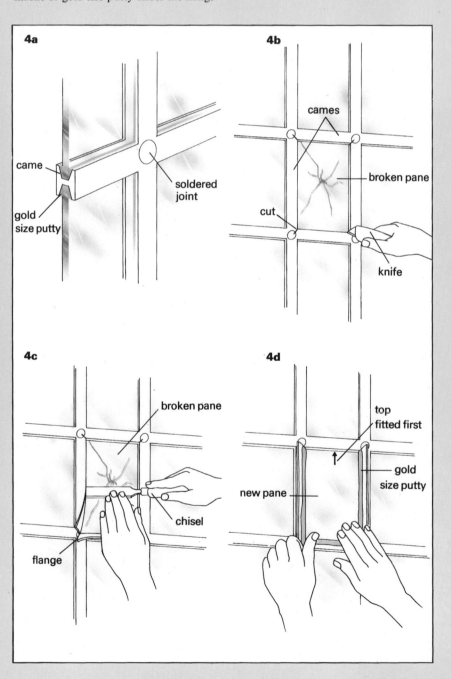

Working with glass

Glass is such a fragile and potentially dangerous material that most people understandably prefer to have it cut to size and delivered by their supplier. It can be difficult to manoeuvre a large sheet of glass from the supplier's to your home without the aid of the glazier's specially adapted van. However, it is often impossible to give the supplier complete instructions for cutting and drilling before the glass is delivered. Once you understand the elementary procedures for working with glass, you will find there are many jobs you can handle with both confidence and safety.

Cutting the required size from a large piece of glass presents problems and there is little that can be done with offcuts – unlike timber and similar sheet materials. But there are occasions when it is useful to know the basic techniques of working with glass, whether you want to cut a straight or curved line, to finish edges or to drill holes in glass.

Warning Always wear thick, preferably leather, gloves when handling glass and put on protective spectacles before cutting. When you carry glass hold it either vertically or horizontally midway along the long edges.

Cutting straight edges

Glass is cut by scoring a line on the surface with a glass-cutter and applying pressure on each side of the line to make a clean break. A glass-cutter is a delicate instrument and must be stored carefully when not in use. Hardened steel cutters are suitable for most types of glass, but you need a diamond cutter for harder high-silica glass. Before use, wet the cutter with a light oil or paraffin.

Place the sheet of glass on a level surface covered with a thick layer of clean felt. Score a line along the surface of the glass by drawing the cutter across it under pressure. Patterned and rolled glass should always be cut on the smooth side. Use a try square to ensure you score at right-angles to the edge of the sheet. To cut irregular shapes, make an accurately shaped template and run the cutter against this.

There are various ways of breaking the glass along the scored line. One is to tap the underside of the glass with the cutter along the scored line and then place your fingers under the glass – with the thumbs on top – and press down firmly. Alternatively you can lay the glass over a straight edge with the scored line immediately above it and apply gentle pressure. Too much pressure may cause the surface of the glass to splinter or flake as it breaks.

Cutting holes

A special cutting tool is used to score a circle. It consists of a suction pad, a cutting edge that rotates on a pivot and a radius scale. First establish the

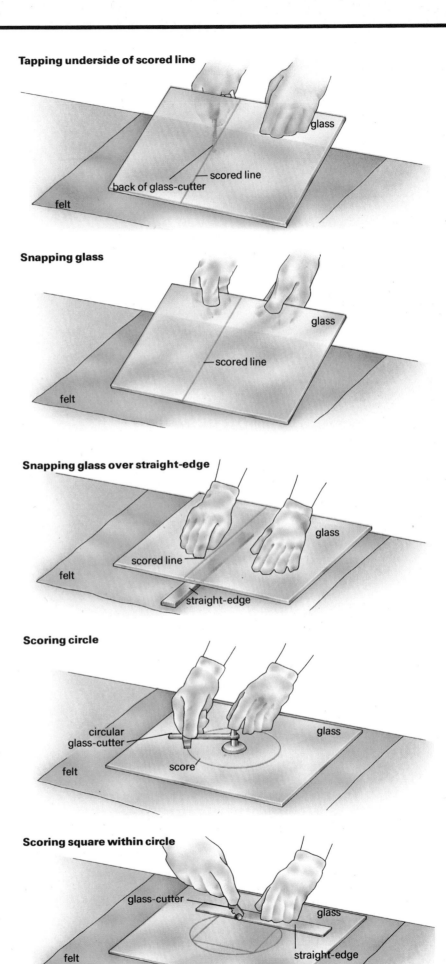

Tapping underside of scored line

glass
scored line
back of glass-cutter
felt

Snapping glass

glass
scored line
felt

Snapping glass over straight-edge

glass
scored line
felt
straight-edge

Scoring circle

circular glass-cutter
glass
score
felt

Scoring square within circle

glass-cutter
glass
felt
straight-edge

centre of the circle you intend to cut. Set the cutting edge at the correct radius and rotate it to score the circle outline. Lightly tap the underside of the glass and, unless you are cutting a fixed piece of glass, lay it on a flat, felt surface. Score the largest possible square within the circle, then score several smaller squares within each other. Finish scoring with a series of criss-cross lines within the area of the circle. This will help to provide a clean break when the glass is tapped out from the underside (or the outside of a pane already in a window). Start tapping out from the centre and work outwards towards the circumference in all directions.

This method is only suitable if you are working on a small area of glass. If you do break the glass, it will not cost too much to replace and the supplier can also cut out the circle for you.

Finishing edges
Straight cut edges can be smoothed by placing the glass on the bench with a slight overhang and rubbing a wet smooth emery block along the entire length of glass. Fine glasspaper can also be used but it must be wrapped round a support block for safety. Curved cut edges can be smoothed in a similar manner.

Drilling holes
Never use a masonry bit to drill holes because it could easily shatter the glass. Use a special spear bit and try to keep the holes at least 25mm (1in) from the edge, since the chances of the glass breaking are increased the closer to the edge you drill. The absolute minimum distance is 13mm ($\frac{1}{2}$in).

Having decided on the position of the hole, place a ring of putty or plasticine around it to form a well and place a few drops of white spirit or paraffin in the middle. If you are drilling a mirror, use water to prevent the silvering from staining.

Ideally use a multi-speed drill because it is important to start drilling as slowly as possible to prevent the bit skating across the surface. Maintain light pressure and continue drilling as slowly as possible to keep the point of the bit cool.

Start drilling mirrors from the back to make a clean cut through the backing and silvering. Once the drill makes a pinhole on the other side, turn over the mirror to complete the drilling from the front and ensure you have a clean hole on both surfaces.

When drilling bottles, fill the bottle with sand and place it in a bed of sand to keep it in position. Drill slowly through the glass, stopping frequently to lubricate the glass with a brush or dropper and white spirit or paraffin. Alternatively lubricate the bit from time to time.

Basic items
thick gloves, protective spectacles
glass-cutter
circle glass-cutter
try square
carborundum stone, smooth emery
  block or fine glasspaper
multi-speed electric drill, spear bit
putty or plasticine
paraffin, white spirit or light oil
sand (if drilling bottles)

equipment

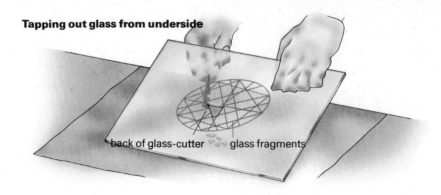

Tapping out glass from underside

back of glass-cutter   glass fragments

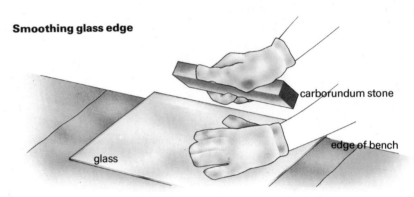

Smoothing glass edge

carborundum stone

edge of bench

glass

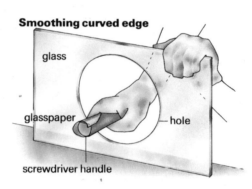

Smoothing curved edge

glass

glasspaper   hole

screwdriver handle

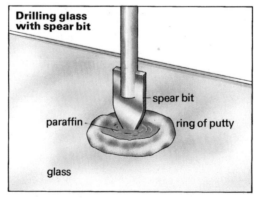

Drilling glass with spear bit

spear bit

paraffin   ring of putty

glass

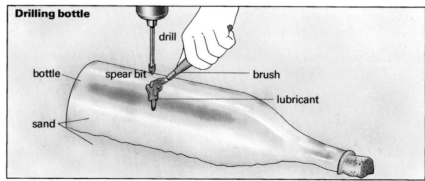

Drilling bottle

drill

bottle   spear bit   brush

lubricant

sand

Replacing windows in solid walls

You can remove and replace all types of window yourself as long as you adopt the right procedure. But make sure you can finish the job in a reasonable amount of time to avoid leaving openings exposed.

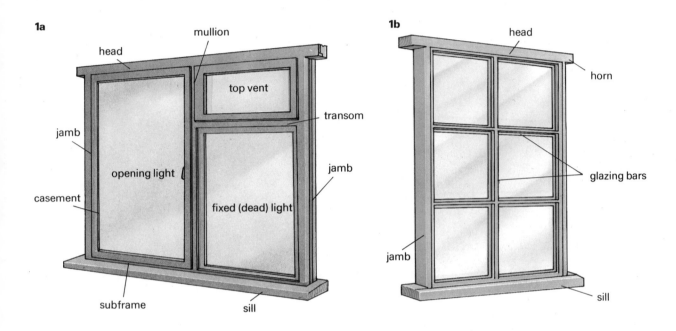

1a
head
mullion
top vent
transom
jamb
opening light
jamb
casement
fixed (dead) light
subframe
sill

1b
head
horn
glazing bars
jamb
sill

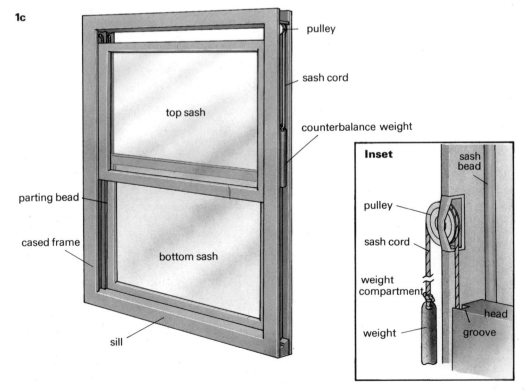

1c
pulley
sash cord
counterbalance weight
top sash
parting bead
cased frame
bottom sash
sill

Inset
sash bead
pulley
sash cord
weight compartment
weight
head
groove

Before you begin removing a window, identify the various parts from our diagrams
1a Casement window with fixed light, opening light and top vent
1b Fixed window
1c Sash window and its operating mechanism (**inset**)

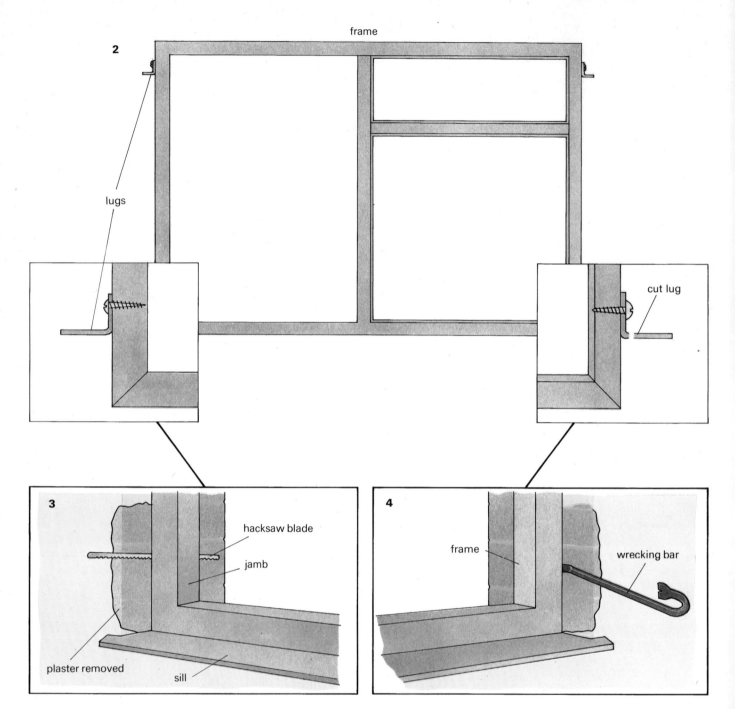

2 The position of the fixing lugs on a casement window

3 You can remove the frame relatively intact by severing the fixings with a hacksaw blade threaded between the frame and the brickwork

4 Lever the frame away from the wall with a wrecking bar

Having decided on the style of window you want, you may need to have it made instead of simply choosing one from a catalogue. In either case, measure the size of the opening (checking all angles are 90 degrees) and deduct 6mm (¼in) from the height and width measurements. Make sure your figures are accurate; while it is possible to trim a timber frame if it arrives over-size, there is nothing you can do about a metal one. When you take delivery, make sure the size and quality are as specified. Refuse to accept the frame if the wood is bruised, split or has developed shrinkage cracks, or if there are numerous large or loose knots, badly cut joints or the frame is out of true.

Never begin removing a window before you have the new one delivered; it is not only inconvenient to have to cover a gaping hole with polythene for a night or longer, but also a positive invitation to intruders.

Replacing timber frames

Take down window hangings and curtain tracks and remove any window fittings, including security catches. Remove the glass from the frame, preserving as much of it as possible; even if it is not suitable for your replacement window, you may be able to use it at some point in the future.

Removing casement windows

Start by removing hinged lights; when taking off the casements, it is easier to remove screws from the top hinge last – but be prepared for the weight when it comes free.

Frames are fixed with metal lugs or ties which are built into the mortar joints of the brickwork, although screws or spikes (long nails) are sometimes used. There are usually two fixings in each upright jamb. If you want to remove the frame relatively

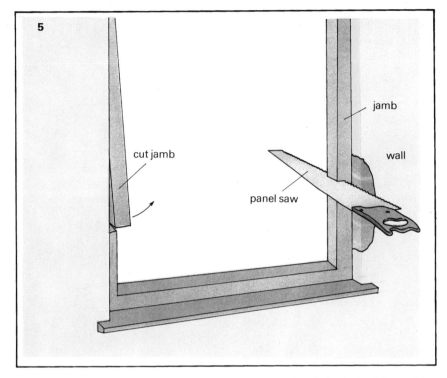

5

cut jamb

panel saw

jamb

wall

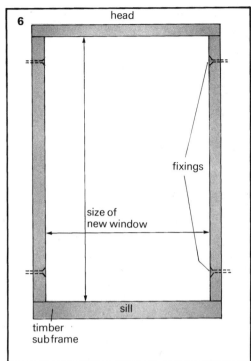

6

head

fixings

size of
new window

sill

timber
subframe

5 If you do not wish to keep
the frame, cut through the
jambs with an old panel saw
and lever them out with a
wrecking bar

6 If you are replacing a sash
window with another type,
you will probably have to
install a subframe first so
the new frame will fit
snugly into the opening

undamaged, try cutting through the fixings with a
general purpose saw or a hacksaw blade threaded
between the brickwork and the frame. First you
will have to remove the mastic seal between the
frame and the wall and you may need to hack away
plaster from interior walls around the window and
some exterior pointing.

Check whether there are fixings at the head and
sill of the frame (it is unlikely you will find any in
small domestic windows, but you can put them in
when installing the new frame).

After severing the fixings, use a wrecking bar to
lever out the frame. If you are dealing with a ground
floor or basement window, you can push the frame
outwards, but on upper storeys you must lever it
into the building. If you have any doubts about
which way to take the frame, remember damage to
interior plasterwork is easier to repair than brickwork. Whichever way you go, use even leverage all
round, otherwise you may jam the frame in the
opening.

If you do not wish to save the frame, you can
remove it quickly by sawing through the jambs
(using an old panel saw because the teeth are
certain to grate on the bricks). When the jambs (and
mullion, if there is one) are out of the way you can
lever out the head and sill.

Installing the new frame
Prime timber frames on all surfaces before you
install them, using a lead-based primer for best
results. Make good any damage to the brickwork
and, if you are using screws or spikes, check the
plugs in the wall (often just hardwood) are sound
and tight. You may be able to use them again by
knocking slivers of hardwood into the holes left by
the old screws.

Mark the position of the plugs on the frame, drill
fixing holes, put the frame in position and, using
packing pieces to keep it central, fix with countersunk screws or spikes. It is important to keep
checking the angles are at 90 degrees – using a
spirit level and plumb line – because screwing can
force the frame out of true and any distortion will

make it difficult to hang the opening lights. Using a
trowel or putty knife apply a non-hardening mastic
to the gaps between the frame and the walls.
Finally hang lights and casements, glaze and paint
the frame and replace fittings, security catches or
locks. Lightly oil moving parts.

Using metal lugs or ties If you are fixing the frame
with metal lugs or ties, screw them to the frame so
they coincide with mortar joints in the brickwork.
Remove the mortar from the brickwork with a
chisel and hammer, or with a masonry router bit in
an electric drill, and cement the lugs or ties into
position. Allow the cement to set before hanging
lights and casements.

Using masonry bolts Another method is to wedge
the frame into position, drill through the timber
into the brickwork and secure the frame with loose-
type expanding masonry bolts. First drill a flat-
bottomed hole with a power bore bit deep enough
to recess the bolt head and wide enough to allow it
to be tightened with a box (or socket) spanner.
Continue drilling through the frame with a twist
drill slightly larger than the expanding bolt.
Finally use a masonry bit of the same size to drill
into the brickwork to the correct depth for the
fitting.

Double-hung sash windows
With sash windows it is not always necessary to
replace the whole frame. Where the sashes themselves have become mis-shapen, it is possible to
replace only these, but it is likely the box frame
(containing the mechanism) is in the same condition. You can discard the sashes, retain the
framework and install a fixed window, a casement
or a steel sash. This involves lining the frame with
plywood and fixing your new window to this, which
may not be satisfactory because you will not know
the real condition of the bricks and mortar behind
the box. It would be better to replace the entire
frame.

Replacing sashes These will almost certainly have
to be made to order and must be of the same
specification as the originals: the same thickness

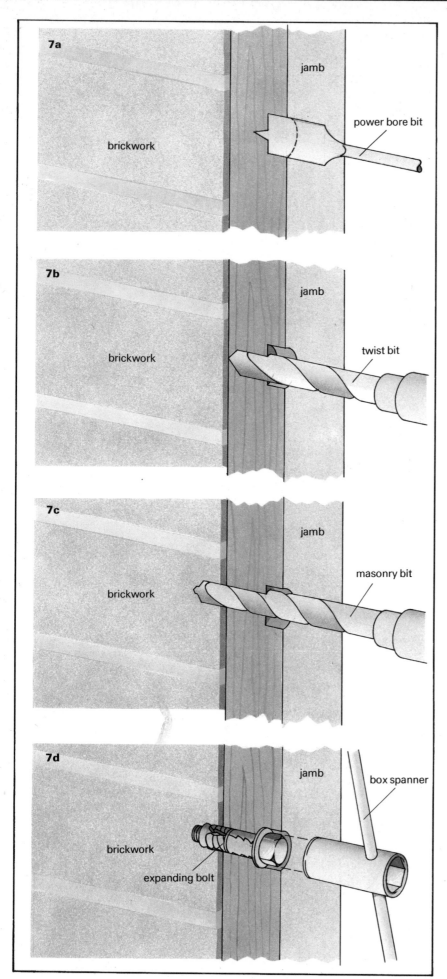

7a brickwork | jamb | power bore bit

7b brickwork | jamb | twist bit

7c brickwork | jamb | masonry bit

7d brickwork | expanding bolt | jamb | box spanner

glass and sash stuff (timber), otherwise the weights will not counterbalance the sashes.

Use a chisel to lever out the staff (or inside) bead all round the window, taking care not to damage the wood. Lower the inside window and, holding the cord in one hand, cut it with a knife close to the top of the sash and lower the weight to the bottom of the box. Repeat for the other side. Remove the inside sash then lever away the parting beads from the framework, cut the outside sash cord in the same way and remove the outside sash.

Lift the pockets on each side of the frame and remove the four weights (two for each sash) and the cord attached to them. Mark which weights are for which sash – those for the upper sash are heavier to keep it in the fully up position. Measure your pieces of cord to give the length of the new cord. Check the condition of the pulleys: if they are sound, oil them lightly to ensure they run freely. If the pulleys are rusted, unscrew them and buy new ones; take the originals with you to the dealer to ensure you buy the right size.

Reassembly Always begin replacing sashes and cords in the reverse order – the outside sash must go in first. The cord may be fixed to the sashes by nails or with a system of slots and wedges: follow the previous fixing method where possible.

Begin the reassembly by taking a length of twine and attaching one end to a cord. Attach a heavy nail to the other end of the twine and run it round one outside sash pulley into the frame box. Retrieve the nail and twine through the pocket and tie the cord end to one of the counterbalance weights, checking you have the right weight for the sash. Measure the distance between the top of the sash and the bottom of the cord position or groove and mark the frame at this distance down from the top.

Pull the cord until the weight is about 50mm (2in) from the bottom of the box and cut the free end of the cord level with the mark you have made. Pull the cord again until the weight touches the pulley and wedge a piece of wood between the frame and the pulley, making sure it will not slip. Repeat with the second cord and secure the cords to the sash grooves with nails or fixing wedges. At this stage the job will be easier if you have help, especially when dealing with large, heavy sashes. Check the sash slides properly and the weights do not hit the bottom of the box: if they do, you will have to shorten the cords.

When replacing the inner sash, follow the same method until you have inserted the weight and cord. This time, mark the frame at the lowest cord position with the sash down. Pull the weight almost to its top position and cut the cord at the mark on the frame. Then follow the procedure for fitting the outer sash. Finally replace the pockets and parting bead and the staff bead.

Replacing sash windows

If you are replacing the entire window with a new double-hung sash or with another type, remove the sashes as described above. Then, using a chisel, remove the architrave (moulding), taking care not to damage it since you may want to use it again. Lever out the whole frame and make good by cleaning up and repointing. In the case of a replacement of the same type, put the window straight in.

If you are installing a different type of window, such as a casement, shop around to see whether you can find a ready-made frame which will fit the opening; if not, you may find it cheaper in the long

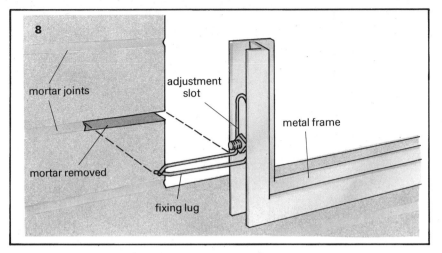

8

mortar joints

mortar removed

fixing lug

adjustment slot

metal frame

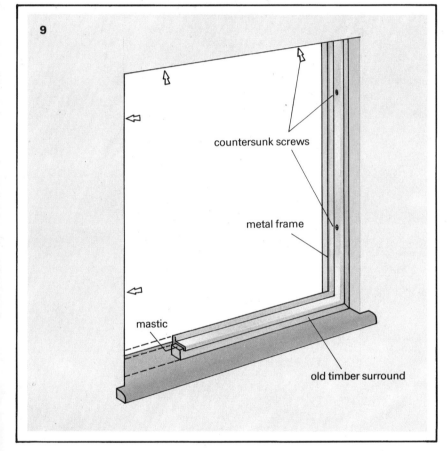

9

countersunk screws

metal frame

mastic

old timber surround

run to have one made to measure, since filling in the opening so the frame fits does take a lot of time and materials. When fitting a casement window in place of a sash one, it is important to set the frame further forward in the opening so the casement will clear brickwork when you open it, otherwise there is a danger of smashing the glass.

Unless you are having a window specially made you will probably have to build and install a subframe first. The type of timber used will depend on the type of window, but in any case you must make the internal dimensions offer a snug fit to the actual frame. Fix the subframe as for installing timber windows: put the head and sill parts (or surround) in first, then the jambs which act as wedges and strengthen the structure. The final stage is to install the frame.

Replacing metal frames

Start by removing the opening lights; if the hinges are stiff, it is best to remove them with a hacksaw. Take the glass out of fixed lights and remove fixing screws. If the screws are rusted solid or if the heads break off, you must drill the screws out. Wear goggles as a precaution and use a centre punch and a hammer to make a starting point for a twist drill with a tungsten hardened tip (the diameter should be slightly larger than that of the screw.) Continue drilling until the screw no longer holds the frame.

If the window is not attached to a timber surround, tap all round the edge of the frame with a cold chisel and hammer to loosen the grip of the mortar and plaster. If a screw is stubborn and you do not want to drill it out, cut through the jamb with a hacksaw and lever it out with a wrecking bar. **Warning** Some large windows may be made up of several standard units using coupling bars and these occasionally provide support for the lintel and are built into the structure. If this is a possibility, never hacksaw through them but seek advice from an expert.

If you are dealing with a metal frame fixed in a timber surround, remove the glass; this should reveal countersunk fixing screws. Where metal windows are fitted by lugs or ties, deal with them as for removing timber windows.

Installing the new window

If there is an old timber surround which is in good condition, you can set the frame in a bed of non-hardening mastic and secure it with countersunk screws. When fixing directly to brickwork, clean off any projections of mortar or plaster and repoint where necessary. Pay particular attention to any instructions from the manufacturer, but generally you will install the window with lugs cemented into the mortar joints, as explained for timber windows; the lugs are attached to the metal frame with screws and can be adjusted to meet the joints. Again, bed the frame on a layer of mastic before fixing.

Despite the claims made by manufacturers of the increasingly popular aluminium alloy frames, these frames are not entirely free from corrosion problems, and it may be advisable to paint them. If you do paint them, first apply a coat of zinc chromate primer, then at least three coats of paint; brush the paint well into the hinges to prevent problems with rusting and oil the hinges lightly after they have dried.

7a If you are fixing the frame with expanding masonry bolts, first drill a hole in the timber with a power bore bit
7b Change to a twist bit and continue drilling through the frame
7c To drill into the brickwork, use a masonry bit
7d Fit the bolt and tighten it with a box spanner
8 To fix a metal frame directly to brickwork, cement the lugs into the mortar joints
9 With a timber surround, set the frame in mastic and fix with countersunk screws

Basic items
screwdriver, chisel
general purpose saw or hacksaw
wrecking bar, old panel saw
electric drill
spirit level, plumb line
trowel or putty knife, trimming knife
masonry router bit or cold chisel and hammer (to remove mortar)
power bore bit, twist drill and masonry bit, box or socket spanner (for expanding masonry bolts)
twine, heavy nail (for replacing sashes)
centre punch, tungsten twist drill, protective spectacles (for metal frames)

equipment

Replacing windows in cavity walls

When serious decay of a window frame makes complete replacement necessary, many people turn to the professional builder. However, if you tackle the job systematically, there is no reason why it should be beyond the skill of the handyman. Nevertheless, windows in houses with cavity walls will present the handyman with extra problems making care essential.

Replacing windows in cavity walls involves similar procedures as replacing windows in solid walls, but in this case you must take particular care not to disturb or damage the damp proof course which surrounds the frame, otherwise moisture will penetrate to the inside of the house and cause damp. In older buildings the dpc consists of strips of lead, copper or zinc; in modern buildings more flexible materials – bituminous felt or plastic – are used.

Before you remove your existing window, discover how it was installed and whether it was built into the walls or fixed after the walls were completed. Built-in windows are propped into position and the walls built up on each side. This is more usual with softwood windows with a paint finish because accidental damage or repeated soaking and drying during bricklaying can be made good after the wall is finished. These windows are usually fixed by metal lugs or ties screwed or nailed to the frame and cemented into the joints.

Hardwood windows with a varnish finish are usually installed after the brickwork is finished because damage to these cannot be made good. They are usually secured by countersunk screws or spikes through the frame and into hardwood plugs built into the joints. Fixings at the heads of both types of window are often into dovetailed wood plugs cast into the concrete lintel when it is built.

Removing the frame
Begin by taking off any hinged lights and casements. Remove the glazing from fixed lights to

1 A window opening in a cavity wall; damp proof courses bridge the cavity horizontally top and bottom and vertically at the sides
2 If the window was built into the wall, it should be secured with fixing lugs cemented into mortar joints
3 The head of the window is usually fixed with dovetail wood plugs set in the lintel
4 If you find the vertical dpc is nailed to the frame, cut it close to the jamb before you remove the frame

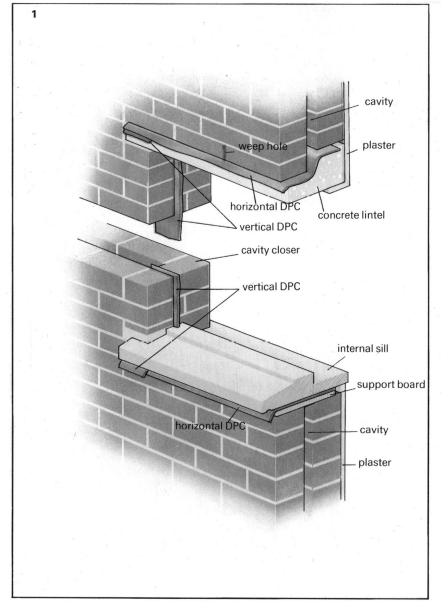

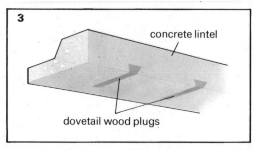

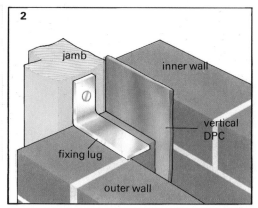

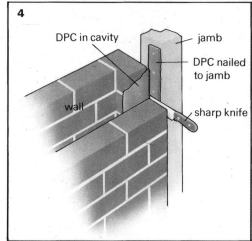

reveal any screw or spike fixings. You can either undo the screws or cut through them (this also applies to spikes, lugs and ties) by sliding a hacksaw blade or general purpose saw between the brickwork and the frame. It is at this point you must take great care not to damage the damp proof course or pull it out of the cavity.

A vertical dpc lines the interior of the cavity wall at each side of the frame. It is sometimes nailed to the frame itself and you should be able to see this when you begin to remove the frame. Use a sharp knife to trim the dpc as close to the jambs as possible (whatever you do, don't pull it out of the cavity), then continue removing the frame.

There should be a horizontal damp proof course under the sill unless a non-porous sill was built into the wall; the course at the head will have been laid above the lintel at the time of construction – neither needs your attention.

Fitting the new frame

Once you have made good any damage to brickwork and plaster caused by removing the frame, you can install your new window. The manufacturer may specify the type of fixing and you should always follow his instructions, but usually the window will be fixed with lugs attached to the frame and cemented into the brick joints. Clean out the required joints to a depth sufficient to slide in the frame, apply non-hardening mastic to the sides and bottom of the opening and place the frame in position. The frame must sit squarely over the wall cavity and cover the end of the vertical dpc to ensure an effective barrier against moisture penetration. Cement with a fairly dry mix of about one part cement to three parts sand.

Other methods of fixing are by nailing the frame into hardwood plugs built into the brick joints, or with screws and plugs. Position the frame on a bed of mastic as before and secure it in place with wedges between the wall and the frame. Check with a spirit level to ensure the frame sits squarely in the opening and fill any gaps between the wall and frame with more mastic. Hang any casements, glaze, replace fittings and paint with undercoat and top coats. Finally lightly oil moving parts.

5a When installing a frame which is secured with fixing lugs, first rake out the appropriate mortar joints
5b Apply non-hardening mastic to the sides and bottom of the opening so the dpcs are covered
5c Place the frame in position, sliding the fixing lugs into the raked joints; make sure the frame sits squarely over the cavity
5d Finally cement the lugs into the joints with a fairly dry mortar mix

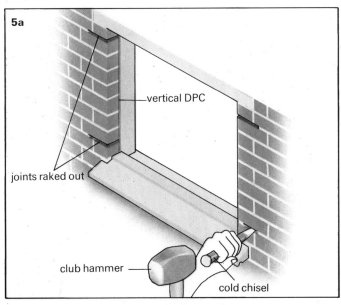

5a

vertical DPC

joints raked out

club hammer

cold chisel

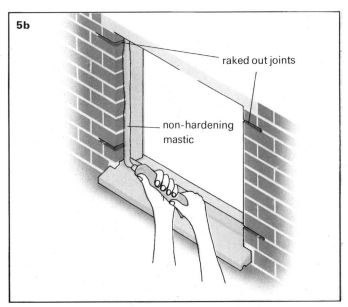

5b

raked out joints

non-hardening mastic

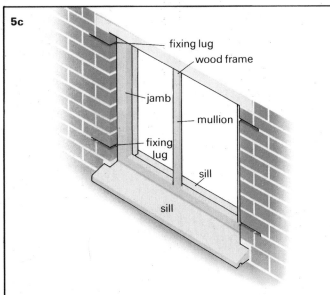

5c

fixing lug

wood frame

jamb

mullion

fixing lug

sill

sill

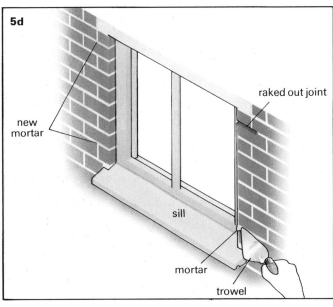

5d

raked out joint

new mortar

sill

mortar

trowel

Repairing external window sills

Timber window sills

Flaking paintwork is one of the first signs of rotting wood, but even an outwardly sound paint surface can, on closer inspection, be hiding a multitude of troubles. If you suspect rot in a sill strip off the paint and cut back any rotting areas until you reach sound timber. If the exposed timber looks grey it is suffering from surface decay, which you must skim away before repainting. When removing affected areas take out any nails or screws in the surface and plane down until you reach clean, healthy timber.

Don't forget to check the underside of the sill as well. Dig a sharp penknife into the wood; if it goes in easily these soft parts will have to be dug out and stripped back as before.

An important part of the sill is the drip groove, a U-shaped channel running the length of the underside. This ensures a free passage for rainwater and must therefore be kept free of dirt.

If you have discovered rot in its early stages you will have only small cavities to fill. This operation is carried out using a hard stopping such as an exterior wood filler or waterproof stopping.

Warning If you use putty instead of a hard stopping, when the sill has been repainted the oil content trapped beneath the surface of paint film could cause blistering when the paint is subjected to excessive heat.

Let the stopping set according to the manufacturer's instructions and sand smooth. Where resinous (sticky) knots are revealed apply a coat of shellac knotting and leave to dry before painting. Repaint the entire surface with primer, undercoat and top coat.

Where it has been necessary to remove a large chunk of rotten timber, to repair by filling would not only be impractical but unsound. Here you will need to make good by cutting a new piece of timber with a panel saw to the same size as that removed. Position the new piece of timber and mark a drip groove in pencil, following the line of the existing groove. Remove and tenon saw the groove to the required depth and width, gouging out the waste timber with a narrow chisel. Glasspaper smooth for a clean finish.

Fix the new piece of timber in position with exterior adhesive and galvanized nails. Sink the nail heads below the surface with a nail punch and fill the cavities with exterior filler or waterproof stopping. Repaint as before.

The most troublesome timber is oak which, because of its open grain, tends to encourage breakdown of the paint. Here strip back to bare wood and rub fine surface filler well down into the grain with a piece of clean rag. Let it set and then smooth with glasspaper, working only with the grain. Finally apply a coat of aluminium primer, then undercoat and top coats of paint.

Ideally oak is best left in its natural state and protected by coating with boiled linseed oil or a timber preservative. So when you strip the sill decide which finish you want – natural or painted.

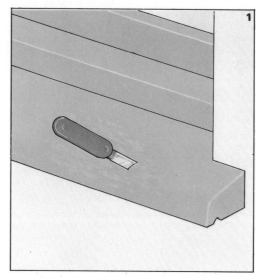

replacement section

drip groove

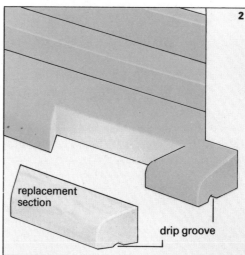

galvanized nails

1 Checking for decay in timber window sill with sharp knife
2 Extensive rot removed and new piece of timber cut to fit gap with drip groove to match existing one
3 New timber fixed into place with exterior adhesive and galvanized nails

Opposite page
4 Badly rotted timber sill cut away to be replaced with new one cast in concrete
5a Timber shuttering box supported on batten screwed to wall below window frame. Sash cord stretched along base of box and knotted through holes in box ends gives line of drip groove **(see 6)**
5b Cast concrete sill is smoothed level to top edges of timbers with steel float
6 Detail of drip groove at side of sill, with knotted cord in place. Remove cord when concrete is set

For timber sill
plane, claw hammer
penknife
medium coarse glasspaper
panel saw, tenon saw (for cutting
   drip groove)
chisel
galvanized nails 150mm long
nail punch
filling or putty knife
lint-free rag
50mm (2in) paint brush
exterior wood filler or waterproof
   stopping
knotting liquid (for sealing
   resinous surfaces)
primer (aluminium for oak)
undercoat and top coat paint
timber offcuts (for replacement)
exterior adhesive (for offcuts)

surface filler
boiled linseed oil or wood preservative (for natural finish)

For concrete sill
chisel, mallet
50mm (2in) paint brush
claw hammer
nails 150mm long
screwdriver, bradawl
hand or electric drill
wood and masonry bits
shovel, steel float
acrylic primer
timber (for shuttering box, batten)
No 8 countersunk screws 40mm long
length of cord
concreting mix as required
concrete paint

equipment

Making a concrete sill

In extreme cases of rotting, where the sill has to be removed completely, it is worth casting a new one of your own in concrete. This is not difficult or expensive and removes forever the possibility of rot.

Chisel out all remaining pieces of the old sill. Apply one coat of acrylic primer to the bare wood of the frame for protection and apply a second coat immediately prior to casting the sill. To reinforce the concrete, drive a row of 150mm (6in) nails, 150mm apart and a third of their length, into the timber along the bottom of the window frame.

You must then construct a shuttering box from 25mm (1in) thick timber, screwed together, into which you pour the concrete. The tops of the sides of the box should slope slightly downwards away from the wall to prevent rainwater from collecting on the sill and causing possible rotting of the window frame. To support the shuttering box screw a batten to the wall below the window frame, ensuring the screws are well anchored. Remember to make the top of the box the level you intend as the top surface of the sill, and that the inside measurements of the box will be the outside measurements of the sill.

For your drip groove, stretch a length of stout cord – sashcord is ideal – along the base of the box and through specially drilled holes in the side pieces, knotting at both ends to keep it taut.

Mixing the concrete

Using one part fine shingle, two parts clean sharp sand and one part cement, add water gradually until you have a buttery, rather than sloppy, consistency. Shovel the mix into the shuttering box and smooth level with the top edges of the timbers with a steel float. Care will be needed to maintain an even downward slope in the centre of the new sill. Before you remove the box frame, cord and wall batten, allow a few days for the concrete to set thoroughly. The job is completed by painting with a proprietary concrete paint.

4

drip groove

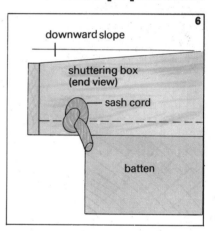

6

downward slope

shuttering box
(end view)

sash cord

batten

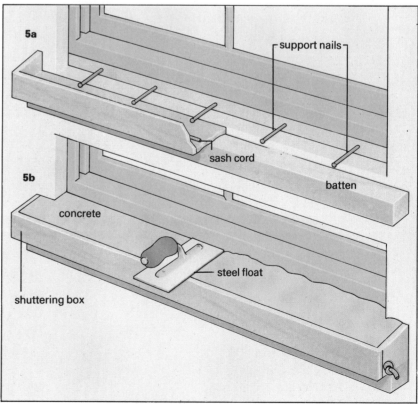

5a

support nails

sash cord

batten

5b

concrete

steel float

shuttering box

Internal window sills

Internal window sills were traditionally made of timber, although many modern houses now have quarry tiled sills. Their obvious advantage is that they will stand up to far greater wear and tear and do not suffer from the same deterioration as their timber counterparts. However most of the problems surrounding timber sills stem from the fact that they are now made from inferior quality timber.

Timber sills

The depth of the average window sill recess is 150–225mm (6–9in) and a length of 25mm (1in) thick timber is commonly used. In houses built before 1939 the material was of a high standard and has mainly stood the test of time. Properly maintained, these sills will remain sound for many more years.

The growing trend for central heating has, however, highlighted the problems of timber sills, especially those in newer houses where inferior quality material has been fitted. The sills dry rapidly, causing splits and warping along the timber, faults often accelerated by priming and painting on the top, visible surface only. These cracks and splits are then vulnerable to moisture resulting from excessive condensation from the windows.

Any attempts to repair a sill in this condition and keep it in a reasonable state of decoration are eventually doomed to fail and the only certain remedy is to remove the offending timber and replace it with good quality material.

Removing old sill

Timber sills are often nailed into timber blocks in the masonry below them and into the base of the

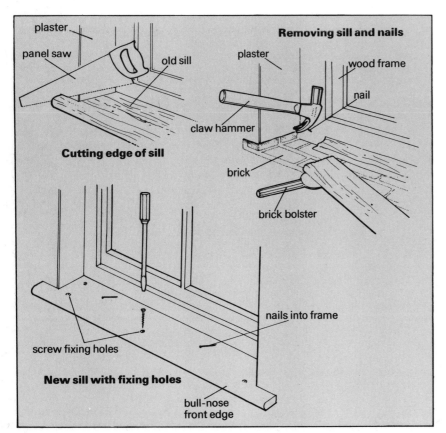

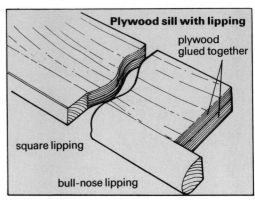

window frame. The ends of the sill are also secured – by the plaster which is laid tight to the sill when it is in position.

It is quite a simple operation to remove the sill. With a sharp chisel and hammer chop through the ends and then drive a brick bolster under the front edge to lever the sill up. You may find it easier to lever the overlap onto the wall surface at either end of the sill using a chisel; alternatively you can free the timber from the plaster with a small saw. Make sure you remove any nails that are left, levering them up with a claw hammer, and clean out any ragged corners with the chisel so the new piece of timber will sit flush in position.

Making new sill

When you fit a new piece of timber, make sure it is well seasoned and of good quality. Measure carefully the area left by the old sill – depth, thickness and length; it is safest to buy the timber slightly over-sized and trim for an exact fit, in case you make a mistake and otherwise find your new sill is too small. Mark up the new timber carefully with a pencil and straight-edge and cut just to the waste side of these lines with a tenon saw. Smooth down the cut edges with medium, then fine, glasspaper until the timber fits exactly. If you want a half-rounded bull-nose finish on the front edge, plane the area carefully with a small block plane and rub smooth with medium, then fine, glasspaper. Alternatively you can buy bull-nose lipping which should be glued and pinned into position on the front edge.

If there are already fixing points in the masonry, mark accurately corresponding positions on the new sill and drill clearance holes ready for fixing later. Alternatively drill a set of clearance holes in the new sill at about 400mm (or 15in) intervals along the front and back edges of the sill and, laying the sill in position, mark through these holes where to drill into the masonry to take plugs and countersunk screws. Remove the sill and complete these fitting points in the masonry. Before fitting the new sill make sure all faces and edges are well-primed. Apply two coats of proprietary wood primer to the back edge where it meets the window frame, since this is one area particularly prone to attack from moisture.

Fitting new sill

To secure the new piece of timber, countersink the clearance holes and screw through these into the masonry fixing points. For extra strength hammer in two or three nails at an oblique angle into the window frame. All nail and screw heads must be primed with a rust-resistant primer before they are filled in with cellulose filler, or matching plastic wood if you want a natural finish. When fitted, the sill can be decorated as you want in the usual way, either painted or given a natural finish.

Using plywood

The best alternative to natural timber is a good quality plywood. To get the required thickness for the sill you may find it easier to glue together two 9 or 12mm ($\frac{3}{8}$ or $\frac{1}{2}$in) thicknesses. For added protection it is worth sticking a timber lipping to the outer edge of the plywood – and if you want the edge shaped you can pin and glue on bull-nose lipping. Prime all the edges carefully and fix using the same method as for timber. Then complete the decoration. A good resin-bonded plywood will give

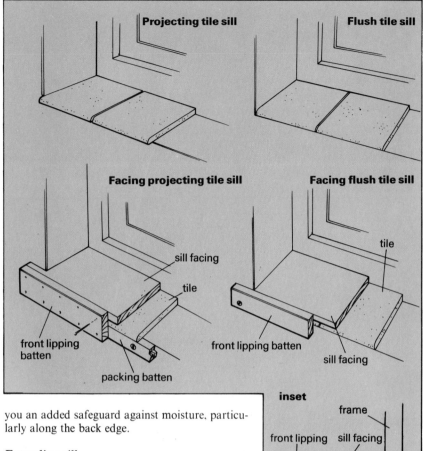

you an added safeguard against moisture, particularly along the back edge.

Extending sill

If you are lining the walls around a window for insulation, you will probably have to extend the existing sill (or make the new one) to sit flush with or, if you prefer, overhang the new wall surface. If cutting out a new sill, allow for the extra when measuring the new piece of timber. If your old sill is in good condition you can simply fix on a new piece of lipping of the correct thickness and length as the original timber and of the width required. All you have to do is glue and pin the lipping into position, but make sure the edge of the old sill is trimmed square for a flush fitting and that all paint or other covering is cleaned off to ensure a firm bond.

Tiled sills

Because of the problems already described with timber sills, many builders have tended to favour quarry tiles on sills in new houses. Although hard-wearing and needing little maintenance, they can be chipped or work loose, in which case you will have to refix them with a tile adhesive, if necessary clearing away the surface below to ensure a flush finish – or replace them with new tiles. If you think quarry tiles do not suit the room decoration, you can face over the tiles and have a painted or laminate finish.

Facing tiles

If you want a painted finish, the best facing to use over tiles is either plywood or blockboard.

For painted finish The plywood or blockboard facing should be approximately 13mm ($\frac{1}{2}$in) thick and taken to the front edge of the tiles. If the tiles are flush to the wall, a lipping batten should be fixed to the front edge of the new facing so a strong fixing can be made into the wall below the tile line.

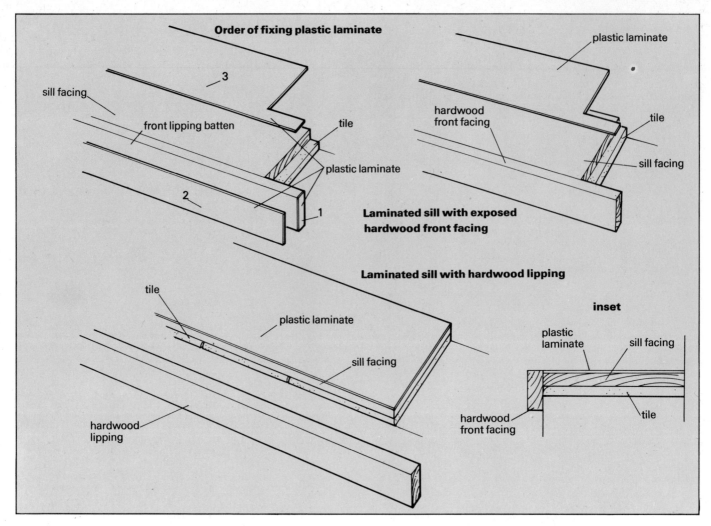

Order of fixing plastic laminate

sill facing

front lipping batten

tile

plastic laminate

3

2

1

plastic laminate

hardwood front facing

tile

sill facing

Laminated sill with exposed hardwood front facing

Laminated sill with hardwood lipping

tile

plastic laminate

sill facing

hardwood lipping

inset

plastic laminate

sill facing

hardwood front facing

tile

If the tiles project in front of the wall line, you will have to fix a packing batten below them to make up the level. This batten must be screwed into the wall with countersunk screws at 400mm (or 15in) intervals; the facing batten can then be glued and pinned to the packing batten and the edge of the sill facing board above. The packing batten is not needed if the tiles are flush to the wall line, since the facing batten can be fixed (in the same way) to the wall below the tiles and glued and pinned to the edge of the facing board as before.

For laminate finish Chipboard can be used here as the facing board, one advantage being that it is cheaper than plywood or blockboard. It is, however, extremely vulnerable; if you do use it, make sure all edges and faces not being covered with laminate are thoroughly sealed with two or three coats of a proprietary wood primer. If you do use laminate on all the surfaces, it has the advantage of concealing the fixings.

Having assembled the facing boards, cut out strips of laminate to cover the areas you want. If covering the whole facing, first stick the laminate with an impact adhesive onto the underside and ends of the front lipping batten, then the face of this batten and finally the top of the sill facing board, including the top edge of the lipping batten. If using hardwood on the front facing and leaving it exposed, fix it with the same adhesive, which will save you having to plug it to the board facing.

When lipping with hardwood, fix the top edge as flush as possible to the laminate surface on the sill to cut down the need for trimming afterwards; a really flush finish can be achieved by carefully planing the top edge. To protect the hardwood, treat it with teak oil or apply a thin coat of clear polyurethane with a lint-free rag. One advantage of hardwood as lipping is that if the edge of the sill is damaged, you can plane the hardwood smooth again. The only way to repair laminate-covered lipping is to strip away the damaged material and reface with a new piece.

Extending sill

It is a very difficult job to extend a quarry-tiled sill, since the tiles are difficult to lift and you will have great trouble trying to make rows of even-shaped tiles. The best way is to face the tiles, as described above, making sure the new facing extends far enough out to sit flush or overlap the new wall surface if you are lining your walls for insulation. Fit the facing as before.

Wall, floor and ceiling repairs

Repointing bricks

Good quality brickwork is generally a maintenance-free structural material; but as a building ages the exposed surfaces of the mortar joints may show signs of decay and need repointing. There are a number of reasons why this may happen.

Poor mix The original mortar mix may have been of incorrect proportions.

Moisture Driving rains, a faulty damp proof course or leaking gutters and downpipes may have allowed water to penetrate the mortar.

Frosts Any moisture in the mortar or bricks will freeze, expand and break up the surface if subjected to heavy frosts.

Pollution In heavy industrial areas, sulphates in the atmosphere will cause deterioration.

Structural movement Inadequate foundations or a poor standard of building will break up the stability of the mortar.

Where the cause of mortar failure can be diagnosed, it should be remedied, if possible, before repointing, which itself should not be carried out during cold weather because of the possibility of frost affecting the new mortar before it has dried. If winter working is unavoidable, you must use plenty of waterproof sheeting to keep off icy winds, rain and frosts.

1 Raking out old mortar. **2** Repointing tools: cold chisel for removing old mortar **(top)**; plugging chisel, with groove same width as mortar, ideal for raking out **(centre)**; frenchman made by bending end of old kitchen knife **(bottom)**

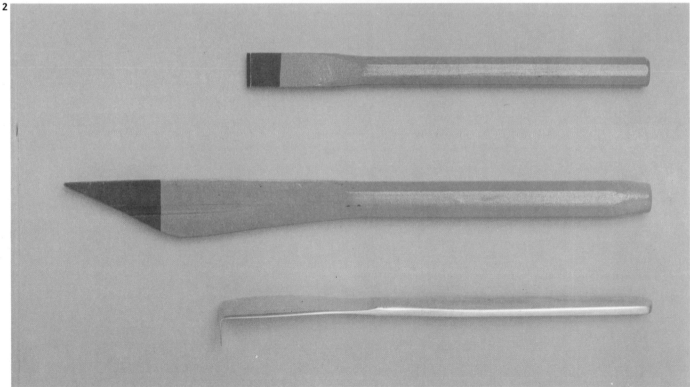

How to repoint

You should always start repointing at the top of the brickwork and work downwards, covering about two square metres (21sq ft) at a time. Scrape any moss or lichen from the surface and then rake out mortar joints to a depth of about 15mm (or ½in), taking care not to damage the brickwork. The recess must be left square (otherwise the mortar may fall out); this can be done with a cold chisel or with a tool you make yourself by filing one end of a square section length of steel. After raking out, ensure the brick edges are free from old mortar and brush out all traces of dust with a fibre bristle brush.

Dry brickwork should be dampened, not soaked, with clean water before repointing; this is important in hot weather when bricks store heat. Water will reduce any suction from the old mortar and brickwork, but too much on the surface could cause the freshly applied mortar to run down the face of the bricks. An old distemper brush is ideal for dampening.

What mix to use

The mortar should be chosen carefully to suit the existing brickwork and the amount of exposure it is likely to undergo. A general mix, suitable for most brickwork, consists of one part cement, one part lime and six parts of washed builder's sand. For a soft facing brick a mix of one part cement, two parts lime and nine parts sand would be satisfactory. Where hard, dense bricks are used in situations of extreme exposure a mix of one part cement, a quarter part lime and three parts sand should be used. This richer cement mix is more likely to

3 Brushing away dust after raking out mortar. **4** Dampening brickwork with distemper brush. **5** Applying mortar with pointing trowel. **6** Forming weathered joint with frenchman and timber straight-edge. **7** Mortar levelled with face of bricks above and below. **8** Making rounded or tooled joint. **9** Forming recessed joint with square timber

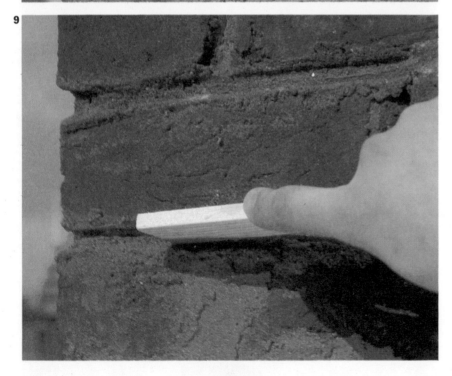

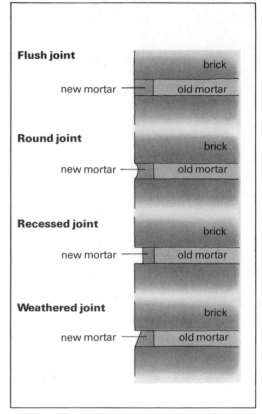

Flush joint

brick

new mortar — old mortar

Round joint

brick

new mortar — old mortar

Recessed joint

brick

new mortar — old mortar

Weathered joint

brick

new mortar — old mortar

shrink and there is a possibility of hairline cracks forming between the bricks and mortar.

As each batch is used, the joints already filled should be tooled or cut and loose material brushed away. When the colour of mortar is important, a ready-mixed coloured mix should be used to maintain consistency.

Warning Make small amounts of mortar at a time and discard it as soon as it begins to dry.

Types of pointing

Different pointing effects can be employed, depending on the type of brickwork and the style of joint used when the house was built.

Weathered The most effective way of shedding rain away from the bricks. Apply the mortar firmly with a small pointing trowel. Push the blade edge at the top of the joint to form a slight recess that slopes forward to meet the top edge of the brick below. You can form this angle using a straight-edge with the edge of the trowel or use a small tool called a 'frenchman' together with the straight-edge; this tool can easily be made by bending the end of a long thin kitchen knife.

Flush Usually employed when matching old brickwork, it is formed by applying the new mortar level with the face of the bricks above and below.

Round or tooled joint A variation on a flush joint, it is also used mainly when matching old brickwork. First form the flush joint and then run a thin rounded piece of timber along the mortar face.

Recessed joint Used solely when matching existing recessed joints in brickwork. After forming a flush joint, the recess is raked back by using a square section piece of timber of the exact width of the mortar joint.

Having finished pointing, remember to remove carefully any remaining deposits of mortar from the face of the brickwork – before the mortar is thoroughly dry – with a fibre bristle brush.

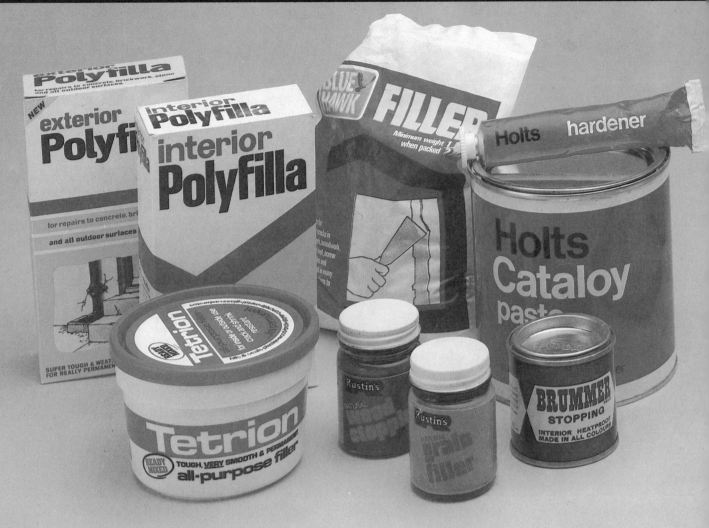

Fillers and fillings

Fillers are used to make good any defective area in wood, concrete, brick, plaster, metal or any other material. In wood and metal where rot or rust has been removed, leaving an irregular indentation, a filler can be worked into the recess and then shaped to blend in with the surface of the work.

There are certain circumstances in which fillers should not be used. Large holes in sheet materials such as metal, plywood and laminates cannot be filled since there is no proper key, base or reinforcement. It is also inadvisable to try to make good any weakness in the structure of any work since a filler will only provide a temporary remedy and will undoubtedly break or collapse at some future date.

The chief disadvantage of fillers is they cannot easily be made to match in appearance or colour the original work and therefore require a paint or rendered finish. If the final appearance is critical and paint or rendering is not applied, fillers should not be used and replacement parts or sections will have to be fashioned out of the original material and grafted on – an extremely difficult and time-consuming task. Fortunately this rarely arises and a paint or rendered finish is perfectly adequate.

Types of filler

Fillers used for repair work around the home are available in two forms. Both contain a mixture of filling substances and chemicals as well as a bonding agent to help them retain their form when set. Some brands of filler are described as elastic, which means they can absorb a small amount of movement without working loose and falling out.

One-part These general-purpose fillers come in a powder or ready-mix form and are used mainly for wood, plaster, brickwork and masonry. Some brands are water and weather-resistant, which makes them suitable for exterior as well as interior use.

Two-part These fillers are used almost exclusively for repairing metal, such as car bodywork, and begin to harden immediately they are mixed.

Interior fillers

These are all of the one-part type and should be used for the materials specified by the manufacturer; these chiefly include wood, plaster and some plastics. The most popular are ready-mix, although the unmixed varieties are a little cheaper. All are said to be 'shrink' or 'sink' resistant and most can be dyed, stained or painted. Some are claimed to be heatproof, which means they will maintain their form even when exposed to above normal temperatures – as when used near fires or cookers. All interior fillers will tolerate the normal range of domestic temperatures including those created artificially by central heating or air conditioning.

Above Various fillers in powder, ready-mixed and two-part form. Some types are more suited to a particular job than others, so before you buy always check the manufacturer's instructions to ensure you choose the right type of filler for the work in hand

103

Above With powder filler, you will need a mixing board or hawk and a filling knife
Top right To mix filler, form it into a heap and make a well in the centre; add water and mix until smooth
Above right Spread filler as evenly as possible to avoid rubbing down later

Exterior fillers

These fillers have been developed to resist all weathering without shrinking, cracking or working loose. The toughest type are cement-based and are best suited for use with concrete, bricks, masonry, asbestos and glass fibre (wood requires a more flexible filler which can tolerate the movements that take place in exterior woodwork). Some of the fillers are suitable for use on marine structures, although none is suitable for surfaces which are constantly under water.

Wood fillers

These fillers are used in joinery and carpentry before the final finish is applied to a particular item. They fall into two general categories – those used for filling cracks and abrasions and those used for filling the grain.

The former are supplied in many shades and with specifications by the manufacturers as to which finishes (eg oil, polish, polyurethane) they can be used with. The latter are available ready-mixed (or as powders which are mixed with water into a fine slurry) to fill the grain and seal the surface of porous woods such as oak and ash.

Metal fillers

These fillers are mostly of the two-part type. They are of a thick paste consistency and can be quite difficult to work with, since they are relatively quick-setting. But once rubbed down and painted they are almost impossible to detect. When set, they maintain their form under all conditions, including vehicle vibration and bad weather.

Application and storage

The method of application is simple and usually all that is required in the way of equipment is a filling knife and board. Tins or containers should be resealed after use to prevent drying out and care should be taken to use up all the filler well within the manufacturer's stated drying time before any more is mixed for use or taken out. Partly set filler and fresh filler should never be mixed since the stated drying time will be shortened. Regular cleaning of your filling knife is very important.

Spread the filler as evenly as possible to avoid any extra work in rubbing down afterwards. This can be achieved when using water-based fillers by dipping the knife in cold water at regular intervals during use. With large cavities build up the filler in layers and always work carefully and slowly, otherwise air bubbles may be trapped round the bottom of the hole which can result in the filler working loose at some later stage. Always read the manufacturer's instructions and never use fillers when proper repairs are required.

Few homes will escape damage to wall plaster. Settlement of the main structure over the years, penetration by damp, excessive heat or just general wear and tear will all lead to damaged plaster surfaces. Not only do imperfect patches look unsightly, they can also grow into a major problem if they are not dealt with promptly. By tackling the job at an early stage, both time and expensive will be saved in the long run: reason enough to get cracking.

The thought of repairing damaged or flaking plaster may be fairly daunting to some people, but tackled in the right way with the right materials it is a relatively straightforward operation. Obviously it is quite a different matter if you have to replaster an entire wall or ceiling, in which case this is probably best left to the professional. But most of the small repairs normally required in the home are well within the capabilities of the DIY enthusiast.

Ceiling cracks These are caused by the movement in roofing and flooring joists, leading to the plasterboard (where fitted) parting at the joints. Repairs, which are quite simple, are discussed later in the book.

Wall cracks These are more likely to occur in new houses and are caused by the settlement of the main structure. The area most likely to be affected is the angle between the wall and the ceiling. Apart from filling in these cracks, which are likely to reopen later, one of the most effective methods is to fix cove over the gaps round the room. Plaster cove can be bought from DIY suppliers.

Unsightly cracks across the wall may also be caused by settlement and normally only affect the plaster. If, however, you get a wide diagonal crack appearing not only in the plaster but also in the wall, this could be a major problem and professional advice should be sought immediately. When this happens it is usually on external walls and is clearly visible from the outside as well.

Filling cracks

Common hairline cracks can be repaired simply and quickly. Rake out the affected area with a sharp knife or the edge of a paint scraper. Cut a 'V' shape into the wall along the crack so that it is widest at the deepest point of the crack. This allows you to push the filler into the cavity dovetail fashion to prevent it falling out on drying. Apply cellulose filler with a flexible steel filling knife. Use either a 75 or 100mm (3 or 4in) filling knife, the larger size being preferred since you can work quickly over large areas. Don't confuse this knife with a paint stripping knife, which looks similar, but must not be used as a substitute. The blade, which will bend about 90 degrees, should be perfectly straight and undamaged. Correctly used the knife can be used to give a smooth finish and make the job of rubbing down later unnecessary. Otherwise rub down with medium fine, then fine, glasspaper when the filler has completely dried, before redecorating.

Replacing loose plaster

Plaster often comes away from the surface around fireplaces. It can work loose due to vibration such as excessive hammering near the affected area – possibly when fitting a door or window frame. One simple test for loose plaster is to tap the suspect surface with the handle of a knife or a small blunt instrument. A hollow sound indicates poor adhesion between the plaster and substrate. Lift all the loose pieces with a broad knife and clean the surface beneath with a soft brush.

Repairing plaster

Filling cracks
sharp knife or paint scraper
cellulose filler
flexible filling knife
medium fine and fine glasspaper

Replacing loose plaster
knife or blunt instrument
broad knife and soft brush
undercoat plaster
finishing plaster
wood float, plasterer's trowel
cellulose filler and flexible filling knife (if needed)

Repairing external corners
cellulose filler, flexible filling knife and medium fine glasspaper (if needed)
undercoat plaster
finishing plaster
soft brush, timber batten
plasterer's trowel or wood float

Recessing fittings and cables
cold chisel
brick bolster
plaster or cellulose filler

equipment

Filling deep cavity

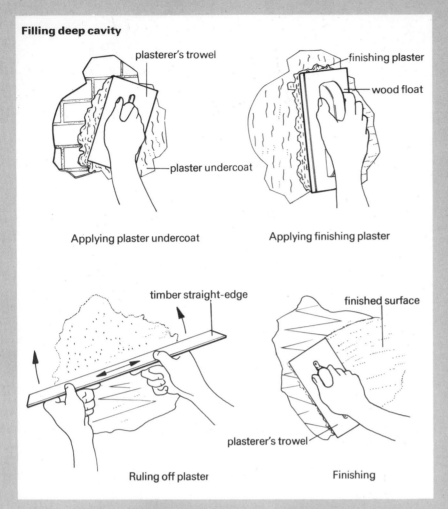

Applying plaster undercoat

Applying finishing plaster

Ruling off plaster

Finishing

If you are dealing with only a small cavity you will probably get away with filling the area with fresh finishing plaster. In the case of a deep cavity, first apply a plaster undercoat. Wet the wall thoroughly, then roughly fill the cavity to within about 3mm ($\frac{1}{8}$in) of the original plaster surface, applying the undercoat with a plasterer's trowel. The undercoat will dry with a rough texture which will provide a key for the finishing plaster. You will find a small 'hawk' useful to carry the plaster to the wall area after mixing it; make one by nailing a square of plywood to a short length of broom handle.

When the undercoat is quite dry, mix up enough finishing plaster to a creamy consistency to complete the job. In powder form it does not keep that long and old plaster will often set too quickly to enable you to spread it properly; in this case the application will just crack and fall away. If you find the plaster is hardening before you have a chance to use it, take it back to your supplier for replacement.

To complete filling, go over the undercoat surface with a dampened brush, put a generous amount of plaster onto the bottom of a wood float or plasterer's trowel and apply it into the remaining cavity. When the cavity is filled you can rule off the plaster. Using a timber straight-edge, which must be longer than the area being repaired, start from the bottom and work upwards over the new plaster with a sawing action, making sure both ends of the timber keep in contact with the surface of the existing plaster. This method ensures high spots are removed and low spots are built up as excess plaster is pushed up the wall, giving a level finish. When the plaster has almost set, rub a plasterer's trowel over the new surface to give a smooth, polished finish. Lift the front edge of the trowel away from the wall

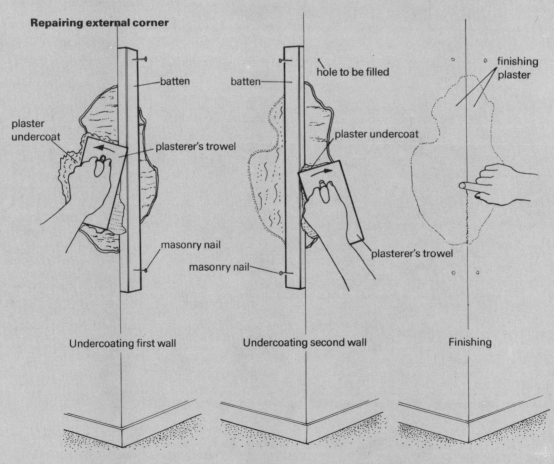

Undercoating first wall

Undercoating second wall

Finishing

so only the back edge is in contact; this will prevent the trowel cutting into the new plaster. Alternatively wait until the plaster has set completely and apply a layer of cellulose filler over the fresh plaster using a filling knife.

Repairing external corners

In any room it is the plaster on external corners that is the most vulnerable to damage. You can repair small holes and chips with cellulose filler as described earlier. When making good these small areas, apply the filler with a flexible filling knife working in each direction away from the corner. When dry the filler can be rubbed down lightly to form an edge to match the rest of that corner.

With a badly damaged corner you will make the best repair by building up the corner with a plaster undercoat, then applying a layer of finishing plaster. Remove any loose plaster and clean back the area with a soft brush. Fix a batten, which must be longer than the affected area, to the wall so its edge is in line with the existing front wall plaster – and flush to the corner. Either hold the batten in position as you work or tack it lightly to the wall with masonry nails, knocking the points of the nails through the batten before fixing. You can screw it into position by drilling the necessary holes in the batten and the wall, plugging the wall and inserting screws through the batten. Make sure you fix the batten well clear of the affected area or you may cause further damage.

Build up the level by applying the undercoat plaster with a trowel or float, always working away from the corner. On one side, plaster the area to within about 3mm (⅛in) of the original surface, then move the batten to the other wall to complete the undercoating. When this is dry, complete the repair with finishing plaster, using the batten on each wall as before.

If you nailed or screwed the batten to the wall, fill the holes with any plaster you have left over or with cellulose filler. Before the plaster sets hard, round off the corner by rubbing your fingers over the plaster to form an edge to match that on the rest of the corner. Use glasspaper if the plaster has set really hard.

Recessing fittings and cables

When new socket outlets have to be fitted or wiring extended along walls or ceilings, you will have to cut a channel in the plaster to conceal the cable. You will also have to chop out some of the brickwork to house the steel box for the socket.

Cut through the plaster cleanly with a sharp cold chisel (or fit a specially designed router to an electric drill and work at slow speed), making the grooves and openings as wide as necessary. Chop through the brickwork with a sharp brick bolster, making the hole deep enough for the front edge of the box to lie flush with the wall surface. Screw the box into position, feed in the cable and fill any surrounding gaps with plaster or cellulose filler, finishing the surface as before. When you have made the necessary repairs you can then connect up the socket and screw it onto the box.

Plastering large areas is physically demanding work best left to a skilled professional, who can apply large amounts of plaster before the mixture begins to harden. If you employ a contractor to insert a new damp proof course, an estimate for replastering internal walls should be included if hacking away old plaster is involved.

Cutting recess for socket
Chanelling plaster

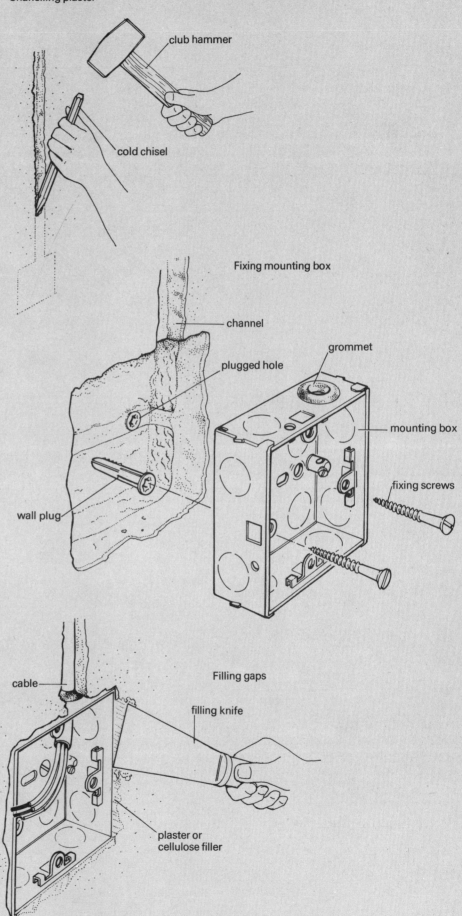

club hammer

cold chisel

Fixing mounting box

channel

grommet

plugged hole

mounting box

wall plug

fixing screws

cable

Filling gaps

filling knife

plaster or
cellulose filler

Repairing a fireplace

An open fire provides real comfort in cold weather; if not being used, a screen or large plant placed there can provide an attractive focal point for the room. If your fireplace is showing signs of wear or damage, you can carry out repairs quite easily.

Repairing hearth and surround
Heat and smoke from an open fire can cause tiles in the hearth and surround to crack or the pointing between bricks to deteriorate. If a tile becomes damaged and you manage to find a suitable replacement, remove the old tile by chipping it out with a cold chisel and hammer, starting at the centre and working outwards. Fix the replacement tile with mortar, making sure it lies flush with the existing ones.

Brickwork For repointing, rake out the old mortar to a depth of about 13mm (½in), remove dust and

1a When replacing a brick, insert small pieces of wood at each corner to hold it in position
1b Use a straight-edge to check the brick is in line with the existing bricks
2 Use fireclay cement to repair a cracked fireback
3 To remove a fireback, break it up with a club hammer and bolster chisel

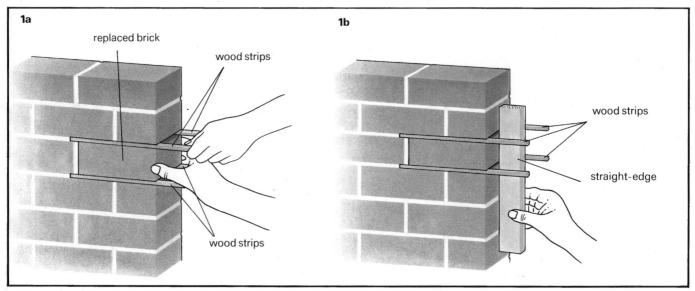

1a replaced brick / wood strips / wood strips
1b wood strips / straight-edge

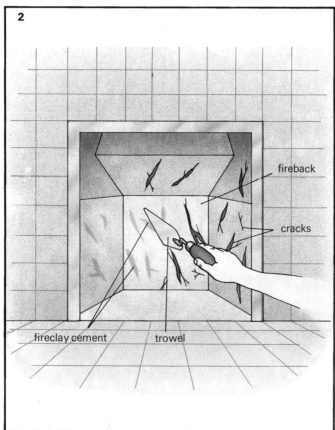

2 fireback / cracks / fireclay cement / trowel

3 bolster chisel / club hammer

debris, brush water over the bricks and fill the joints with a new mortar mix of one part Portland cement, three parts hydrated lime and ten parts silver (heat-resistant) sand; if the fireplace is no longer in use, a mix of one part cement to three parts clean builder's sand is suitable. It is best to repoint the whole fireplace to ensure a uniform effect. To replace a loose brick, use a bolster chisel and club hammer to remove the brick and clean mortar from the cavity and any adjoining bricks. Soak the brick in clean water and apply a layer of mortar (three parts sand to one part cement) to the back and sides. Replace the brick, using small wood strips of equal size top and bottom to hold it in line with the existing bricks. Once the cement has set, remove the strips of wood and repoint.

Repairing fireback

Cracks sometimes develop in firebacks and the chimney structure may eventually be weakened due to the penetration of heat and smoke. Repair work is easy, using fireclay cement (available from builders' merchants). The surround should be cold when the work is done, so don't light a fire for at least 24 hours beforehand. Clean away any soot or dirt from the surface with a stiff brush. Undercut the crack slightly, using a bolster chisel and a club hammer, to ensure the filling is well anchored and rake out any loose material. Soak the cracks thoroughly with water and, before the water dries, trowel in the fireclay cement, making sure the crack is well filled and levelling off as the work proceeds. Allow at least 24 hours before lighting a fire.

Replacement When a fireback is badly cracked or otherwise damaged it must be removed and a replacement unit fitted. Lever out the fireback with a crowbar or use a club hammer and bolster chisel to break it up. Remove the rubble from behind the base section and hack off the cement, on which the base was bedded, to the concrete below.

On many old firebacks, there will be a manufacturer's name or reference code which will help when ordering a new unit. The traditional fireback has a central protruding portion called a 'knee'; on some the knee is too low and causes problems in the final stages of installation when shaping the area which forms the throat to the flue of the chimney. When ordering your new fireback, ask for one which complies with British Standards – this will ensure the unit supplied has a high knee and is made to modern dimensions to suit a modern open fire. The quality of the fireback is another important factor. The old unit may have cracked or suffered general deterioration through age.

Although single-piece firebacks are available, they are best avoided because the fireplace surround must be removed to fit them and they are heavy and awkward to handle. Also, cracking is often caused by heat expanding the lower part of the fireback while the cooler upper part does not expand; in a single-piece unit without space for expansion, cracks will develop. Two-piece units are the most popular, although there are four and six-piece versions. With the two-piece unit, the lower half is free to expand without the rest of the fireback being affected.

Check if there is asbestos rope clipped to the back edges of the fireplace surround. If not, hold two lengths of 13mm (½in) asbestos rope, equal to the height of the lintel above the hearth, against the back edges of the surround and place the lower half of the fireback squarely and centrally in the open-

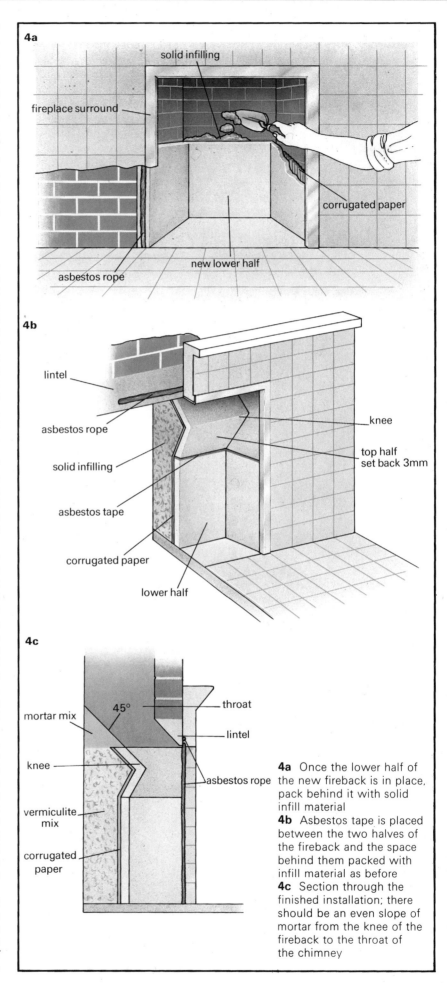

4a Once the lower half of the new fireback is in place, pack behind it with solid infill material

4b Asbestos tape is placed between the two halves of the fireback and the space behind them packed with infill material as before

4c Section through the finished installation; there should be an even slope of mortar from the knee of the fireback to the throat of the chimney

ing so the asbestos rope is slightly compressed and held in position. To allow for a small amount of expansion, line the back of the new fireback by pushing corrugated paper or thin strawboard up against it and pack infill material behind it to provide insulation between the fireback and the wall. You will need a solid infilling, not loose rubble; a mix of one part lime, two parts sand and four parts broken brick is suitable. (Don't use cement in the mix since it would be too strong for this function.) Alternatively use a mix of six parts vemiculite and one part lime, mixed to a paste with water; this has better insulating qualities and is especially useful against an outside wall, through which you could otherwise lose an excessive amount of heat.

Place a length of flat asbestos tape along the top edge of the lower half of the fireback. Unlike fire cement, which is sometimes used to make the joint between the top and bottom pieces of the fireback, asbestos tape will not fall out and it allows for the expansion difference between the two halves. Hold the asbestos rope in place against the back of the fireplace surround, check there is a third length across the top of the fire opening between the lintel and the back of the fireplace and place the top half of the fireback flush on the lower portion or set it back by 3mm ($\frac{1}{8}$in) to avoid its lower edge being burned. On no account should it protrude forwards. Fill in behind the top half with the same mix as before, smoothing the filling level with the top. Fill the space all round the top of the fireback within the chimney with a mortar mix of four parts sharp sand to one part cement (using broken brick as a filler if the space is large) to give an even slope of at least 45 degrees from the knee to the throat – you should end up with a smooth line running from the knee to the back of the flue. You can leave the asbestos rope exposed or hide it by applying a very thin layer of fire cement to smooth out the surface.

Lining the fireplace opening

At a time when electricity supplies can be cut off with little advance warning, it is useful to keep those old fireplaces in good repair for use in an emergency. However, if you decide to abandon coal fires, there is an alternative to briking it up.

If your fireplace is disused, instead of filling it in with bricks or a panel you can turn it into an attractive alcove by providing a panelled lining. For this, tongued and grooved panels, veneer plywood, melamine faced boards or plasterboard are suitable materials.

To prevent dust and soot falling into the alcove, you should block off the chimney. Since this cuts off ventilation to the chimney, knock out a brick in the fireplace above the lintel, replace it with an air-brick and screw on a fixed ventilation grille. Use plugs and screws to fix 50 × 25mm (2 × 1in) battens to the sides and back of the fireplace opening so the bottom edges of the battens are flush with the bottom of the fireplace lintel, and screw a piece of resin-bonded plywood to the battens to seal off the chimney. Install a framework of 50 × 25mm (2 × 1in) battens (using plugs and screws) in the fireplace opening and fix decorative panels to the framework with impact adhesive.

Warning Don't attempt to leave out the timber framework and glue the panels directly to the bricks, since the sooty surface of the bricks prevents secure fixing and the panelling in the recess will not stay in place.

Basic items
bolster and cold chisels, club hammer
mortar mix, wood strips (for replacing brick)
stiff brush, crowbar, fireclay cement (for repairing cracked fireback)
asbestos rope, corrugated paper or thin strawboard, infill material, asbestos tape, mortar mix (for replacing fireback)
airbrick, 50 × 25mm (2 × 1in) battens, plugs and screws, resin-bonded plywood, decorative panels, impact adhesive (for lining opening)

equipment

5a When lining a disused fireplace with decorative panels, first block off the chimney by fixing resin-bonded plywood to a timber batten framework
5b Screw a batten framework to the walls of the fireplace opening and fix the decorative panels to this with impact adhesive; remember to install an airbrick above the lintel to provide ventilation to the chimney. If you don't, damp may set in and spoil wall decorations

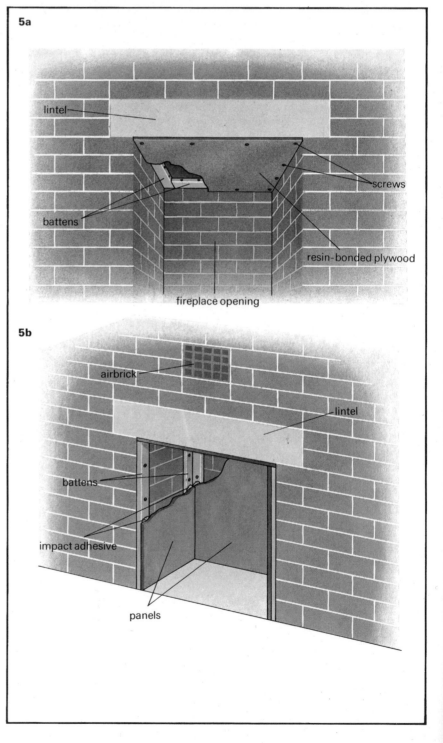

5a
lintel
screws
battens
resin-bonded plywood
fireplace opening

5b
airbrick
lintel
battens
impact adhesive
panels

Levelling a solid floor

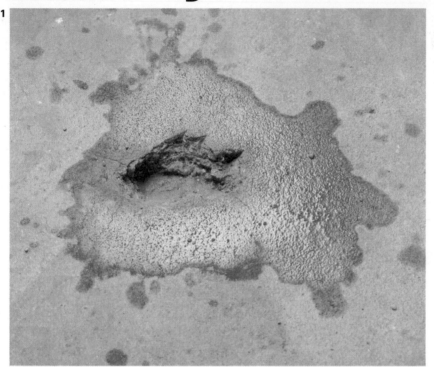

How you deal with an uneven or sloping solid floor depends on the degree to which it is out of true. Check this with a spirit level placed on a long straight board, using it over different areas of the floor and pointing in a number of directions. If the floor slopes more than about 6mm (or ¼in) you will have to level it with a sand and cement surfacing layer, or screed. Where the irregularity is no more than 6mm (or ¼in) you can make the floor level with one or two layers of a self-smoothing screeding compound. This is a mixture like runny cement which sets in a few hours to form a hard surface suitable as a base for any type of floor covering.

If the floor is old it may be badly cracked and very uneven and it is best to remove it and lay a new concrete floor with a damp proof membrane. (You can use the same method to replace a downstairs timber floor which has rotted.) Where the floor is damp but otherwise sound, you do not need to replace it; simply paint the floor with a damp-proofing sealer.

1 Fill any holes in the floor. **2** Pack with cement mortar and trowel smooth. **3** If necessary brush on a liquid damp proof membrane. **4** Pour on the levelling compound, mixed to a creamy paste

Laying a self-smoothing screed

Clean, dust-free concrete is the ideal surface for a self-smoothing screed and it is best to remove any existing floor covering before starting treatment. You should always remove wood blocks or any type of sheet covering (vinyl, carpet etc.), but you can use screeding compounds on quarry tiles, flagstones, slate and bricks. Some compounds are suitable for application over hard surface vinyl tiles provided these are securely fixed and properly prepared.

Preparing the surface Remove any flaking or crumbling sections with a metal scraper. Sweep the floor and wash it thoroughly with a strong sugar soap solution. Remove stubborn oil and grease patches with caustic soda or a proprietary floor cleaner and take off polish with medium grade wire wool and cleaning powder. Rinse with clean water and, when dry, sweep the floor again.

Indentations more than 6mm (or $\frac{1}{4}$in) deep must be filled with cement mortar (one part Portland cement to three parts clean, coarse sand). To make sure the mortar adheres firmly in these hollows paint the affected area with a PVA bonding agent diluted according to the manufacturer's instructions. Allow this to dry before applying another coat and, before the second coat dries, trowel on the cement mortar.

Prepare reasonably absorbent surfaces, such as cement mortar or concrete, by lightly dampening the surface with water using a garden syringe or spreading with a wide brush. Prime quarry tiles and other non-absorbent surfaces – and very dusty ones such as sandy screeds – with a PVA bonding agent; allow this to dry before applying the compound.

Vinyl tiles These need special preparation: wash them thoroughly with a proprietary floor cleaner or with sugar soap. Don't use abrasive or solvent-based cleaners. Fill small depressions in the surface with a mixture of two parts of a special water-mixed screeding compound and one part clean sharp sand.

Vinyl tiles also need special priming treatment: use an acrylic floor primer mixed with water (one part primer to one part water). When the primer has dried, brush a thin coat of a suitable bonding agent over the floor (never a PVA bonding agent). Allow the bonding agent to set for up to two hours or until you can walk on it without it sticking to your feet.

Applying the compound Screeding compounds are usually supplied in powder form, which you mix with water to a creamy paste. Pour a little of the paste onto the floor and spread it out as evenly as possible with a steel float. No finishing off is needed since the marks made by the float disappear within a few seconds. Work from the corner farthest from the door to allow an easy exit. You can use the compounds in layers from 1.5 to 3mm (or $\frac{1}{16}$ to $\frac{1}{8}$in) thick, making one or two applications. If two coats are necessary, apply the second as soon as the first has dried hard enough to walk on. The screed sets quickly and can be walked on usually after about one or two hours. You can lay the floor coverings the following day, although the screed does not harden thoroughly for a week.

5 Smooth the levelling compound with a steel float; no finishing is needed
6 Before laying a sand and cement screed, position battens over the floor
7 Draw a levelling board across the screed using the battens as a guide

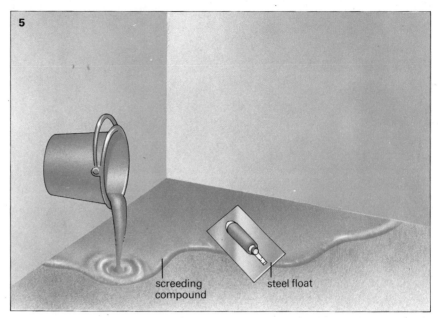

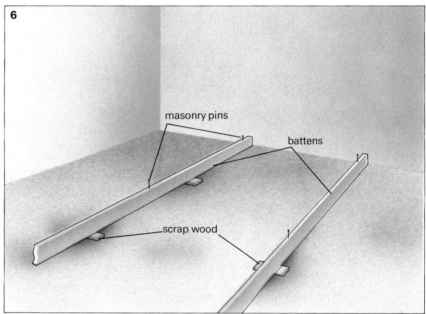

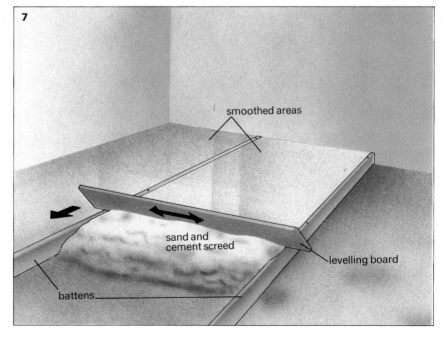

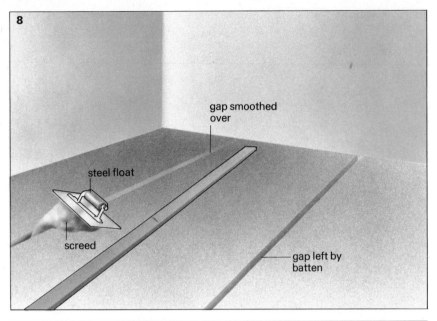

gap smoothed over

steel float

screed

gap left by batten

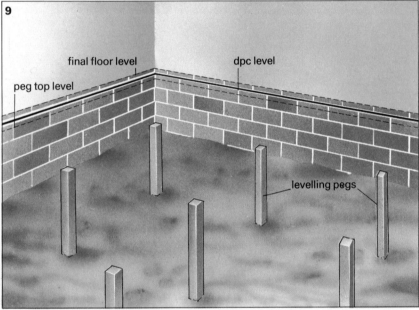

final floor level

peg top level

dpc level

levelling pegs

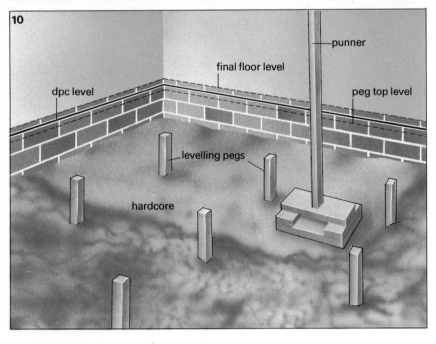

punner

final floor level

dpc level

peg top level

levelling pegs

hardcore

Laying a sand and cement screed

The technique you use for laying a sand and cement screed is very similar to laying a self-smoothing screed, but this type is thicker and it takes more effort and skill to get a smooth level surface. Since the finished surface will be slightly higher than before, it will be necessary to plane a small amount from the bottom of doors and perhaps refix skirting boards.

Preparing the floor Clean the floor as previously described, then apply a PVA bonding agent and allow it to dry. To ensure the new floor surface will be smooth and level, you will have to lay battens on the floor; the screed is spread between these battens and levelled off by drawing a board along them. The thickness of the battens will govern the thickness of the screed which, for maximum strength, should be 25 to 50mm (1 to 2in) – and no less than 6mm (or $\frac{1}{4}$in) – thick.

Lay the battens a convenient distance apart: about 1m (or 3ft) is ideal because it allows you to place the screed in strips. Use a spirit level and a straight-edge to get the battens level in all directions and position pieces of scrap wood to pack them out at the low spots. Fix the battens temporarily to the floor with masonry pins and apply another coat of slightly diluted bonding agent, allowing it to dry partially.

Applying the screed Mix the cement screed (one part Portland cement to three parts clean coarse sand), making sure the mixture is not dry or crumbly nor too wet so puddles form on the surface when the screed is smoothed over. If the screed will be less than 25mm (1in) thick, add a bonding agent to the mix according to the manufacturer's instructions.

Roughly spread the screed between the battens with a steel float. Pull the edge of the levelling board, which should be long enough to rest easily on the battens, over them to give a level finish and smooth the screed with the steel float, checking the surface frequently with your spirit level.

When the surface of each strip of screed is slightly firm, prise up the battens and fill the resulting gaps with screed mixture, smoothing it out to maintain the level surface. Leave the finished screed to cure for at least three days before walking on it. If it is essential to cross the floor before this time, lay duckboards of timber planks or chipboard or plywood sheets.

Warning It is essential thin section screeds do not dry out too rapidly or the cement will not cure and harden properly. Cover them with polythene sheets or wet newspapers or sacking during curing.

Laying a new solid floor

Putting down an entirely new floor allows you to control exactly the height of the finished floor surface. It can line up with existing floors, or be at a lower level to give extra height to the room. This is particularly useful if you are modernising an old cottage, since you can make it meet building regulation requirements which lay down a minimum ceiling height of 2.3m (or 7ft 6in). Always consult your local building control officer before making a new floor to ensure the work complies with current regulations.

8 When the surface is firm, remove the battens and fill the gaps with more screed
9 Set out levelling pegs for a new floor
10 Compact the hardcore with a punner

Preparing the surface Remove the old floor by breaking it up with a sledgehammer and pickaxe or a heavy duty electric hammer, all of which you can hire. Dig out the base to a depth of 300mm (or 12in) below the finished floor level. Remove plaster from the walls until you find the level of the damp proof course.

Insert a series of stout levelling pegs made from 50 × 50mm (or 2 × 2in) timber at regular intervals over the entire area. The tops of the pegs should be level and 50mm (or 2in) below the finished floor surface. Use a long straight-edge and a spirit level to set the pegs accurately.

Constructing the floor Place a layer of hardcore (the broken segments of the old floor can be used for this) about 100mm (4in) thick between the pegs. Ram it well down and bind the surface with a layer of sand. Then spread concrete to the top of the levelling pegs to give a concrete depth of about 150mm (6in). A suitable concrete mix is one part Portland cement, two-and-a-half parts concreting sand and four parts coarse aggregate. You can use ready-mixed concrete if a large area is involved.

Damp proof membrane Most local authorities will accept a damp proof membrane consisting of two coats of a heavy damp-proofing liquid, but some may prefer a plastic membrane sheet. A plastic membrane sheet is usually laid over the concrete before the finishing screed. Fold it up the walls to link with the existing damp proof course.

A liquid bitumen rubber damp proof membrane is brushed over the surface after the concrete has hardened. Start in the corner furthest from the door and apply an even coat, taking care not to miss any areas. Again, make sure you take the membrane up the wall to link with the damp proof course. When the first coat has dried apply a second one and cover it with clean coarse sand while it is still wet to provide a good key for the screed (which you will lay next) and to protect the membrane when it is walked on.

Laying the screed Finish the floor by laying a 50mm (or 2in) thick sand and cement screed (one part cement to three parts sharp, washed sand) over the damp proof membrane.

Because the concrete sub-floor is level and smooth you do not need to nail guide battens over the surface in the same way as when a screed is laid on an uneven floor. Instead, make two guide battens 2m (or 6ft) long and 50mm (2in) thick and lay them fairly close to each side of the room with a levelling board placed across them. Spread the screed mix around the battens using the levelling board as a guide.

Smooth the surface with a steel float and check with a spirit level to make sure the surface is level. Draw back the battens and make good the surface before laying another screed strip. Work backwards to the doorway, changing the direction of work if necessary.

To avoid damage to the screed before curing is complete, it is advisable to allow a three-day curing period before you walk on the floor.

If walking over a freshly laid screed is unavoidable, it should be protected by laying duckboards or planks or boards to spread the load over as wide an area as possible.

11 Put a plastic membrane sheet over the newly laid concrete
12 Apply screed on top of the sheet
13 Remove the battens and fill the gaps

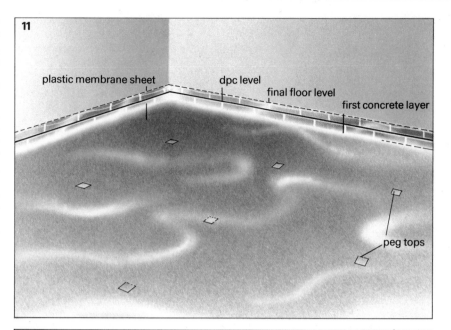

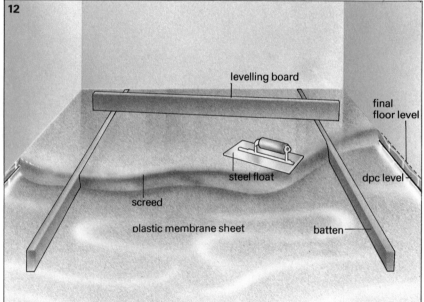

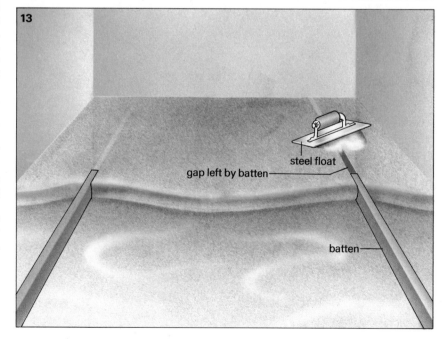

Repairing timber floors

Most homes have timber floors in upstairs rooms, but in houses built in Britain since 1945 – and in recent extensions to older houses – you will often find that the ground floor rooms have solid floors. As both timber and solid floors can be covered with wood blocks or plastic tiles it may not be immediately obvious which type you are dealing with. So always check first what sort of floor you have.

Timber floors downstairs consist of boards or sheets of chipboard nailed over sturdy timber joists, which are often supported on low walls (called sleeper walls). Upstairs the joists may be built into opposite walls or supported in galvanized steel brackets (joist hangers).

As they are supported on joists, timber floors are also called suspended floors. Unlike solid floors, they make a hollow sound when stamped on and also have a certain amount of bounce. Another means of recognizing a timber floor downstairs is the presence of airbricks on the outside walls just above soil level. These bricks allow air to circulate beneath the floor to keep it dry and free of rot. Solid floors at ground level do not have airbricks.

Fixing loose and squeaky boards

Loose boards move when you walk on them and will increase wear on any floor coverings laid over them. They may also develop annoying squeaks and creaks as two faces of timber rub together. To cure this, refix the boards by nailing them down properly. Possibly not all the nails were replaced the last time the boards were lifted; more likely the nails are loose. Renailing with cut floor brads or round head nails slightly to one side may solve the problem, but there is a danger this will cause the end of the board to split. It is better to drill small pilot holes and refix the boards, using No 10 countersunk screws 38mm (1½in) long. The screws must pass into the joists, the position of which can be seen by the line of nail heads on the surface of the boards.

If the boards are properly fixed but still squeak because they are flexing, the problem can be temporarily overcome by dusting the crack between the boards with French chalk or talcum powder. If the squeak returns, one of the boards must be lifted and the edge planed to give slight clearance.

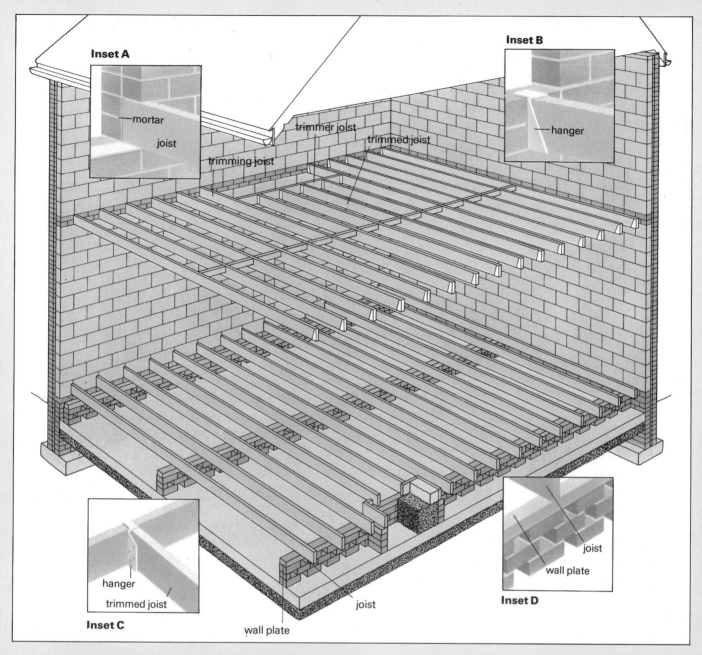

Inset A

mortar

joist

trimming joist

trimmer joist

trimmed joist

Inset B

hanger

hanger

trimmed joist

Inset C

joist

wall plate

joist

wall plate

Inset D

Sometimes boards which have been properly fixed to the joists still spring up and down, usually because the joists themselves are not properly secured. The only way to check this is to lift some boards in the affected area and examine the joists.

Lifting floorboards

Because of the way floors are made, lifting a floor-board is not always as straightforward as it may appear. Older houses usually have square-edged boards (see 1). These are not too difficult to lift, although some force may be needed.

Square-edged floorboards To lift these, check the surface of the board to see if it is secured with nails or screws; the screw slots may be filled with dirt, so look carefully. If it is held with screws, the board will come up easily once the screws are removed; if nailed, it must be levered up.

Start near the end of a conveniently placed board and insert a strong lever, such as a long cold chisel, car tyre lever or flooring chisel, into the gap between the boards (see 2a). Hammer the chisel to prise up the end until another lever, for example a

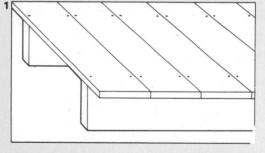

claw hammer, can be inserted under the board (see 2b). Work the two levers along the board until it is free. Alternatively, put a batten under the board, resting on boards either side, and hammer it along to avoid splitting the board or marking the next.

Another method is to slip a length of steel pipe or rod under the end which has been lifted. Stand on the loose end and the leverage of the rod will force up the board further along its length. Keep moving the rod forward until the entire board comes up (see 2c).

Above Example of timber floor construction in two-storey house, with joists and struts exposed
Inset A End of joist embedded into wall with mortar
Inset B End of joist supported by hanger in wall
Inset C Trimmed joist supported on trimmer joist by hanger
Inset D Joist supported by wall plate on sleeper wall
1 Square-edged floorboards

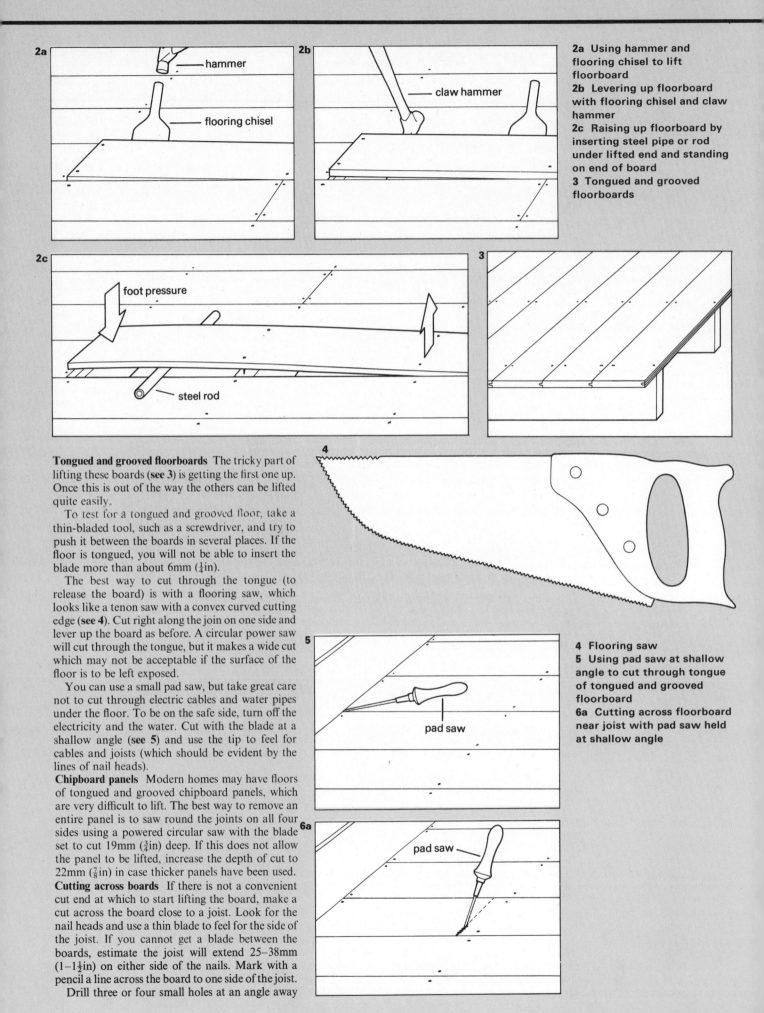

2a Using hammer and flooring chisel to lift floorboard
2b Levering up floorboard with flooring chisel and claw hammer
2c Raising up floorboard by inserting steel pipe or rod under lifted end and standing on end of board
3 Tongued and grooved floorboards

2a hammer / flooring chisel
2b claw hammer
2c foot pressure / steel rod

Tongued and grooved floorboards The tricky part of lifting these boards (**see 3**) is getting the first one up. Once this is out of the way the others can be lifted quite easily.

To test for a tongued and grooved floor, take a thin-bladed tool, such as a screwdriver, and try to push it between the boards in several places. If the floor is tongued, you will not be able to insert the blade more than about 6mm ($\frac{1}{4}$in).

The best way to cut through the tongue (to release the board) is with a flooring saw, which looks like a tenon saw with a convex curved cutting edge (**see 4**). Cut right along the join on one side and lever up the board as before. A circular power saw will cut through the tongue, but it makes a wide cut which may not be acceptable if the surface of the floor is to be left exposed.

You can use a small pad saw, but take great care not to cut through electric cables and water pipes under the floor. To be on the safe side, turn off the electricity and the water. Cut with the blade at a shallow angle (**see 5**) and use the tip to feel for cables and joists (which should be evident by the lines of nail heads).

Chipboard panels Modern homes may have floors of tongued and grooved chipboard panels, which are very difficult to lift. The best way to remove an entire panel is to saw round the joints on all four sides using a powered circular saw with the blade set to cut 19mm ($\frac{3}{4}$in) deep. If this does not allow the panel to be lifted, increase the depth of cut to 22mm ($\frac{7}{8}$in) in case thicker panels have been used.

Cutting across boards If there is not a convenient cut end at which to start lifting the board, make a cut across the board close to a joist. Look for the nail heads and use a thin blade to feel for the side of the joist. If you cannot get a blade between the boards, estimate the joist will extend 25–38mm (1–1$\frac{1}{2}$in) on either side of the nails. Mark with a pencil a line across the board to one side of the joist.

Drill three or four small holes at an angle away

4 Flooring saw
5 Using pad saw at shallow angle to cut through tongue of tongued and grooved floorboard
6a Cutting across floorboard near joist with pad saw held at shallow angle

5 pad saw
6a pad saw

from the joist, just inside the pencil line, to enable **6b** you to insert a saw blade. Using a pad saw or powered jig saw cut across the board (see **6a**), keeping the handle of the saw tilted towards the middle of the joist so the board will be supported when it is replaced. Give the board some additional support when you replace it by gluing and nailing a piece of scrap wood ($50 \times 25mm/2 \times 1in$) to the side of the joist with **clout** nails 38mm ($1\frac{3}{4}$in) long so its top is flush with the top of the joist (see **6b**).

Securing loose joists

When floorboards have been lifted, the exposed joists can be tested for movement. If the ends have rotted, it is best to check with a flooring expert to remedy the problem. Dampness in the supporting walls is the usual cause – or blocked or insufficient airbricks.

If the joists and floorboards show signs of woodworm attack (neat round holes surrounded by fine sawdust), brush them free of dust and cobwebs and spray with woodworm killer applied with a garden-type insecticide sprayer. If the attack is widespread, you should get professional advice.

The joists may be loose because the mortar which holds them firmly in place in the wall has dropped out (see **floor construction diagrams**). In this case the joist should be repacked with new mortar.

If the joist end is supported on a wall plate or in a metal joist hanger (see **floor construction diagrams**), you may be able to secure it by wedging it in place with a piece of scrap wood or by packing pieces of slate under it.

If the joists bounce, it is because they are fitted across too wide a span. They can be stabilized with timber struts fitted between them midway from the support points. Lengths of floorboard about $125 \times 25mm$ ($5 \times 1in$) nailed into the joists are the easiest to fit (see **7**).

Levelling boards

Uneven surfaces of old floors result in extra wear on floor coverings and could be a hazard, causing people to trip over raised sections.

Correcting surface levels If the floor surface is uneven in only a few places and is to be covered, lift the offending boards and pack them with pieces of scrap hardboard or plastic laminate to the correct level.

When the boards are high, the securing nails should be punched well below the surface, tacks should be pulled out and the surface of the boards levelled with either a plane or a coarse sanding disc attached to an electric drill.

Alternatively you can cut a rebate in the underside of the offending floorboard where it sits on the joists. Measure the depth of board to be trimmed, lift and hold it at right-angles to the floor. Mark on the underside the exact position of the joists, allowing 12mm ($\frac{1}{2}$in) on either side of each joist (see **8a**). With a try square complete your marks across the width of the board and shade in the rebate area. Measure and mark the depth of the rebate on both edges of the board (see **8b**) and tenon saw along the pencil lines to the depth marked on the edges (**8c**). Clamp the board and chisel out the rebate area, taking care not to chisel below the required depth (see **8d**). Replace the floorboard, check it is the same level as the other boards (see **8e**) and nail it to the joists with 63mm ($2\frac{1}{2}$in) cut floor brads or round head nails.

Warning Floorboards are usually 22mm ($\frac{7}{8}$in)

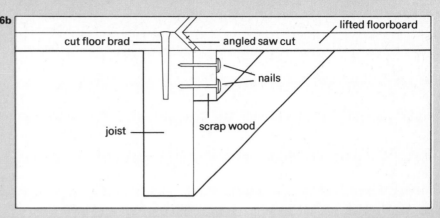

6b

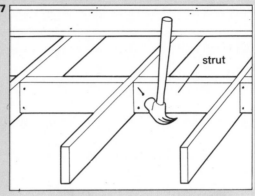

7

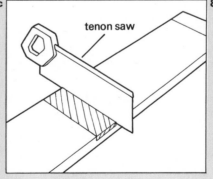

6b Section of lifted board replaced and supported
7 Fixing plain struts between joists

Below Levelling a thick floorboard 8a Marking rebate on underside of floorboard. 8b Measuring and marking depth of rebate. 8c Sawing rebate depth. 8d Chiselling out rebate. 8e Thicker board now lies at correct level

8a

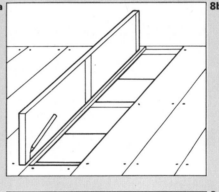

8b

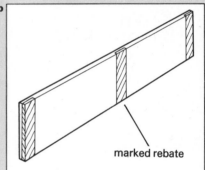

8c

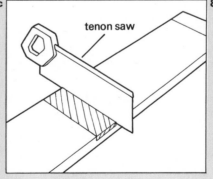

8d

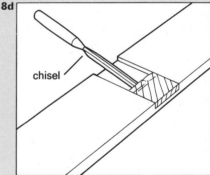

8e

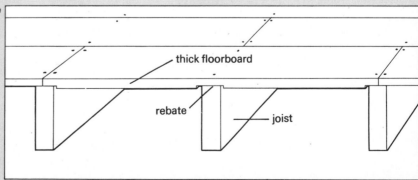

thick. It is dangerous to remove more than 3mm ($\frac{1}{8}$in) from the thickness of the board. Pay special attention to this when making the saw cuts.

Resurfacing Where a number of boards are uneven, resurface the entire floor by sanding it with an industrial-type electric floor sander, which can be hired. This has a large drum covered with a belt of tough abrasive paper.

The machine will remove about 3mm ($\frac{1}{8}$in) of the surface without difficulty, but nail heads must first be sunk well below the surface or they will tear the abrasive paper. Move the sander up and down the length of the floorboards or slightly at an angle. Most of the dust is collected in a bag, but some will escape into the air so you must wear a mask when sanding.

The alternative to sanding is to lay sheets of hardboard on the floor surface. If there are any serious undulations, these should first be corrected by lifting and relaying the offending boards.

Usually 3mm ($\frac{1}{8}$in) standard hardboard is suitable for resurfacing, but use 5mm ($\frac{3}{16}$in) board if the floor is in a very poor state and there are gaps of more than 6mm ($\frac{1}{4}$in) between the boards. If the hardboard is to be laid in a kitchen, bathroom or where it could be subjected to damp, tempered hardboard should be used since it is resistant to moisture.

Conditioning hardboard To avoid buckling, hardboard must be conditioned before it is laid. Separate the boards and stand them on edge in the room where they will be fixed for up to 72 hours before laying. In new houses, and in kitchens and bathrooms, where there is likely to be more moisture, sprinkle the rough side with water – about 1 litre per 2440 × 1200mm sheet (2 pints per 8 × 4ft sheet). Stack the boards flat, back to back, and leave for 48 hours (standard hardboard) or 72 hours (tempered).

Laying hardboard sheets The boards should be laid as soon as they have been conditioned. If working with full 2440 × 1200mm (8 × 4ft) sheets, cut each one in half or quarters with a fine tooth saw since smaller sheets are much easier to handle. Either get someone to help hold the sheet or clamp and support where possible to keep the sheet firm when cutting.

If varnishing the hardboard and using it as a decorative surface (or if laying thin vinyl floor tiles on it) lay the shiny side uppermost; for any other decorative floor covering lay the rough side upwards.

The hardboard sheets should be laid, as far as possible, in staggered brickwork fashion so the joints do not align. Fix down the boards with hardboard nails 25mm (1in) long at 100mm (or 4 in) intervals along the edges and at 150mm (or 6in) intervals over the whole board surface (**see 9**).

Where floorboards may have to be lifted from time to time to give access to cables and pipes, the hardboard should be fixed in small panels with No 6 countersunk screws.

Relaying a floor

If the boards are badly worn and there are a lot of wide gaps between them, it is best to relay the floor. You can then refix worn boards upside down to give a new surface. It is possible to fill gaps between boards with papier mâché, wood filler or wood strips, but this is generally too time-consuming except where there are only a few gaps to fill.

If you are relaying the floor, it is a good oppor-

tunity while the boards are lifted to check for damp, rot and woodworm – and carry out treatment if necessary. You may also decide it is worth while insulating under the floor, if working downstairs.

Normally gaps between boards can be eliminated by pushing the boards together as they are renailed. If they are warped, however, you will have to fill the gaps with wedges or plane the edges level.

Nail the first board into place with 63mm ($2\frac{1}{2}$in) cut floor brads or lost head nails, then position four or five boards together. Place folding wedges at intervals against the boards and nail pieces of scrap timber to the joists against the wedges to stop them moving. Hammer the wedges together to close the gaps in the boards, then nail the boards to the joists when the boards are in the correct position (**see 10**).

Replace damaged boards with new timber or with second-hand floorboards, which are usually available from demolition yards. All second-hand timber should be carefully examined for rot and woodworm damage. It is advisable to take a sample of the existing floorboards to compare for width and thickness.

You can make a very hard and smooth floor by replacing the timber floorboards with flooring grade chipboard panels. The tongued and grooved type makes an exceptionally smooth floor, but because it is difficult to lift make sure to leave small, screwed down access panels over cables and pipes which may have to be reached from time to time.

9 Order of laying cut hardboard sheets to level uneven floor surface
10 Using folding wedges and nailed blocks to close gaps between boards when relaying timber floor

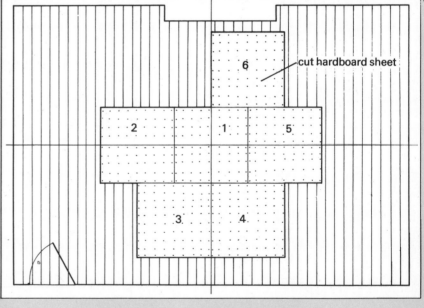

9

cut hardboard sheet

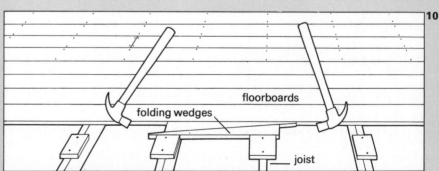

10

floorboards

folding wedges

joist

Use 19mm ($\frac{3}{4}$in) chipboard for joists up to 450mm (or 18in) apart and 22mm ($\frac{7}{8}$in) chipboard for joists from 450–600mm (or 18–24in) apart. Fit the panels together and nail in place through the tongues with round head nails.

Ceiling problems

Patchy ceilings are not just an eyesore; the smallest defect may eventually grow into a major problem. Never try to hide them or they'll soon become expensive headaches. There are lots of small repair jobs you can do yourself, so start now while it still involves just filling in cracks and removing bubbles in the plaster.

There are two main types of ceiling: plasterboard or lath and plaster. Most ceilings in modern properties are composed of plasterboard sheets butted closely together and nailed to the joists above, covered with a skim or thin coat of plaster. The lath and plaster type of ceiling is no longer constructed, so will only be found in older buildings. The laths (thin strips of timber) were nailed to the joists with narrow gaps between them. Plaster was pressed onto the laths and forced up between (and above) them; when set, this formed the ceiling. A setting coat of plaster was sometimes applied to give a smooth finish.

If you are not sure which type of ceiling you have, look in the loft to see whether there is a plain surface of plasterboard or plaster keyed between the laths. And before you make any repairs to a top floor ceiling make sure there is nothing wrong with your roof. If it leaks, any repair work will be wasted.

Types of ceiling filler

Cellulose filler and plaster are the main types of material used in repairing ceilings.

Cellulose Comes in powder form for mixing with water to a workable consistency, or ready-mixed in tubs and tubes. When filling really deep cracks you may have to build up the surface gradually. Leave each layer to dry thoroughly before making the next application. If you have not done this job before you may find you have to use fine glasspaper on the final layer to obtain a really smooth flush finish.

Plaster More economical than filler when making large repairs. To achieve a smooth finish either level the plaster with a timber straight-edge or, much easier, fill the bulk of the hole with plaster and finish with cellulose filler.

Repairing general damage

Before you start work on any type of ceiling make sure you have a secure platform on which to stand to make the job less tiring and to reduce the risk of accident. If only a small area is involved a step ladder is sufficient. For large repairs use a scaffold board supported both ends on step ladders, trestles or stout boxes. You will be able to move around freely and adjust the height to suit your needs.

Protect all floor coverings and furniture preferably with polythene dust sheets but take care not to spill liquids on the polythene, making it slippery. If you are dealing with a large area, it is best to clear the room completely or stack the furniture well away from the working area.

Bubbles in ceiling paper These often occur when emulsion has been applied over ceiling paper. To remove one or two bubbles, cut them with a sharp knife, daub wallpaper paste on the ceiling and push the flaps back into place. Once repainted the cuts should be invisible.

Bubbles and loose areas may also appear through insufficient pasting of the paper or, particularly in older houses, papering over soft distemper. Temporary repairs are unlikely to be satisfactory and you will do better to repaper the whole ceiling. Soak the paper with water and pull it off, using a flat wallpaper scraper on stubborn areas. To find out if the surface has originally been distempered, rub wet fingers over the ceiling; if you find heavy deposits of white powder on your hand then the ceiling has been distempered. Remove thin layers of distemper with a coarse cloth and plenty of water; thick layers will need to be well soaked before they can be scraped off. To reduce mess, catch as much as possible of the old distemper in a dustpan as it falls. Rinse the ceiling with clean water and, when dry, apply a sealer or size before repainting or papering the surface.

Stains Most ceiling stains are caused by water from leaking pipes or overflowing tanks. Once you have rectified the plumbing fault and the ceiling has dried out, cover the area with aluminium primer to prevent the stain showing through and redecorate as usual.

Tobacco smoke can leave a yellowish film on a painted ceiling. Wash the area thoroughly with a solution of water and sugar soap and rinse well.

Narrow cracks Cut along to form 'V' shape in the surface (this is known as undercutting). The point of the 'V' should be at the surface so the cut is widest at its deepest point. Clear the crack of dust and force filler into the cavity, using a flexible filling knife for a smooth, flush finish.

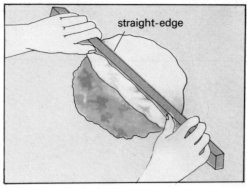

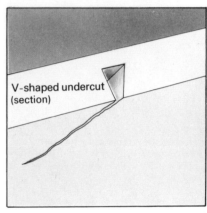

Repair major damage to ceiling with layers of plaster and go over surface with timber straight-edge to ensure smooth finish

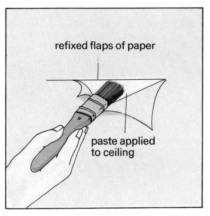

Cut bubbles in ceiling paper with sharp knife. Lightly paste ceiling and smooth paper back into place

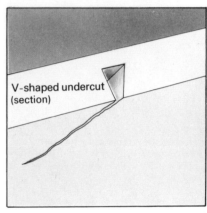

Cut back surface of shallow cracks in 'V' shape and apply enough filler to ensure strong repair

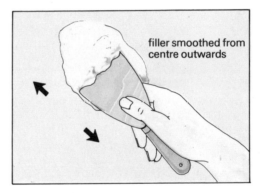

Pack wide shallow cracks with filler. Use knife in both directions, working outwards from centre, for smooth flush finish

Thin springy blade of flexible filling knife draws filler smoothly over surface

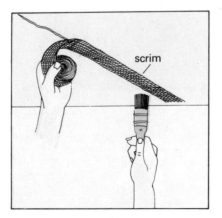

To repair reopened cracks in plasterboard ceilings, fill cavity and paste scrim over length of crack

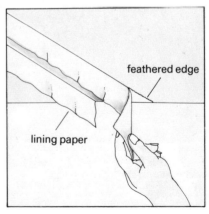

Paste lining paper over scrim; leave sides free. Tear off sides to give feathered edge. Mask with filler

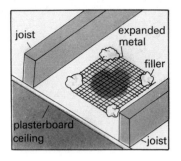

joist
expanded metal
filler
plasterboard ceiling
joist

Before filling, support large holes with expanded metal

Wide, shallow cracks Apply the filler and smooth the surface by drawing the knife outwards from the centre of the cavity, working in alternate directions.

Plasterboard ceilings

Certain types of damage are found specifically with plasterboard and can be made good by using the following methods.

Reopened cracks These are usually caused by seasonal movement of the ceiling joists supporting the plasterboard. If you use just filler the cracks are likely to recur; so you must make a stronger reinforced repair with a build-up of filler, scrim and lining paper. Scrim resembles a coarse bandage and acts as a keying material to prevent the cracks reopening. Lining paper provides a good surface for repainting.

Fill the crack in the usual way and, with wallpaper paste, fix a strip of scrim along the crack. Cut a piece of lining paper to the same length as the crack and about 300mm (or 12in) wide. Paste the middle section of the paper and brush it over the filled crack, leaving the unpasted edges hanging. When the paste is dry, tear off the hanging paper to give a fine feathered edge. Apply a thin film of filler to the edges to mask the paper and finish off with two coats of emulsion.

Sizeable holes Here you will have to gain access from above. This will be simple enough if you are working in an upstairs room with a loft space above; but if the room is downstairs, you will have to lift the relevant floorboards from the room above.

Strengthen the hole with a piece of expanded metal (a type of wire mesh), fixing it to the back of the plasterboard above with dabs of filler. From below, fill the cavity with plaster, building it up in two or three layers. Finish off by applying filler with a flexible filling knife.

Major damage The only way to repair major damage is to insert a new section of plasterboard the same thickness as the existing board.

Cut back around the damaged area to the joists above. Nail softwood battens to the insides of the joists to form a support framework, making sure the bottom edge of the joists and framework are flush. Cut the replacement board to the size of the hole and use galvanized nails to fix it to the framework, sinking the nail heads below the surface with a nail punch. Cover the nail holes and the edges of the new plasterboard with filler. You may need to apply a skim of board-finish plaster to the repair to make up the level to the surrounding ceiling.

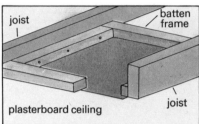

joist
batten frame
plasterboard ceiling
joist

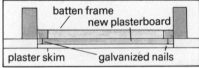

batten frame
new plasterboard
plaster skim
galvanized nails

Repair major damage with new section of plasterboard fixed to batten framework and nailed to joists

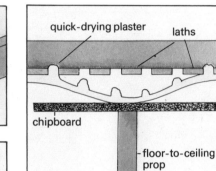

quick-drying plaster
laths
chipboard
floor-to-ceiling prop

To remove bulges from lath and plaster ceiling, prop up ceiling and apply new plaster from above

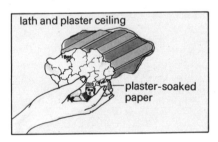

lath and plaster ceiling
plaster-soaked paper

For backing support, line large holes in lath and plaster ceilings with wedges of plaster-soaked paper

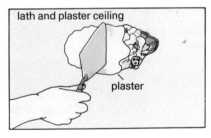

lath and plaster ceiling
plaster

Build up repair with layers of plaster. When set, dampen edges and apply last coat of plaster or filler

Lath and plaster ceilings

For removing bulges and repairing major damage with this type of ceiling use the following methods.

Bulges These are caused when the plaster keying the ceiling to the laths cracks up and no longer provides any support. It may occasionally be possible to make a temporary repair by pushing the bulge into place from below with a square of wood supported by a floor-to-ceiling prop and screwing through the bulge into the laths. But we recommend you cut out the bulge and repair as for holes.

With access to the ceiling from above there is another method of repair. Push the bulge into place and prop up from below with a piece of chipboard or plywood as before, rake out the blobs of plaster from the laths and pour in some quick-setting plaster (like plaster of Paris) so ridges are formed above the laths. Don't remove the prop until the plaster has set.

Major damage Repair small holes just with plaster or cellulose filler, but for holes more than 75mm (3in) wide you will need to provide a backing support before filling. Either nail expanded metal to the laths or wedge plaster-soaked paper into the hole. Fill the bulk of the cavity with plaster using a trowel, gradually building up the layers to within 6mm ($\frac{1}{4}$in) of the surrounding area. Leave this to set, dampen the surface with water and apply a last layer of plaster or filler. Finally, go over the edges of the repair with a dampened brush to give the necessary smooth finish.

Basic items
step ladders or scaffold board supported on ladders, trestles or stout boxes
polythene dust sheets

For bubbles in paper
sharp trimming knife
wallpaper paste and brush
flat wallpaper scraper
coarse cloth, sealer or size (for distempered ceilings)

For stains
aluminium primer
sugar soap (for smoke stains)

For cracks
cellulose filler
flexible filling knife

For plasterboard ceilings
cellulose filler, wallpaper paste and brush, scrim, lining paper (for reopened cracks)
filler, expanded metal, plaster, flexible filling knife (for sizeable holes)
softwood batten framework, plasterboard, galvanized nails 38mm (1$\frac{1}{2}$in) long, nail punch, hammer, board-finish plaster (for major damage)

For lath and plaster ceilings
square of wood, floor-to-ceiling prop, filler, quick-setting plaster (for bulges)
expanded metal or plaster-soaked paper, plaster, plastering trowel (for major damage)

equipment

Appendix

Metric conversion charts

Metric prefixes and abbreviations

The metre is used as an example below. The same prefixes apply to litres (l or lit) and grams (g). The abbreviation lit is used for litre when unqualified to avoid confusion with the numeral 1.

millimetre (mm)	0.001	one thousandth metre
centimetre (cm)	0.01	one hundredth metre
decimetre (dm)	0.1	one tenth metre
metre (m)	1	one metre
decametre (dam)	10	ten metres
hectometre (hm)	100	one hundred metres
kilometre (km)	1000	one thousand metres

Length (linear measure)

Fractions of 1 inch in millimetres

Thirty-seconds, sixteenths, eighths, quarters and one half

in	mm
1/32	0.8
1/16	1.6
3/32	2.4
1/8	3.2
5/32	4.0
3/16	4.8
7/32	5.6
1/4	6.3
9/32	7.1
5/16	7.9
11/32	8.7
3/8	9.5
13/32	10.3
7/16	11.1
15/32	11.9
1/2	12.7
17/32	13.5
9/16	14.3
19/32	15.1
5/8	15.9
21/32	16.7
11/16	17.5
23/32	18.3
3/4	19.0
25/32	19.8
13/16	20.6
27/32	21.4
7/8	22.2
29/32	23.0
15/16	23.8
31/32	24.6
1 inch	25.4

Twelfths, sixths and thirds

in	mm
1/12	2.1
1/6	4.2
1/4	6.3
1/3	8.5
5/12	10.6
1/2	12.7
7/12	14.8
2/3	16.9
3/4	19.0
5/6	21.2
11/12	23.3
1 inch	25.4

Note

Find the Imperial figure you wish to convert in the **heavy** type central column and read off the metric equivalent in the right-hand column and vice versa.
For example:
10 inches = 254 millimetres and 10mm = 0.39in.

Conversion from inches is only taken up to 40 in the chart below, see next chart for continuation.

Inches/millimetres

in		mm
0.04	**1**	25.4
0.08	**2**	50.8
0.12	**3**	76.2
0.16	**4**	101.6
0.20	**5**	127.0
0.24	**6**	152.4
0.28	**7**	177.8
0.31	**8**	203.2
0.35	**9**	228.6
0.39	**10**	254.0
0.43	**11**	279.4
0.47	**12**	304.8
0.51	**13**	330.2
0.55	**14**	355.6
0.59	**15**	381.0
0.63	**16**	406.4
0.67	**17**	431.8
0.71	**18**	457.2
0.75	**19**	482.6
0.79	**20**	508.0
0.83	**21**	533.4
0.87	**22**	558.8
0.91	**23**	584.2
0.94	**24**	609.6
0.98	**25**	635.0
1.02	**26**	660.4
1.06	**27**	685.8
1.10	**28**	711.2
1.14	**29**	736.6
1.18	**30**	762.0
1.22	**31**	787.4
1.26	**32**	812.8
1.30	**33**	838.2
1.34	**34**	863.6
1.38	**35**	889.0
1.42	**36**	914.4
1.46	**37**	939.8
1.50	**38**	965.2
1.54	**39**	990.6
1.57	**40**	1016.0
1.97	**50**	
2.36	**60**	
2.76	**70**	
3.15	**80**	
3.54	**90**	
3.94	**100**	
7.87	**200**	
11.81	**300**	
15.75	**400**	
19.68	**500**	
23.62	**600**	
27.56	**700**	
31.50	**800**	
35.43	**900**	
39.37	**1000**	

Imperial measurements are expressed below in yards, feet and inches rather than in decimals for convenience if converting with rulers or measuring tapes which do not include decimal readings.

Feet/metres					Yards/metres				
ft	in		m	yd	ft	in		m
3	3	**1**	0.30	1	0	3	**1**	0.9
6	7	**2**	0.61	2	0	7	**2**	1.8
9	10	**3**	0.91	3	0	10	**3**	2.7
13	1	**4**	1.22	4	1	1	**4**	3.7
16	5	**5**	1.52	5	1	5	**5**	4.6
19	8	**6**	1.83	6	1	8	**6**	5.5
23	0	**7**	2.13	7	2	0	**7**	6.4
26	3	**8**	2.44	8	2	3	**8**	7.3
29	6	**9**	2.74	9	2	6	**9**	8.2
32	10	**10**	3.05	10	2	10	**10**	9.1
65	7	**20**	6.10	21	2	7	**20**	18.3
98	5	**30**	9.14	32	2	5	**30**	27.4
131	3	**40**	12.19	43	2	3	**40**	36.6
164	0	**50**	15.24	54	2	0	**50**	45.7
196	10	**60**	18.29	65	1	10	**60**	54.9
229	8	**70**	21.34	76	1	8	**70**	64.0
262	6	**80**	24.38	87	1	6	**80**	73.2
295	3	**90**	27.43	98	1	3	**90**	82.3
328	1	**100**	30.48	109	1	1	**100**	91.4

Quick conversion factors – length

Terms are set out in full in the left-hand column except where clarification is necessary.

1 inch (in)	= 25.4mm/2.54cm
1 foot (ft)/12in	= 304.8mm/30.48cm/0.3048m
1 yard (yd)/3ft	= 914.4mm/91.44cm/0.9144m
1 mile (mi)/1760yd	= 1609.344m/1.609km
1 millimetre (mm)	= 0.0394in
1 centimetre (cm)/10mm	= 0.394in
1 metre (m)/100cm	= 39.37in/3.281ft/1.094yd
1 kilometre (km)/1000m	= 1093.6yd/0.6214mi

Quick conversion factors – area

1 square inch (sq in)	= 645.16sq mm/ 6.4516sq cm
1 square foot (sq ft)/144sq in	= 929.03sq cm
1 square yard (sq yd)/9sq ft	= 8361.3sq cm/ 0.8361sq m
1 acre (ac)/4840sq yd	= 4046.9sq m/0.4047ha
1 square mile (sq mi)640ac	= 259ha
1 square centimetre (sq cm)/ 100 square millimetre (sq mm)	= 0.155sq in
1 square metre (sq m)/ 10,000sq cm	= 10.764sq ft/1.196sq yd
1 are (a)/100sq m	= 119.60sq yd/0.0247ac
1 hectare (ha)/100a	= 2.471ac/0.00386sq mi

Quick conversion factors – volume

1 cubic inch (cu in)	= 16.3871cu cm
1 cubic foot (cu ft)/ 1728cu in	= 28.3168cu dm/0.0283cu m
1 cubic yard (cu yd)/ 27cu ft	= 0.7646cu m
1 cubic centimetre (cu cm)/ 1000 cubic millimetres (cu mm)	= 0.0610cu in
1 cubic decimetre (cu dm)/ 1000cu cm	= 61.024cu in/0.0353cu ft
1 cubic metre (cu m)/ 1000cu dm	= 35.3146cu ft/1.308cu yd
1cu cm	= 1 millilitre (ml)
1cu dm	= 1 litre (lit) See **Capacity**

Area (square measure)

As millimetre numbers would be unwieldy for general use, square or cubic inches have been converted to square or cubic centimetres. Conversion from square inches is only taken up to 150 in the first chart below; see next chart for continuation.

Square inches/square centimetres

sq in		sq cm
0.2	1	6.5
0.3	2	12.9
0.5	3	19.4
0.6	4	25.8
0.8	5	32.3
0.9	6	38.7
1.1	7	45.2
1.2	8	51.6
1.4	9	58.1
1.6	10	64.5
3.1	20	129.0
4.7	30	193.5
6.2	40	258.1
7.8	50	322.6
9.3	60	387.1
10.9	70	451.6
12.4	80	516.1
14.0	90	580.6
15.5	100	645.2
17.1	110	709.7
18.6	120	774.2
20.2	130	838.7
21.7	140	903.2
23.3	150	967.7
31.0	200	
46.5	300	
62.0	400	
77.5	500	
93.0	600	
108.5	700	
124.0	800	
139.5	900	
155.0	1000	

Square feet/square metres

sq ft		sq m
10.8	1	0.09
21.5	2	0.19
32.3	3	0.28
43.1	4	0.37
53.8	5	0.46
64.6	6	0.56
75.3	7	0.65
86.1	8	0.74
96.9	9	0.84
107.6	10	0.93
215.3	20	1.86
322.9	30	2.79
430.6	40	3.72
538.2	50	4.65
645.8	60	5.57
753.5	70	6.50
861.1	80	7.43
968.8	90	8.36
1076.4	100	9.29

Square yards/square metres

sq yd		sq m
1.2	1	0.8
2.4	2	1.7
3.6	3	2.5
4.8	4	3.3
6.0	5	4.2
7.2	6	5.0
8.4	7	5.9
9.6	8	6.7
10.8	9	7.5
12.0	10	8.4
23.9	20	16.7
35.9	30	25.1
47.8	40	33.4
59.8	50	41.8
71.8	60	50.2
83.7	70	58.5
95.7	80	66.9
107.6	90	75.3
119.6	100	83.6

Volume (cubic measure)

Cubic inches/cubic centimetres

cu in		cu cm
0.06	1	16.4
0.12	2	32.8
0.18	3	49.2
0.24	4	65.5
0.31	5	81.9
0.37	6	98.3
0.43	7	114.7
0.49	8	131.1
0.55	9	147.5
0.61	10	163.9
1.22	20	327.7
1.83	30	491.6
2.44	40	655.5
3.05	50	819.4
3.66	60	983.2
4.27	70	1147.1/1.15cu dm
4.88	80	1311.0/1.31cu dm
5.49	90	1474.8/1.47cu dm
6.10	100	1638.7/1.64cu dm
12.20	200	3277.4/3.28cu dm
18.31	300	4916.1/4.92cu dm
24.41	400	6554.8/6.55cu dm
30.51	500	8193.5/8.19cu dm
36.61	600	9832.2/9.83cu dm
42.72	700	11470.9/11.47cu dm
48.82	800	13109.7/13.11cu dm
54.92	900	14748.4/14.75cu dm
61.02	1000	16387.1/16.39cu dm
122.05	2000	32774.1/32.77cu dm

Cubic feet/cubic decimetres

cu ft		cu dm
.04	1	28.3
0.07	2	56.6
0.11	3	85.0
0.14	4	113.3
0.18	5	141.6
0.21	6	169.9
0.25	7	198.2
0.28	8	226.5
0.32	9	254.9
0.35	10	283.2
0.71	20	566.3
1.06	30	849.5
1.41	40	1132.7/1.13cu m
1.77	50	1415.8/1.42cu m
2.12	60	1699.0/1.70cu m
2.47	70	1982.2/1.98cu m
2.83	80	2265.3/2.27cu m
3.18	90	2548.5/2.55cu m
3.53	100	2831.7/2.83cu m

Cubic yards/cubic metres

cu yd		cu m
1.3	1	0.8
2.6	2	1.5
3.9	3	2.3
5.2	4	3.1
6.5	5	3.8
7.8	6	4.6
9.2	7	5.4
10.5	8	6.1
11.8	9	6.9
13.1	10	7.6
26.2	20	15.3
39.2	30	22.9
52.3	40	30.6
65.4	50	38.2
78.5	60	45.9
91.6	70	53.5
104.6	80	61.2
117.7	90	68.8
130.8	100	76.5

Capacity

Fluid ounces/millilitres

fl oz		
0.04	1	28.4
0.07	2	56.8
0.11	3	85.2
0.14	4	113.6
0.18	5	142.1
0.21	6	170.5
0.25	7	198.9
0.28	8	227.3
0.32	9	255.7
0.35	10	284.1
0.70	20	568.2
1.06	30	852.4
1.41	40	1136.5/1.136 lit
1.76	50	1420.6/1.421 lit

Pints/litres

pt		lit
1.8	1	0.6/568ml
3.5	2	1.1
5.3	3	1.7
7.0	4	2.3
8.8	5	2.8
10.6	6	3.4
12.3	7	4.0
14.1	8	4.5
15.8	9	5.1
17.6	10	5.7

Gallons/litres

gal		lit
0.2	1	4.5
0.4	2	9.1
0.7	3	13.6
0.9	4	18.2
1.1	5	22.7
1.3	6	27.3
1.5	7	31.8
1.8	8	36.4
2.0	9	40.9
2.2	10	45.5
4.4	20	90.9
6.6	30	136.4
8.8	40	181.8
11.0	50	227.3
13.2	60	272.8
15.4	70	318.2
17.6	80	363.7
19.8	90	409.1
22.0	100	454.6

Weight

Ounces/grams

oz		g
0.04	1	28.3
0.07	2	56.7
0.11	3	85.0
0.14	4	113.4
0.18	5	141.7
0.21	6	170.1
0.25	7	198.4
0.28	8	226.8
0.32	9	255.1
0.35	10	283.5
0.39	11	311.8
0.42	12	340.2
0.46	13	368.5
0.49	14	396.9
0.53	15	425.2
0.56	16	453.6
0.71	20	567.0
1.06	30	850.5
1.41	40	1134.0
1.76	50	1417.5
2.12	60	1701.0
2.47	70	1984.5
2.82	80	2268.0
3.17	90	2551.5
3.53	100	2835.0

Pounds/kilograms

lb		kg
2.2	1	0.5
4.4	2	0.9
6.6	3	1.4
8.8	4	1.8
11.0	5	2.3
13.2	6	2.7
15.4	7	3.2
17.6	8	3.6
19.8	9	4.1
22.0	10	4.5
44.1	20	9.1
66.1	30	13.6
88.2	40	18.1
110.2	50	22.7
132.3	60	27.2
154.3	70	31.8
176.4	80	36.3
198.4	90	40.8
220.5	100	45.4

Quick conversion factors – capacity

1 fluid ounce (fl oz)	= 28.4ml
1 gill (gi)/5fl oz	= 142.1ml
1 pint (pt)/4gi	= 568.2ml/0.568 lit
1 quart (qt)/2pt	= 1.136 lit
1 gallon (gal)/4pt	= 4.546 lit
1 millilitre (ml)	= 0.035fl oz
1 litre (lit)	= 1.76pt/0.22gal
1ml	= 1 cubic centimetre (cu cm)
1 lit	= 1 cubic decimetre (cu dm) See **Volume**
1 US pint	= 5/6 Imperial pt/473.2ml/0.473 lit
1 US gallon	= 5/6 Imperial gal/3.785 lit

Quick conversion factors – weight

1 ounce (oz)	= 28.35g
1 pound (lb)/16oz	= 453.59g/0.4536kg
1 stone/14lb	= 6.35kg
1 hundredweight (cwt)/ 8 stone/112lb	= 50.80kg
1 ton/20cwt	= 1016.05kg/1.016t
1 gram (g)	= 0.035oz
1 kilogram (kg)/1000g	= 35.274oz/2.2046lb/ 2lb 3.274oz
1 tonne (t)/1000kg	= 2204.6lb/0.9842 ton

Index